"Equitable employment is vital if we want to transform lives of persons with disabilities. This is an enthralling contribution to the disability debate, benefitting from a grounding in empirical social science. I warmly welcome it."

- **Tom Shakespeare,** *Professor of Disability Research, London School of Hygiene & Tropical Medicine*

"This is the very first book to present a holistic perspective on the scope of practices in disability employment inclusiveness. It distinguishes itself by exploring the erstwhile uncharted territory in how psychosocial assumptions undergird employment access and practices, drawing from the broader and emerging scholarship on disability work inclusion to guide local adaptations and practices. Readers will find this book to be an invaluable landmark guide to understanding their evolving disability inclusion employment practices in the diversifying world of work."

- **Elias Mpofu,** *Professor of Rehabilitation and Health Services, College of Health and Public Service, University of North Texas*

"At a moment when social justice issues are at an all-time high in focus, it is most timely to have a book on this topic. Employment equity for people with disabilities, particularly those with intersectional identities and often multiply marginalized, is a critical topic for inclusion in this discourse."

- **Susanne Bruyère,** *Professor of Disability Studies, Academic Director, Yang-Tan Institute on Employment and Disability, School of Industrial and Labor Relations, Cornell University*

Disability in the Workplace

This book introduces the difference model of disability. Framed within an affect-based understanding of the relationships between those living with impairments and others, this new model offers a reconsideration of the construct of disability itself. Disability is flexible, relational, and perceived through an acognitive lens.

At a practice level, the difference model offers a framework for creating more positive and successful relationships between people with disabilities (PWDs) and others within the workplace. This includes two new tools, the Co-Worker Acceptance of Disabled Employees (CADE) Scale and the Perceived Barriers to Employing Persons with Disabilities (PBED) Scale. Designed to measure workplace attitudes, and changes to these attitudes, each of these scales provides empirical evidence in support of strategic planning and, ultimately, an increased representation of PWDs. Finally, this book considers the effects of language and technology on workplace attitudes toward disability.

Jonathon S. Breen is a Postdoctoral Fellow of the Department of Occupational Science and Occupational Therapy (Faculty of Medicine) at the University of British Columbia in Vancouver, Canada. His research interests focus on the theoretical and practical understandings of disability, particularly as these apply in the workplace. Dr Breen's academic work follows an extensive career in both the public and the private sectors.

Susan J. Forwell is a Professor and Head of the Department of Occupational Science and Occupational Therapy at the University of British Columbia (UBC) and a Research Associate with both the UBC MS clinic and the International Collaboration of Research and Discovery. Her occupation-focused research and teaching address employment among populations with disability, occupational implications of life transitions, and functional difficulties among those with progressive neurological conditions.

Routledge Studies in Employment and Work Relations in Context

Peter Fairbrother and Tony Elger

The aim of the *Employment and Work Relations in Context Series* is to address questions relating to the evolving patterns and politics of work, employment, management, and industrial relations. There is a concern to trace out the ways in which wider policy-making, especially by national governments and transnational corporations, impinges upon specific workplaces, occupations, labour markets, localities, and regions. This invites attention to developments at an international level, marking out patterns of globalisation, state policy, and practices in the context of globalisation and the impact of these processes on labour. A particular feature of the series is the consideration of forms of worker and citizen organisation and mobilisation. The studies address major analytical and policy issues through case study and comparative research.

Contesting Inequality and Worker Mobilisation
Australia 1851–1880
Michael Quinlan

Trade Unions and Regions
Better Work, Experimentation, and Regional Governance
Edited by Christian Lévesque, Peter Fairbrother, Blandine Emilien, María C. González and Lucie Morissette

International Trade, Labor Relations, and Bargaining Power
International Strawberry Commodity Networks
Matthew M. Fischer-Daly

Disability in the Workplace
The Politics of Difference
Jonathon S. Breen and Susan J. Forwell

For more information about this series, please visit: https://www.routledge.com/Routledge-Studies-in-Employment-and-Work-Relations-in-Context/book-series/SE0840

Disability in the Workplace

The Politics of Difference

Jonathon S. Breen and Susan J. Forwell

Routledge
Taylor & Francis Group
NEW YORK AND LONDON

First published 2023
by Routledge
605 Third Avenue, New York, NY 10158

and by Routledge
4 Park Square, Milton Park, Abingdon, Oxon, OX14 4RN

Routledge is an imprint of the Taylor & Francis Group, an informa business

Library of Congress Cataloguing-in-Publication Data
Names: Breen, Jonathon S., author. | Forwell, Susan J., author.
Title: Disability in the workplace : the politics of difference / Jonathon S. Breen and Susan J. Forwell.
Description: 1 Edition. | New York, NY : Routledge, 2023. |
Series: Routledge studies in employment and work relations in context |
Includes bibliographical references and index.
Identifiers: LCCN 2022055629 | ISBN 9781032116068 (hardback) |
ISBN 9781032116112 (paperback) | ISBN 9781003220695 (ebook)
Subjects: LCSH: People with disabilities--Employment. |
Work environment. | Work--Psychological aspects. |
Interpersonal relations--Psychological attitudes.
Classification: LCC HD7252 .B74 2023 | DDC 362.4/0484--dc23/eng/20221117
LC record available at https://lccn.loc.gov/2022055629

ISBN: 978-1-032-11606-8 (hbk)
ISBN: 978-1-032-11611-2 (pbk)
ISBN: 978-1-003-22069-5 (ebk)

DOI: 10.4324/9781003220695

Typeset in Bembo
by MPS Limited, Dehradun

Contents

Tables and Figures

Tables

Figures

Author Biographies

Jonathon S. Breen, PhD, MSW, BA, is a Postdoctoral Fellow of the Department of Occupational Science and Occupational Therapy (Faculty of Medicine) at the University of British Columbia in Vancouver, Canada. His research interests focus on the theoretical and practical understandings of disability, particularly as these apply in the workplace. Dr Breen's academic work follows an extensive career in both the public and the private sectors. He has served as the Executive Director of a supported employment agency, the principal of a private consultancy within the field of employment and disability, and as the Yukon government manager of disability employment services.

Susan J. Forwell, PhD, OT, FCAOT, is a Professor and the Head of the Department of Occupational Science and Occupational Therapy at the University of British Columbia (UBC), a Research Associate with both the UBC MS clinic and the International Collaboration of Research and Discovery. Her occupation-focused research and teaching address employment among populations with disability, occupational implications of life transitions, and functional difficulties among those with progressive neurological conditions. She is also well known for holding numerous leadership positions (i.e. Past president, Canadian Association of Occupational Therapists; associate editor, *International Journal of MS Care*; chair, International Society of Occupational Science; and chair, Inaugural World Occupational Science conference).

Preface

The purpose of this book is to offer a way forward within the ongoing struggle to achieve fair and equitable employment opportunities for people with disabilities (PWDs). The underrepresentation of PWDs in the workplace, both in number and in hierarchical location, is commonly accepted. To meet this challenge, we present a new, affect-based theoretical perspective – the difference model – to the understanding of workplace relationships between PWDs and others.

In a transition from theory to practice, we describe how we have applied this model to the development of tools that measure workplace attitudes. We also consider how the information generated from these measures allows for strategic shifts in workplace interventions and in individual vocational planning on the part of PWDs.

In support of the difference model of disability, we examine and critique the several factors that are held to influence the relationship between PWDs and others within the workplace. These include a description and comparison of the arguments and assumptions that are relied upon by the several extant models of disability and by those that underpin the difference model. We also examine the effects that a range of technological developments, from stair-climbing wheelchairs to thought-controlled prostheses, have on others' perceptions of PWDs. Finally, we consider the topic of disability itself; particularly in terms of who is counted, what effects the various definitions of disability have on the perceptions of others, and to what extent these general perceptions influence workplace relationships.

We describe how this paradigm shift from current models of disability will provide PWDs, students and teachers of disability studies, corporate champions, and vocational rehabilitation practitioners, with new insights in support of the strategic planning required to reach a wide range of employment goals.

Several additional points require comment at this early juncture. The first is the language that we have decided to employ with reference to individuals living with disabilities and to others without disabilities. As noted above, we have adopted the more North American *people with disabilities* (PWDs) description rather than the UK description of *disabled people.*

The arguments in favour of each of these are relatively well-known. The former, employing what is described as "people first" language, is often used to signify that the individual is paramount, with the disability understood to be an aspect of that individual. The latter is commonly used to represent disability as a construct forced upon individuals living with impairments by an ableist society.

We have determined that *people with disabilities*, and, in particular *PWDs*, which has to some extent taken on the mantle of a semiotic representation of disability, is most appropriate in the context of this book. Although we recognize that we may be open to criticism on this point, this designation appears to us to be the more ontologically neutral of the available options. As described next, this positioning fits in well with the difference model of disability.

We have also introduced the acronym of IWOD to refer to *individuals without disabilities*. Our intent is to present a term that is quite different in tone from other indicators such as TAB (i.e. temporarily able-bodied) in reference to individuals who are not currently considered to be PWDs. IWOD is intended to be more neutral and less easily perceived as a politically charged term. Its purpose is to be descriptive but, similar to PWD, an ontologically neutral representation.

Second, the first several chapters of this book are intended, in part, to provide a degree of contextualization within which to frame our description of the difference model of disability. We recognize that some readers will have some or most of this information already in hand. In those instances, those readers may wish to first review Chapter 5 and then return to those earlier chapters as required.

Third, prior to your consideration of the arguments and analyses that we have put forward throughout this book, we would like to draw your attention to an overarching trope that has informed much of this work. It is best described as an effort to consider and describe the socially generated assumptions that have contributed to the present employment status of PWDs. We believe that these have, to various degrees, influenced broad concepts such as the relationship between the construct of validity and the efficacy of measures of attitudes toward PWDs, while others have been unwarrantedly applied within several practice frameworks associated specifically with PWDs. It is our intent, throughout this work, to describe and consider the effect that these several normative assumptions have had on the employment of PWDs. In addition, we look beyond these assumptions to reveal and explicate underlying motivations and attitudes in an effort to provide a more grounded understanding of the relationship that exists between PWDs and the larger community.

Our final point at this juncture is to state, at the onset, that the purpose of this book is to provide a contribution to the enormous efforts being made by many to create more equitable employment opportunities for PWDs. We trust that the following considerations of disability, from both a theoretical and praxis perspective, will make that intended contribution. We offer space for both critique and further validation of these arguments.

We would like to acknowledge and thank Viviana Shiffman, PhD student at the University of British Columbia, for her editorial and proofreading contribution to this work.

1 Introduction – Employment of People with Disabilities

Policy makers, researchers, and disability activists all maintain that employment is a central tenet of the social inclusion of people with disabilities (Shah & Priestley, 2011). The United Nations Convention on the Rights of Persons with Disabilities (CRPD) recognizes the right of people with disabilities (PWDs) to employment that is inclusive, accessible, and free of discrimination (United Nations, 2006). However, as is widely acknowledged, employment rates for PWDs are significantly lower than those of the general population (Saleh & Bruyère, 2018; Turcotte, 2014) and this discrepancy continues to grow (Burke et al., 2013).

In high-income countries, PWDs are typically employed at a rate that is approximately half that of the general population. Unemployment rates, which consider only those individuals who are actively seeking work, are more than double those of the general population (Burke et al., 2013). In low- and medium-income countries, these rates of employment are significantly lower (Saleh & Bruyère, 2018). The United Nations committee engaged in the development of the CRPD observed that the unemployment rates for PWDs were "nearly 60% in Peru, 67.75% in Morocco, 76% in Jordan and a staggering 99% in Kenya" (Harpur, 2019, p. 45). Similarly, Ndzwayiba and Ned (2017) note that, according to the 2014 South African Commission on Employment Equity Report, employees with disabilities accounted for less than 1% of that country's workforce.

The relationship between PWDs and employment has been a topic of critical concern by researchers and scholars for at least the past 40 years (Goodley, Hughes, & Davis, 2012). Shah and Priestley (2011), citing the Union of the Physically Impaired Against Segregation [UPIAS] (1976), state that "all other situations from which physically impaired persons are excluded are linked … with the basic exclusion from employment" (p. 119).

In this book, we describe and evaluate a new model of disability – the difference model – to provide a theoretical framework to support positive employment outcomes for PWDs (Breen, 2017; Breen & Forwell, 2020). We also consider how applications of the difference model have demonstrated early successes in addressing this critically important component of full citizenship for PWDs. We do this through a pragmatist lens (Peirce, 1923;

DOI: 10.4324/9781003220695-1

Rorty, 1966); therefore, this framing of disability will ultimately be evaluated through the scope of its contributions to social change related to employment, not solely to its contribution to academic discourse (Vernon & Swain, 2002).

We offer a revised understanding of disability as it pertains to employment; one that relies on an affect-based relationship between those of us considered to be PWDs and the IWOD community. We contend that the attitudes of others are the single, most critical determinant of employment success for PWDs. We also describe how these attitudes toward individuals living with impairments drive the creation of the construct of disability itself.

To contextualize the difference model, we examine several other theoretical frameworks that describe disability and consider their individual and common characteristics purporting to address the global challenge of welcoming and maintaining PWDs in the workplace at a rate that is at parity with the general population. The difference model is compared and contrasted with these several other models, each of which is held out by many authors as being relatively contradictory and mutually exclusive (Beaudry, 2016). We demonstrate that each of these models of disability, as currently applied to strategies designed to enhance employment opportunities for PWDs, share a cognitively driven perspective that is insufficient to meet these goals.

> We wish to state that the materials presented and conclusions drawn in this book are based on data generated principally from within several of the high-income countries. As will be noted throughout, these data have been drawn predominantly, although not exclusively, from the United States, Canada, the United Kingdom, and Australia – *Breen & Forwell.*

It should be noted that the theoretical frameworks described below are not to be construed as a comprehensive list. Others, including the affirmative model (Swain & French, 2003) and variations of a cultural model (Priestley, 1998; Hughes, 2019) have been articulated elsewhere. However, these latter models are concerned, respectively, with the perspective of PWDs themselves and the variations of 'differencing' inherent to various social conditions. Although these, and others, provide valuable insights into the lives of PWDs, they are somewhat tangential to our purpose, which is to explore and influence the attitudes of others toward PWDs within a workplace environment. Our purpose is not to argue that one of these models, including the difference model, is true and the others are false. Rather, we present the difference model as being most suitable for a specific purpose, that of enhancing employment opportunities for PWDs.

We also describe the practical supports that we have developed to meet these employment challenges. The difference model of disability, based on an affect-driven relationship between PWDs and others, provides a theoretical basis for understanding and remediating these employment disparities. Based on this model's application at a practice level, we describe two self-report measures that we have developed to gauge workplace attitudes toward PWDs. We include a description of their creation, validation data, and their potential to determine attitude change following a range of workplace interventions.

Finally, we consider the construct of disability itself; from who "counts" as a PWD to how this group, or groups, are affected by this designation within the workplace. We examine the effects of these descriptions of disability – both within an academic context and by the more public media.

Our goal is to present a framework that can be utilized to enhance employment opportunities for PWDs. In support of this goal, the content of this book provides theoretical and practical information throughout its several chapters. In terms of method, several premises and strategies are of note. Principal among these is our position that quantitative analyses are strengthened and supported by qualitative influences (Creswell, 2013; Maxwell, 2012) and that discourses such as those offered within this book presuppose an underlying ontology or general understanding of the world (Bhaskar, 1989). Consequently, we provide a relatively personal approach, in both style and content, and make efforts to delineate our individual and professional understandings of disability, and PWDs, that have provided the impetus and support for our theoretical and empirically derived positions. To this end, we have included several Text Box illustrations to link these analyses with circumstances of lived experience in an effort to integrate theory with practice.

By taking this approach, we have attempted to explicate not only the definitions and arguments that we put forward but also to look more deeply at why we have chosen this path. We agree with Young (1990) who states that, without such a consideration and articulation of an informing worldview, comparisons and evaluations of any theoretical and practical constructions are of a diminished value. This argument is extended by Hacking (1999). That author notes, in a consideration particular to disability, that a clear articulation of the basis of one's understandings is necessary to support any following interpretations or conclusions. Consequently, in an effort to approach 'full disclosure', we have described the ontological framework that we have relied upon in support of our effort to reduce the employment challenges faced by PWDs.

As a final introductory comment, a word about the construct of difference is presented. Making use of this term, and what it implies within the difference model, follows a long list of that construct's cultural and social applications within descriptions and analyses of disability. As such, we do not purport to be in any way novel in our application of the term itself to the disability debate (see, for example, Crow, 1996).

However, as we describe throughout this book, it is our intention to interrogate new options with regard to its justification within this debate. Specifically, it has been our intent to explore more deeply into what difference means and why it has come to represent a significant tipping point between PWDs and IWODs. Following Bhaskar (1989), we have applied a three-step process within this excavation. First, we have built a model. Second, we have subjected that model to empirical scrutiny in order to determine whether it is consistent with a particular phenomenon and that it is a more successful predictor than its competitors. In this case, we refer specifically to issues of employment and PWDs. Third, we have provided an explanation of this status by delineating the reasons, motivations, and premises that support the difference model. To be clear, it is our intent to challenge the most commonly held explanation for the continued divide between PWD and IWODs as one of cognitively based error.

The balance of this introductory section provides a summary of each of the following several chapters.

Chapter 2: Definitions and Research Gaps

We offer pertinent definitions, articulate research gaps, and discuss research-related challenges, including the definition of disability itself, which have contributed to the ongoing low representation of PWDs in the workplace. These challenges include gaps between research efforts that have been undertaken under the general heading of disability studies and other work that has been conducted in organizational management, the agile workplace, and elsewhere. This chapter also draws attention to the challenges associated with research methodologies, communication, common language, and attention to practical applications.

Chapter 3: Attitudes, Acceptance, and Disability

We provide an overview of attitudes, including considerations of how attitudes are formed, the means by which they may be altered, and their relationship to the acceptance of PWDs by others. The chapter describes a model of attitudes that includes components of behaviour, affect, and cognition, as well as an exploration of the relationships that exist between each of these. The various efforts that have been made to measure attitudes, specifically as these apply to disability, are also reviewed. This chapter closes with a description of the effect of attitudes on perceptions of disability, including the potential for significant challenges to these relationships between PWDs and others.

Chapter 4: Models, Theory, and Assumptions

We describe the several models, theories, and assumptions associated with the several lenses through which the construct of disability has been viewed both historically and in the present time. Following a review of the concepts of "theory" and "model," a critical examination is provided of the challenges found within the application of each of these as they apply to current understandings of disability and the limitations of their cognitively based structures.

Chapter 5: The Difference Model

We introduce the difference model of disability as an affective and evidence-based approach that is positioned as an alternative to the several cognitively framed models referenced in the above chapter. We provide a detailed description of the difference model of disability and contrast this model with these other models of disability. Finally, we offer a unique set of strategies, based on the difference model, to reduce barriers to employment success for PWDs.

Chapter 6: Workplace Attitudes toward PWDs

This chapter considers two distinct aspects of workplace attitudes toward PWDs. First, we summarize two training efforts developed to support more positive attitudes within the workplace – one directed toward PWDs themselves and the other toward IWODs.

Second, we examine two self-report tools that have been created to measure these attitudes, and attitude change, within the workplace. These are the Co-Worker Acceptance of Disabled Employees (CADE) Scale and the Perceived Barriers to Employing People with Disabilities (PBED) Scale. The CADE Scale was developed in response to the need to account for attitudes toward PWDs across a broad spectrum of workplace environments and locations (Breen, 2018a; Breen, 2019), while the PBED Scale was developed at the behest of the United Nations Industrial Development Organization to measure attitudes toward PWDs in Armenia (Breen, Havaei & Pitassi, 2019).

Chapter 7: People with Disabilities

In this chapter, we describe and situate the various ways that PWDs are counted, categorized, and defined. We also address workplace considerations such as strategic planning to engage and recruit PWDs, funding opportunities based on disability, the provision of accommodations, self-disclosure and reporting, organizational training, and associated implications.

Second, we consider the impact of a wide range of technological advances and increasingly sophisticated accommodations available to PWDs within the workplace. These considerations focus on the social effects of this new generation of accommodations, particularly as they pertain to various types of disability, general availability, cost, and their impact on the self-image of PWDs. Consideration is also given to the effects that the association of technology and disability has on the perceptions and attitudes of others. These include potential changes in attitudes from acceptance of difference to the rejection of those PWDs who choose not to avail themselves of technological supports.

Finally, we describe the relatively recent phenomenon of an ongoing fracturing of the disability community by those who do not consider themselves as residing within this construct and by others who maintain this identity but who have chosen to separate themselves from the general population of PWDs.

Chapter 8: An Autoethnographic Journey

This chapter is presented as an autoethnographic review of a lived experience that has informed the creation and articulation of the difference model of disability and its location within the PWD employment reality. It is presented in a narrative format, focusing on the personal and professional development of one of us (Breen). This journey provides the reader with a rich description of the world of disability and its relationship to employment.

The account is guided by a series of questions, developed and delivered by the other author (Forwell), to portray a series of visual *moments* that have contributed to this developmental process. We have positioned this autoethnography within an analytic framework.

Chapter 9: Final Thoughts and Next Steps

This final chapter contains a series of reflections on the work and outcomes that have been described throughout this book. In addition, descriptions are provided of the next steps necessary for generating an effective approach to supporting PWDs in the workplace. Based on the difference model of understanding disability and its implications for employment, several new organizational strategies are suggested. Each of these focuses on either the generation of more positive attitudes toward PWDs in the workplace or considerations of methodologies intended to determine whether these efforts are meeting their goals.

2 Definitions and Research Gaps

The purpose of this chapter is to frame and clarify the several terms, processes, and structural challenges that are associated with the various considerations and applications of the difference model of disability. In addition, as described throughout this book (see Chapters 4–6), any strategy intended to successfully address the employment challenges of PWDs requires, inter alia, a degree of theoretical consistency sufficient to allow for testing and analysis.

This consistency applies equally to the currently discrepant understandings of the several associated constructs and a lack of shared information between various academic disciplines, practice environments, and the employment community (Bruyère et al., 2016). These gaps present an avoidable barrier to the effective strategic planning required to remediate the current inequitable state of employment for PWDs.

This chapter seeks to reduce this barrier by offering definitions of these several constructs, and describing the most challenging gaps in information sharing, in an effort to generate and support procedural coherence within the overall strategy of improving employment opportunities for PWDs. It is acknowledged that many of these, including the definition of disability itself, may not be aligned with readers' current understandings. It is also acknowledged that these several definitions may only be applicable specifically within the context of employment and PWDs.

The early successes that have been generated through applications of the difference model of disability and the corresponding construct definitions provided below demonstrate coherence and structural integrity for the purpose of employment. Although further testing and evaluation are still required, initial results suggest at least a provisional success of this approach within a complex social environment that exists, according to Bhaskar and Danermark (2006), within a matrix of physical, psychological, medical, social, and cultural influences.

Finally, we will explore the relative solitudes that exist between quantitative and qualitative examinations of the employment challenges of PWDs and consider how a coordinated approach has been utilized in support of the difference model of disability. For the purpose of employment and PWDs, a critical realism approach, with its focus on complexity,

DOI: 10.4324/9781003220695-2

variations in perception, and the application of creative processes with which to determine relationships between phenomena and explanations, offers a useful theoretical framework within which to consider this ongoing challenge (Bhaskar, 1989). Critical realism recruits the reasoning tools of abduction and retroduction in support of explaining complex social phenomena (Craig & Bigby, 2015). The former, abduction, is considered to be a creative reasoning process within which the connectivity between observed phenomena and possible explanations, including environmental influences, may be considered (Danermark, Ekstrom, Jakobsen, & Karlsson, 2002). The latter, retroduction, is the analytical process applied within a response to the question "What must be true for this to be the case?" (Craig & Bigby, 2015, p. 315, citing Bhaskar, 1989).

Definitions and Descriptions

There are several constructs and terms that require a clear determination of their meaning as applied within this book. The majority of these have been described and critiqued in other writings from within a variety of vantage points across chronological, cultural, and societal locations. Each of these is summarized and includes the particular meaning that will be applied herein. Others are relatively new terms that require definitions to allow for clarity within their applications associated with the difference model of disability.

Disability

The term *disability* has been variously defined and characterized within several models of disability (Haegele & Hodge, 2016). Disability has been considered as – a social construction within a range of cultural contexts (Priestley, 1998); resulting from social forces unwilling or unable to support impairments (Oliver, 1990); a form of oppression based on these social restrictions (Thomas, 1999a); a result of the meanings that perceptions of disability have on social identities (Swain & French, 2000); akin to impairments related to bodily systems (Altman, 2001; Watson, 2012); an interrelation between the biological and the social (Anastasiou & Kauffman, 2013; Shakespeare & Watson, 2001); and a perception by others of insufficiency (Galvin, 2003).

Silvers (2003) acknowledges this broad spectrum of definitions and indicates that the term itself is sufficiently underspecified so as to allow for a host of interpretations based on political values. On the other hand, Shildrick (2012) chooses to withhold a definition of disability, considering that state to be "a shifting nexus of both physical and mental states that resists full and final definition" (p. 3).

Thomas (1999b) indicates that, even within the same manuscript, writers sometimes confuse different interpretations of disability, at times conflating or otherwise misunderstanding a *social relational* interpretation and a *property* interpretation of that term. This author describes the former as a disadvantage or restriction caused by social forces and the latter as a personal characteristic which, when coupled with social factors, results in restricted activity. Thomas maintains that confusion over these differing interpretations, and their appropriate applications, has led to a number of unproductive debates with each side arguing in support of its conclusions based on dissimilar premises.

Similar concerns have been raised about how the rapid and ongoing changes in the meaning of the term disability have caused this term to be understood differently by different groups (Silvers, 2003). These categorical interpretations are considered to be "slippery, fluid, heterogeneous, deeply intersectional, and thus resistant to definition" (Shildrick, 2012, p. 4).

It is also suggested that these differences in interpretation have been purposefully developed to meet specific organizational or structural requirements. For administrative purposes, disability is often considered to be a multidimensional construct subject to change over time; from a medical perspective, disability is typically defined with a focus on impairment as it relates to particular bodily systems; within a scholarly or academic approach, the construct of disability is described through various efforts to provide a conceptual framework that will contain this phenomenon (Altman, 2001).

Researchers have also focused on the relationship between understandings of the term disability and the evolving cultural politics of language (Corker, 1999a). Based on changing perceptions and prejudice, these fluctuations have influenced how PWDs are perceived by others and themselves (Haegele & Hodge, 2016). Priestley (1999) maintains that the evolving nature of the language associated with disability may be inadvertently reinforcing the stereotypes that theorists are intending to eliminate.

The scholarly debate over the construct of disability has also extended to the language itself – whether the term *disabled person* or *person with a disability* is the appropriate descriptor has been ongoing for several decades (Barnes, 1999; Oliver, 1990; Vivanti, 2020; WHO, 2001). However, these debates and descriptions, including their associated subtleties, are likely unknown to most people. Instead, as we describe in detail in Chapter 7, understandings of disability are more typically premised upon personal experience within the workplace and elsewhere, through media representations of PWDs, and through a consistent and repeated exposure to a word that includes a negative prefix.

Finding a new word to represent a minority group or culture has been the obvious choice in other circumstances (Corker, 1999a). And, when a word becomes inappropriately value-laden or pejorative, it is easier to move on. The challenge, according to Shakespeare and Watson (2001), is that "disability is the quintessential post-modern concept, because it is so complex, so variable, so contingent, so situated … it is a multiplicity, a plurality" (p. 19). These changing applications of language are also seen by many individuals living with impairments as being detrimental to their self-images and creating unwanted identities of disability (Priestley, 1999).

There is an emerging discussion among disability theorists over the effect that these several challenges exert on the understanding of disability. In a recent consideration of the several models of disability, Beaudry (2016) states that proponents of the different models may be operating at cross-purposes, being driven more by concerns over supporting pre-existing political positions than by considerations of current topics affecting PWDs. That author recommends that the concept of disability itself should either be left sufficiently broad and inclusive to allow for these considerations or, alternatively, that the concept of disability itself could be abandoned. This latter option would allow for meaningful dialogue "without being hindered by debates about the nature of disability" (p. 210).

Other recommendations regarding the future use of this term have also been put forward. Linton (1998) states that the term should be retained but with a new, albeit unspecified, meaning. Oliver and Barnes (2012) argue that the term should be maintained for its political value, while acknowledging a wide range of understandings across cultures and time. Galvin (2003) recommends that the disability identity be dissolved as a means to avoid confusion based on prior definitional interpretations.

A review of these several interpretations and arguments reveals a continuum of meanings associated with disability, anchored at one end by directly representational understandings. In that instance, disability describes an objectively identifiable state that, based on the observer's available information, is capable of definition (Watson, 2012). Within this location, the observation of a wheelchair user is understood to incorporate previously held expectations of that category of disability with direct observations of the individual.

At the other end of this continuum are those understandings that interpret disability as consequential, resulting from a range of social forces (Oliver, 1990; Thomas, 1999b). Arguments are also put forward along various points of this continuum that suggest that disability is created through a blending, to various degrees, of the representational and consequential, with the relative input of each of these components being moderated by external influences (Anastasiou & Kauffman, 2013; WHO, 2001).

A final consideration associated with the use of the term *disability* is the discrepancy between the understandings that exist within scholarly debate, the general public, and those PWDs who are not actively engaged in following those theoretical discourses. Harpur (2012), in an analysis of the term as a prelude to a further consideration of associated language, draws upon de Bouvoir, Websters Online Dictionary, Roman mythology, Dante, and several linguistic considerations from within the academy to point out that the term itself is historically entrenched and inherently negative.

We agree with those who argue that the term *disability* itself should be abandoned. However, we see this as a longer term project and will maintain the term for purposes of this book. The definition that we employ understands disability as:

> *a consequential, cognitively-framed interpretation of initial, affective responses to individuals perceived to be living with impairments that signal a negatively valenced difference from the social norm.*

Within this framework, the perceptions of those impairments that generate this degree of difference will vary based on social and cultural context. Disability, therefore, is not understood as a pre-existing trait of the individual so perceived; nor does it represent a state of socially imposed oppression or political restriction. Instead, it is a symbolic representation of those pre-cognitive mental processes that are initiated within the sympathetic nervous system (SNS) of the observer upon a perception of difference. Analogous to a range of "evolved preparedness to ancestral threats" that are triggered from within these rudimentary processes, such as fear of heights, snakes, and spiders (Hoehl, Hellmer, Johansson, & Gredeback, 2017, p. 1), these responses do not necessarily require prior learning by the individual (Poulton & Menzies, 2002; Seligman, 1971). Although a wide range of social and cultural influences may serve as mediators, these core perceptions are based on very primitive, acognitive[1] mental processes that scan for basic fight/flight, good/bad, friend/foe determinations. The mental process that determines disability begins with the creation of a representational simulacrum conjured as an immediate affective response to these primitive perceptions and ends with the generation of a cognitively categorized explanation of this same primitive response.

Most significantly, the initial response to these perceptions of difference, including those associated with PWDs in the workplace, is negative. However, as with these other examples, research indicates that these perceptions of disability may be modified through experience, exposure, or training (Barr & Bracchitta, 2012; Kulkarni, Gopakumar, & Patel, 2017). Disability is understood, not as an object, but as a socially and individually malleable subject of the perception of others.

A second set of mediating factors is of a categorical nature. Initial perceptions of a negative difference associated with disability appear to be mediated by gender and age, with younger people, and females in particular, being found to be more accepting of PWDs in workplace environments (Barr & Bracchitta, 2012; Stone & Colella, 1996). Various hypotheses have been advanced to explain these findings, including the effects of more frequent exposure to PWDs by younger people within the school system and the more inherently nurturing nature of women (Hyde, 2006). At a more neurological level, and according to current analyses of the SNS, women tend to be less sensitive than men to excitatory stimuli of the SNS and, correspondingly, more sensitive to inhibitory stimuli (Hinojosa-Laborde et al., 1999). This more limited response could result in a reduced sense of any negative aspect of difference. Activation of the SNS has also been found to be positively correlated to increased age (Esler et al., 2002). Similarly, this heightened level of activation could increase that perception of negativity.

In summary, disability is conceived as a cognitively constructed representation of an affective response to a perceived potential for harm. It is not directly correlated with any particular impairment other than through social influence. Although we have made use of the term *disability* throughout this book, we apply this relational meaning throughout, with the exception of various references to others' use of the term.

> During the drafting of the first published descriptions of the difference model of disability (Breen, 2018a; Breen & Forwell, 2020), we had considered making use of the semiotic *Dif** as a new identifier of and for individuals who live with impairments. There were several reasons, both pro and con, for this consideration. On the pro side, we thought that this would circumvent the ongoing political debate, providing a new and relatively value-neutral descriptor. We agree with Galvin (2003) and others who have noted that the disability identity itself would benefit from its own dissolution.
>
> We had also surmised that this semiotic would provide a definition that implies that *impairment* is neither a devaluing characteristic nor that PWDs are inadequate (Silvers, 2003). As noted by Finkelstein (1991), "disability itself has come to mean 'unable to work'"(p. 8). Finally, we had surmised that this term could be more acceptable to those individuals who live with impairments and who may see themselves as socially excluded or atypical but who do not identify with a label of disability (Watson, 2012). This group includes some seniors with late-in-life impairments, members of the Deaf and Blind communities, some with learning disabilities, and youth, many of whom do not consider themselves appropriately described within the current nomenclature (Priestley, 1999; Shakespeare, 2014).
>
> However, further consideration led us to postpone the introduction of Dif* as a replacement for disability until a more fulsome consideration of the difference model itself has been presented and critiqued. We welcome comments by readers – *Breen & Forwell.*

Attitudes

In very broad terms, attitudes are described as constructs containing a *mental process* that is used to *evaluate* a *stimulus* (Eagly & Chaiken, 1993; Fishbein & Ajzen, 1975). This construct, comprised of behavioural, affective, and cognitive components (Eagly & Chaiken, 1993; Findler, Vilchinsky, & Werner, 2007), is described as residing along a valenced continuum from negative to positive (Findler et al., 2007). Fishbein & Ajzen (1975) indicate that these evaluations can be generated by objects, ideas or psychological constructs.

Acceptance

Definitions of acceptance vary considerably within the research literature. Acceptance has been considered as a means of predicting attitude change (Eagly & Telaak, 1972) and has also been understood as a means to measure changes to specific attitudes (Thurstone, 1928). Within the context of disability, researchers have used the term *acceptance* as a specific, quantifiable measure of attitude, wherein increasingly positive attitudes are understood to be more accepting of disability (Gething & Wheeler, 1992). Similarly, increasingly negative attitudes are understood as being less accepting, with "nonaccepting attitudes associated with a view of these people as separate or different, the usual implication being that the difference implies deficiency or inferiority" (p. 75). Others, although agreeing that acceptance is a means of measuring attitude, argue that the acceptance of PWDs is not necessarily associated with any perceived moral deficiency (Taylor & Bogdan, 1989). Still others suggest that *acceptance* and *attitude* are typically used somewhat interchangeably (Hunt & Hunt, 2004). In a literature review of factors affecting the acceptance of disabled employees, Vornholt et al. (2013) acknowledge this variety of interpretations. These authors also suggest that the term has not been clearly defined within an employment context.

Throughout this book, we distinguish acceptance from attitude and, following Gething and Wheeler (1992), consider the former to be a quantified measure of the latter, with a greater measure of acceptance indicating a more positive attitude toward PWDs in the workplace. In addition, although potentially mediated by personal characteristics unrelated to disability, we understand acceptance to be negatively correlated with perceptions of difference.

Normal or Typical

Within the context of disability, we want to clearly identify the difference in meaning that we ascribe to *normal* and *typical.* The latter term, *typical,* is most often associated with frequency or likelihood, without a defined negative boundary, but which considers examples that are less likely or frequent as *atypical.* Conversely, the former term, *normal,* is a more bounded description, beyond which circumstances, or subjects, become *abnormal* (Linton, 1998). As described below in Chapter 5, the difference model of disability stretches the boundary of *normal* to include those who may currently be described as *atypical,* leaving the construct of *abnormal* as an empty set.

Horizon of Social Notice

Impairments that signal a sufficiently significant degree of negative difference to be interpreted as disabilities are described as those that rise above *the horizon of social notice* (Breen, 2018a; Breen & Forwell, 2021). Within this concept, particular *horizons* correlate with socially influenced factors such as culture, location, and political perspectives. A determination of *social notice* is the tipping point beyond which a neutrally valenced difference becomes negative.

The Difference Model

The name *difference model* was selected for two reasons. First, the name provides a relatively neutral characterization of individuals who identify as having an impairment. It is an attempt to avoid politically contested descriptions such as disabled people, people with disabilities, the disabled, or the impaired (Barnes, 1999). Each of these terms has come to imply, at least to some, that PWDs are inadequate or devalued (Silvers, 2003). The naming of the difference model is our response to Garland-Thomson (2006), who lamented that "people with disabilities and those who care about them flee from the language of *crippled* or *deformed* and have no other alternatives (italics in original)" (pp. 268–269).

Second, the language of the difference model offers an identity to individuals who may see themselves as *different*, not within the currently defined *ingroup* (Goffman, 1963), or merely outside of what today is considered to be *normal*, but who are not necessarily willing or interested in self-identifying as people with disabilities.

Knowledge Gaps, Perspectives, and Limitations

Knowledge gaps within the research associated with employment and PWDs fall within two distinct categories. The first of these is the lack of quantifiable data available through the administration of measures to determine either the causes or valence of attitudes toward PWDs, particularly as these apply in the workplace.

Instrument effectiveness is determined, in large part, by the degree to which a measure demonstrates both empirical and theoretical evidence of validity (Messick, 1995). Without these demonstrations, inferences made from any resulting data are meaningless (Hubley & Zumbo, 1996). Currently available attitude measures are generally considered to be without a suitable degree of psychometric analysis (Antonak, 1988) and lacking in sufficient theoretical coherence to be reliable (Breen, 2018b).

The second principal research gap may more fairly be described as a research stasis that is associated with explorations of the causes of the ongoing employment challenges faced by PWDs. For many researchers, particularly those working within the social model of disability (Oliver, 1990) and its descendants, the questions regarding the underlying causes of this dilemma are considered to be largely answered. These focus on shortcomings within the built environment and ongoing disability-related factual misunderstandings on the part of employers. However, these assumptions are generally untested and contradict the continued reality of the low rates of employment for PWDs that have remained constant for at least the past 40 years (Rioux & Patton, 2014). For example, this consistency in employment rates does not correlate with the significant improvements that have been implemented following legislative reform within the built environment across many societies (see, for example, the Americans with Disabilities Act, 1990; the UK Disability Discrimination Act, 1995; the UK Equality Act, 2010; the Accessible Canada Act, 2019).

Finally, throughout this book, we illustrate and attempt to resolve a procedural gap that exists within the relative solitudes that exist between quantitative and qualitative examinations of the employment challenges of PWDs. We describe an approach that engages both of these modalities in support of the difference model of disability.

Note

1 Where applicable throughout this text, we have used the term acognitive as a means to express that the difference model, although not cognitively-based, is derived from a specific mental process, albeit one that is affect-based. The use of the prefix "non-" is more commonly "used to express negation" (see Oxford English Dictionary (1997, n.p.). This latter form may incorrectly be interpreted to infer a lack of any mental process.

3 Attitudes, Disability, and Employment

As defined in Chapter 2, attitudes are considered to be valenced responses to various stimulus categories. These categories include objects (i.e. people with disabilities [PWDs] in the workplace), ideas (i.e. skills, performance, costs), and psychological constructs (i.e. disability). It is generally agreed that these responses are generated through a mental process. However, the nature of that process itself is the subject of ongoing debate amongst theorists.

For our purposes, we consider one particular aspect of this debate. That is, whether a cognitive analysis of a specific object, idea, or construct generates an affective response which results in a propensity for a specific behaviour (or the behaviour itself); or whether the first step in this procedural chain is a more immediate affective response that stimulates a secondary cognitive process to provide explanation and consonance with other, related attitudes. This determination is critical, not only as a building block within theory development, but also at the level of practice when considering whether to focus on affective or cognitive premises in efforts designed to impact relationships between PWDs and the workplace.

As we describe throughout this book, we ascribe to the second of these options. This choice has been based on a review of practice, as well as theoretical arguments. We first present this argument in summary form and in greater detail throughout this chapter. Specifically, we have applied a retroductive analysis to the ongoing dilemma of low rates of employment on the part of PWDs. In other words, we have considered what reasons can be found that could explain this phenomenon.

We began by considering those reasons that are currently held out within the several current models of disability, examining the premises that uphold these arguments, and then screening each of these in terms of their efficacy in remediating the employment challenges that face PWDs. We arrived at two remainders after eliminating other options that have been demonstrated as ineffective. The first of these remainders was that of workplace attitudes toward PWDs as the principal cause of low employment rates and their accompanying challenges. To reach this remainder, we first eliminated arguments based on cognitive error. That error encompassed two general

DOI: 10.4324/9781003220695-3

categories – those associated with the built environment and those associated with personal workplace-related characteristics of PWDs.

The second of these remainders is that of the *affect first* position that we have adopted with regard to attitude formation. Essentially, these affective responses are what remains if cognitive responses are rejected as first reactions to stimuli. As described in more detail in the following section, we argue that attitudes toward PWDs are created within the IWOD as a function of very basic mental processes that are engaged initially without a cognitive component. These affect-based processes create a valenced response based on a recognition of difference rather than on a specific image of disability.

Understanding Attitude

To provide context for these positions, we first present a summary of the development of various understandings of attitude and then describe their relationships to PWDs and employment. First considered as measurable by Thurstone (1928), attitudes were considered to be "the sum total of a man's [*sic*] inclinations and feelings, prejudice or bias, pre-conceived notions, fears, threats, and convictions about any specified topic" (p. 529). Attitudes were described shortly thereafter by Allport (1935) as a state of "neural readiness" that was based on experience and which influenced individual responses to objects or situations.

Parsons (1951), within a structural functionalist description of society, first presented the relationship between PWDs and the larger community as a cognitive interpretation of social relationships. These relationships included obligations on the part of PWDs to make efforts to abandon what that author deemed to be positions of *social deviance* and return to being productive members of society.

These two determinations, of separating attitudes into component parts and representing attitudes as being most heavily influenced by cognitive processes, have been supported by many researchers (Eagly & Chaiken, 1993). Fishbein and Ajzen (1975) argue that the individual is, essentially, a rational processor of information and that evidence did not support an important role for "emotional or affective factors" (p. 215). This *cognition first* aspect of attitude creation implies a mental exercise resulting in a deliberate choice, regardless of whether that choice may ultimately be considered correct or even rational.

This position is not universally accepted. Other researchers suggest that attitudes are created initially by affect-based associations (Gawronski & Bodenhausen, 2006; Zajonc, 1980, 2000) and that the more sophisticated mental processes associated with cognition occur slightly later chronologically within a complex process designed to maintain a coherent worldview (Damasio, 1999). This latter argument follows from the concept of cognitive dissonance (Festinger, 1963), which points to the psychological reluctance involved in concurrently holding two disparate views. Additional support for this chronological orientation is provided by Fay (1996). Within a philosophical analysis of the relationship between experience and knowledge, Fay states that "experience is like a sign whose meaning must be derived from seeing how it is connected to other experiences and the situations in which it is located" (p. 19).

The *affect first* position has also found support within the field of disability and employment. Quadflieg, Mason, and Macrae (2010) refer to an earlier workplace-related study by Kleck, Ono and Hastorf (1966) in which, in their language, participants interviewed physically disabled and non-disabled applicants. When interviewing applicants with disabilities, participants were found to exhibit increased physical arousal, including galvanic skin responses. These participants also ended interviews more quickly. Blascovich et al. (2001), in a study that paired participants with a work partner, either an IWOD or a PWD with a visible disability, found increased cardiac rates in participants who had been paired with PWDs. Guglielmi (1999), in a review of issues related to prejudice, found nine studies that focused on psychophysiological responses associated with prejudice and disability. Each of these studies recorded various participant responses that were controlled by the autonomic nervous system. Eight of these nine studies found that psychophysiological responses indicated enhanced emotional discomfort on the part of participants in the presence of PWDs.

Two additional points are of note with regard to attitudes and their relationship to PWDs. First, although the debate continues over the roles played by cognition and affect within the formulation of attitudes, each of the current models of disability described in Chapter 4 relies upon a cognitively based perspective in its analysis of the relationship between PWDs and the larger community.

Second, a growing body of research indicates that attitudes, when applied to PWDs, demonstrate significant discrepancies within different contexts, particularly when comparing employment to other social relations. In a review of studies of employer attitudes toward PWDs that had been conducted between 1987 and 2012, it was found that employers indicated generally positive attitudes toward PWDs. However, these same employers were generally reluctant to hire PWDs, indicating concerns over whether PWDs would be able to perform required tasks (Burke et al., 2013). A similar response was given as the principal concern regarding the employment of PWDs by almost three-quarters of 3,797 employers who responded to a national study conducted by the American Department of Labor (Domzal et al., 2008). A recent study of 158 employers in Armenia found that a significant factor within employers' concerns regarding the hiring of PWDs was what was described as the potentially negative perception of PWDs by co-workers and customers (Breen, Havaei, & Pitassi, 2019). Other research has indicated that various cognitively based responses from employers with regard to rationales for not hiring PWDs, including skills deficits and increased employment costs, may well be masking negative affective responses to disability (Darcy, Taylor, & Green, 2016).

As we have described, the debate among researchers regarding whether these initial mental processes are principally representative of cognitive processes (Eagly & Chaiken, 1993; Fishbein & Ajzen, 1975) or affective processes (Damasio, 2010; Zajonc, 2000) has continued for an extended period. Based on a review of academic abstracts, these two perspectives have been relatively evenly represented since 1984 (Fiske, 2004). However, this distribution has not been particularly constant over this period. In a study of implicit reactions to disability, Dovidio et al. (2011) note that emotional reactions have returned relatively recently as an influential theme in research into prejudice. These reactions have been measured making use of functional magnetic resonance imaging, psychophysiological indices of automatic arousal, and response latency measures. These authors also indicate that distinctions between measures of implicit and explicit attitudes have been found to be consistent with similar variations between neuroscientific findings associated with the limbic system and the application of cognitively based models.

In 2016, one of us (Breen) was contracted by the United Nations Industrial Development Organization (UNIDO) to develop a national strategy for enhancing employment opportunities for PWDs in Armenia. This project included travelling to Armenia and working with a diverse group of stakeholders. This group included representatives from the government, non-governmental organizations (NGOs), the disability community, UNIDO, and private employers. This latter group was, however, not well represented in the initial planning sessions. In an attempt to gather additional information from the employer community, arrangements were made to meet individually with a representative from each of two privately owned organizations.

One such opportunity included Breen's attendance at a large manufacturing company, accompanied by two members of the Armenian branch of UNIDO. With Breen using a wheelchair, the delegation arrived at a facility with several stairs and no ramp. Two employees approached, picked Breen and his wheelchair up, and deposited him at the top of the stairs. Breen and his colleagues were ushered into the employer's office where it became clear that this interview had been granted as a formality and there was little interest in the topic of disability and employment.

However, as Breen described the project, it became equally clear that the employer had become interested in observing Breen both as a person with a visible disability and as someone who had been introduced as an international consultant from Canada. By the end of the meeting, this employer stated that he was in the planning process of building a new facility and that he was now going to instruct the architect to install a ramp at the front door. (adapted from Breen, Havaei, & Pitassi, 2019)

Attitude, Disability, and the Workplace

Stone and Colella (1996) posit a three-factor matrix in their analysis of influences on the employment success of PWDs. These factors include the legislative environment; the norms, values, and culture within individual organizations; and the personal characteristics of PWDs and co-workers. These personal characteristics include the type of impairment and the responses offered by PWDs to others' perceptions of disability. The characteristics of co-workers include previous experience with PWDs (Louvet, 2007).

Although we agree with these authors regarding their multi-faceted analysis of workplace factors that affect the employment success of PWDs, we suggest that there is an opportunity to build upon the approach taken by Stone and Colella (1996) through two separate lines of analysis. The first of these is based on the acknowledgement by these authors that much of their model is premised upon hypotheses to be explored in future research. Over the past 25 years, various research projects have been undertaken since that writing. These have generated significant amounts of relevant data that have variously supported, contradicted, or extended these hypotheses.

The second is that a determination of the efficacy of each of these factors may benefit from a reconsideration of their underlying premises. Specifically, each of these three factors is based on an assumption of cognitive error on the part of employers and co-workers that, once recognized, can be remediated through similarly oriented, cognitively based strategies. To illustrate, these authors cite The Glass Ceiling and Persons with Disabilities (Braddock & Bachelder, 1994), a report funded by the American Department of Labor, in suggesting that employers' ongoing and unfounded concerns regarding the "job-related abilities, performance levels, absenteeism, turnover rates and high costs of accommodation" (p. 353) of PWDs, despite clear evidence to the contrary, are a significant source of biasing and stereotyping of PWDs. We suggest that these strategies do not address the underlying affect-based responses to difference; instead, they attempt to respond to a second level of cognitive rationalization that has little effect on those precognitive responses.

Legislation – various supportive legislative regimes have been implemented in many countries, including the United States (e.g. Americans with Disabilities Act, 1990), Canada (e.g. Employment Equity Act, 1986, 1995), and the United Kingdom (e.g. Equality Act, 2010). However, each of these has failed to exert positive influences on these employment numbers (Barnes & Mercer, 2001; Clayton et al., 2011; Kidd, Sloane & Ferko, 2000).

An examination of the employment rates of PWDs within these several jurisdictions that have implemented legislation in an effort to improve rates of employment for PWDs indicates that these rates have remained relatively stagnant since these data were first gathered in the 1980s.

Although legislation that prohibits discrimination may well be a necessary condition for improving employment opportunities for PWDs, it has proven to be insufficient (Bruyère et al., 2016). As described above, legislative support for PWDs in the workplace, as epitomized in the United States by the Americans with Disabilities Act (1990), was anticipated to have a significant impact on the employment rates of PWDs. However, this has not been the case. The discrepancy between anticipated improvements to employment rates for PWDs following such legislated support and the current reality is clear. From 1990 to the present, rates of employment for PWDs have remained relatively stable at levels significantly lower than those for the general population (Rioux & Patton, 2014).

Hunt and Hunt (2004) note that most of the improvements associated with disability that have been initiated through legislative reform have been to structural barriers rather than to attitudinal barriers. However, it is attitudinal barriers that remain as the most significant obstacles to the employment of PWDs. (Kennedy & Olney, 2001; Stone & Colella, 1996).

Others have gone beyond this position of insufficiency, arguing that legislative supports can actually be counterproductive by blunting the political demands of PWDs (Campbell, 2005). A further point, not addressed in the above analysis, concerns the negative response by some organizations and IWODs who may believe that legislative supports provide an unfair advantage to PWDs, especially as this applies to the workplace. Fink (2008), in an analysis of "litigation-induced group bias" (p. 334), suggests that the litigation process itself, as it is associated with disability-related discrimination claims, can exacerbate and expand organizational bias toward PWDs as a group.

Colella (2001), noting that the Americans with Disabilities Act [ADA] (1990) "stipulates that workplace accommodations be provided to persons with disabilities so that they can perform essential job functions" (p. 101), describes how the provision of such workplace accommodations can generate individual perceptions of unfairness among co-workers. Colella creates a model that describes the several factors that influence these considerations, including the degree to which the accommodation is visible, the overall autonomy of the workplace, the general diversity climate, and the relevancy of the accommodation to the individual co-worker. This author indicates that these co-worker judgments of fairness associated with legislated requirements of disability-related accommodations can be of significant organizational impact.

We suggest that legislated means of addressing discriminatory employment practices, while serving as a rules-based framework necessary to support and resolve determinations of the acceptability of specific efforts and practices, cannot by itself bring about the attitude change necessary to generate these efforts and practices. And, as an unintended consequence, legislation has the potential to damage workplace relationships by inadvertently creating an enhanced degree of bias toward PWDs by some co-workers.

Corporate culture – the second contributor to the informing matrix of workplace relationships that exist for PWDs is that of corporate culture. Described by Stone & Colella (1996) as encompassing organizational norms and values, corporate culture is of influence in determinations of policies and practices, including those "associated with equity, standardization, impersonality, and separation of job and job holder" (p. 373). These authors illustrate these relationships by describing a dichotomous set of corporate cultures. On the one hand, bureaucratic organizations such as governments are understood to incorporate values of standardization and impersonality. These are anticipated to be disadvantageous for PWDs who "may be unable to comply with inflexible rules and procedures" (p. 373). In addition, these authors contend that bureaucratic organizations may be unwilling to provide accommodations for PWDs over concerns that others will perceive these personalized treatments as unfair. On the other hand, it is assumed that organizations that uphold values of social justice, cooperation, and helpfulness will be more suitable for PWDs.

More recent analyses of the relationship of corporate culture to the employment success of PWDs indicate that, unlike the assumption that more bureaucratically-oriented organizations, including governments and large corporations, would be more unlikely to engage PWDs, the opposite has been demonstrated. In an analysis of factors affecting employment rates of PWDs in the United Kingdom, Morris (2019) suggests that an overall reduction in employment opportunities within the government has been disproportionately difficult for PWDs "as they are more likely to find employment in the public sector rather than in the private sector" (p. 254). A recent American study of 466 non-government employers indicated that the effect of company size on rates of employment for PWDs was statistically significant. These rates ranged from 3.53% for large companies to 2.81% for medium-sized companies to 1.2% for small companies (Chan et al., 2021). In 2018, the employment rate for self-disclosed PWDs within the American federal government was 9.42% (United States Equal Employment Opportunity Commission, 2022).

As we describe in detail throughout this book, we agree that corporate culture has a significant influence on the success of PWDs within various employment venues. However, we suggest that the characteristics of these cultures are generated as a result of the attitudes toward PWDs that have percolated throughout these organizations, rather than the reverse. In other words, we argue that the overarching affective states of individuals within these organizations influence subsequent individual actions, policy development, and procedural solutions.

Personal characteristics – the influence of the personal characteristics of both PWDs and co-workers face a similar challenge. Stone & Colella (1996) hypothesize that the process begins with IWODs who generate categorical stereotypes of disability that assign initial traits, abilities, and characteristics to the PWD. These analyses are followed by an assignment of beliefs regarding individual PWDs that align with these predetermined characteristics and which are then followed by a comparison of these beliefs with the behaviours exhibited by the PWD. These several steps, according to these authors, culminate in the "subsequent affective responses" (p. 356) of the co-worker. Essentially, it is suggested that cognitively-generated stereotypes of various impairments lead to stereotypical analyses of individuals, followed by affect-influenced behavioural responses. However, these authors acknowledge that there has been little research directed toward understanding the processes that underly the attitudinal biases directed toward PWDs in the workplace. We suggest that the order of this process should be reversed, beginning with acognitive responses to difference, followed by cognitively framed explanatory rationales for these same behaviours. As we describe in detail in later chapters, this latter position is supported by more current research into attitude creation (Gawronski & Bodenhausen, 2006).

Finally, these authors cast PWDs in a light that would now be considered to be inaccurately needy and not particularly representative of disability in the workplace. Stone and Colella (1996) posit a requirement to address a workplace environment wherein PWDs are perceived as generating resentment on the part of co-workers due to various incapabilities. These same PWDs are in need of supervisors who are more able "to cope with the suffering experienced by disabled individuals" (p. 392).

Within this imaginary, it may well be the case where these personal characteristics of PWDs are of significant impact on the overall workplace relationship. However, research consistently indicates that approximately two-thirds of all employed PWDs do not require any procedural, structural, or equipment-related accommodations (Statistics Canada, 2017a). In addition, more than half of all employed PWDs indicate that they live with invisible disabilities. This discrepancy, between the self-declared impairments of employed PWDs and the implied incapability described above, casts significant doubt on the impact of this hypothesized contribution to workplace relationships. However, PWDs may well contribute to these workplace attitudes, not through demonstrations of "incapacity" and "suffering", but rather through the unintended consequences associated with adherence to relatively new models of disability, each of which (see Chapter Four below) posits a positioning of responsibility for disability that is, at least in part, external to individual PWDs. And, as with the more general construct of identity politics, this externalization informs an inherently dichotomous relationship between PWDs and IWODs (Barnes & Mercer, 2001).

Finally, there is an additional set of behavioural characteristics with regard to PWDs that has not yet been addressed but which adds a further level of complexity to the disability-related dynamics that exist in the workplace. These characteristics, resulting from a developing heterogenization of the construct of disability, can influence the range of responses on the part of PWDs within the workplace. Various groups who have previously been understood as PWDs, including those who have never adopted this mantle, and those who identify only categorically within the general rubric of disability, each bring particular perspectives and responses to the IWOD attitudes described above (see Chapter 7).

With little evidence of enhanced employment rates by PWDs to support a continued application of the above *error-driven* three-part model, a consideration of other influences becomes more critical. Over the past 40 years, many researchers have argued that the attitudes of employers, supervisors, and co-workers within the workplace are the most significant determinant of employment success for PWDs (Antonak, 1982; Burke et al., 2013; Copeland, Chan, Bezyak, & Fraser, 2010; Vornholt, Uitdewilligen, & Nijhuis, 2013). It is generally agreed that the degree to which these attitudes are positive or negative will substantially determine the social relationships that exist between PWDs and others within the workplace and that those relationships are of key influence in determining these levels of employment success of PWDs.

Of particular note is a determination that the baseline of employer attitudes toward PWDs is more negative than typically assumed. Kaye et al. (2011) indicate that, although much of the data that have been collected within vocational research have pointed toward "a generally rosy picture of successfully accommodated workers" (p. 526), frequent failures to consider bias based on both employer self-selection and on social desirability have resulted in artificially positive conclusions.

We have hypothesized that these employer attitudes toward PWDs are negatively correlated with what we have termed *observational complexity*. That is, PWDs who appear to be more challenged by their impairment, whether psychologically, cognitively, or physically, are understood to be less competent and skilled.

We further hypothesized that the dichotomous employer attitudes described by Burke et al. (2013), which indicated relatively positive attitudes toward PWDs coupled with a reluctance to hire, may be affected by this observational complexity. In other words, apparent complexities associated with disability could generate more globally positive feelings toward the PWD, especially if these complexities are perceived as being beyond the control of the PWD (Dovidio et al., 2000). However, these positive responses to complexity correspondingly imply more negative responses in terms of capability and employment skills. These positive feelings are associated with descriptions of PWDs being brave and kind, as well as dependent and isolated (Ross, 2001), rather than competent or skilled.

To test the relationship between observational complexity and more generally positive feelings toward individual PWDs, one of us (Breen) who variously relies on forearm crutches or a wheelchair as mobility aids, conducted a brief study wherein he positioned himself as a panhandler on a busy street corner in Victoria, British Columbia, Canada. Taking up a position on the centre median at a traffic light, Breen spent one hour, on two separate occasions, soliciting donations. He held out a ball cap affixed to a stick with a hand-lettered sign that read "Best Wishes" (see Figure 3.1). On the first occasion, using crutches, he received a total of $60.00 as well as three snack bars, an apple, and a banana. The mean donation was $3.00 (maximum donation was $5.00). On the second occasion, using his wheelchair, he received $75.00, one snack bar, and a candy roll. The mean donation was $5.00 (maximum donation was $20.00). On each occasion, the time and day of the week, weather, and clothing were similar. The number of vehicles was also very similar at ~350.

The street corner described above is one that is popular with a variety of people who ask for donations from drivers who stop at these traffic lights. On three separate occasions following this test, Breen stopped at this corner while driving, in order to make $2.00 donations to different individuals. In each instance, he asked the recipient, all of whom were women (and none of whom had a visible impairment), how much they earned in one hour. Each indicated that they received between $20 and $40.

Although undeniably lacking in sufficiently stringent controls, this brief experiment suggested that motorists felt increased compassion for a PWD as compared to an IWOD and that this level of compassion was more pronounced for a PWD who used a wheelchair as compared to the same individual who used crutches. These results appear to support our hypothesis of observational complexity. (*It should be noted that all proceeds obtained through this experiment were subsequently donated to a local charitable agency that provides a variety of supports to PWDs in need of such assistance.*)

Other research indicates that PWDs are perceived by employers as friendly and warm but lacking in competence and generally unsuitable for hiring (Fiske et al., 2002). As outlined above, employers most typically indicate that they believe PWDs are unable to perform the tasks required by

Figure 3.1 Comparing driver reactions – Dr Breen standing on the centre median of a busy street in Victoria, British Columbia, Canada (March 2022).

Source: Photograph courtesy of Vanora Millar.

their organizations (Domzal et al., 2008). In a review of 14 American companies, which generated almost 30,000 employee survey responses, an assumption of employees being able-bodied was a strong indicator of employee success (Schur, Kruse, Blasi, & Blanck, 2008). However, when these attitudes that associate PWDs with incapacity are examined, it is clear that the informing understandings of disability are both overly narrow and inappropriate within considerations of ability relative to specific jobs. Instead, an overarching affect-driven and negative response to disability allows for the acceptance of self-supporting assumptions. As illustrated in the following Text Box, the step from a generalized assumption of incompetence to conjuring up an example that "proves" that incompetence is not difficult to trace. No one would argue that some impairments may limit individual PWDs from participation in specific activities. However, a tendency to apply that generalized attitude of incapacity results in a "fill-in-the-blanks" exercise that becomes a self-fulfilling prophecy.

> One of us (Breen), while employed as the manager of the Workplace Diversity Employment Office with the Yukon government, attended an internal conference to consider issues of equity and the hiring of PWDs. A concern was raised by a department manager who stated that what may appear to be discriminatory behaviour on the part of hiring committees was actually a practical response to the operational needs of the organization. That manager indicated that his department was responsible for, among other things, sending technicians into wilderness locations by helicopter to do various environmental analyses. How, he asked, could a person in a wheelchair get into and out of a helicopter without exposing himself [*sic*] or his team to unnecessary danger? Breen responded by suggesting that the concept of disability was considerably broader than the image the manager had internalized and presented in order to support a prior assumption.

Many authors indicate that employers struggle with the need to provide accommodations for PWDs, whether these individuals are new or existing employees (Schur, Kruse, & Blanck, 2005). These struggles are understood to include employers' perceptions that costs associated with accommodations are significant. However, as noted above, a recent national Canadian survey indicates that approximately two-thirds of all employed PWDs do not require any workplace accommodations (Statistics Canada, 2017a). Furthermore, most required accommodations incur relatively minimal costs (Job Accommodation Network, 2015).

The impact of these negative attitudes as the principal barrier to the employment success of PWDs was supported in a review of 37 employers conducted by Hernandez, Keys, and Balcazar (2000). That review indicated that employers responded with relatively positive global attitudes toward PWDs but were more negative when queried about their hiring intentions and support for workplace accommodations.

The effect of employer attitudes is critical in that this group has the authority to hire and fire; however, co-worker attitudes are also of significance. The attitudes of this larger group of co-workers within the workplace clearly affect opportunities for success on the part of PWDs (Pruett & Chan, 2006). In this context, co-workers include all those "who might interact with or make judgments about disabled individuals" (Stone & Colella, 1996, p. 356).

Workplace attitudes, whether of employers or co-workers, are influenced by the various theoretical perspectives of disability itself. The difference model, as the name implies, understands PWDs as being framed within a *perception of difference* that is sufficiently significant to rise above the horizon of social notice (Breen & Forwell, 2021). Within this context, a particular attribute is viewed as a disability only when that attribute is perceived as a negative or limiting characteristic (Vehmas & Watson, 2014).

Attitude, Disability, and PWDs

As we have described above, the attitudes of others are held out by many theorists as containing various degrees of influence on the employment success of PWDs (Antonak & Livneh, 2000). However, there is little evidence that these attitudes have been parsed in sufficient detail to effectively inform remediative workplace efforts. We suggest that the strategic planning required to develop enhanced employment opportunities for PWDs will benefit from a detailed analysis of those relationships. This includes a separation between relatively positive societal attitudes toward PWDs and those found specifically in the workplace (Domzal, Houtenville, & Sharma, 2008) as well as the attitudes displayed toward disability as an overarching construct and within various categorizations of PWDs (Harpur, Connelly, & Blanck, 2017).

We adapt a technique from Thomas (2012), whose delineation of impairment effects, as both separate from but intermeshed with disablism, has provided theorists with a more nuanced understanding of the relationship between individual impairments and externally imposed limitations. Impairment effects are described as the bio-social and socially constructed impacts that physical, sensory, intellectual, or emotional impairments have on individuals. Disablism is considered to be the set of avoidable restrictions imposed by society on individuals living with impairments and through institutionalized social norms (Thomas, 2012). We recognize that there is a general acknowledgement that there is a separation between generic attitudes toward PWDs and those displayed within the workplace. However, we suggest that a similarly complex, and as yet undescribed, relationship exists between IWOD attitudes toward the generic construct of disability and attitudes toward individual PWDs.

Within this structure, generic attitudes toward disability are generated through relatively linear mental processes that begin with very basic affective responses to stimuli that induce fear, serve as warnings, or induce fight or flight responses (Buller, 2005). These initial responses may, in turn, be either moderated or rationalized by cognitive processes (Damasio, 1999). Over time, these attitudinal responses become homogenized into an overall representation of disability as a construct. This representational interpretation of disability then serves as a filter through which individual PWDs are evaluated. In some cases, the individual PWD becomes essentially invisible apart from that representation.

Susceptibility to Change

Although, as noted by Shildrick (2012) perceptions of disability and PWDs are fluid and may well change over time and location, attitude change is considered to be difficult and dependent upon training, exposure, and evolving social norms. Those who hold with a cognitively informed understanding of attitudes argue that new information generates a new analytical matrix, resulting in an opportunity for this change. Others, who argue for an affect-based understanding, suggest that these new stimuli may act as mediators on pre-existing acognitive, unlearned responses to a range of stimuli that trigger fight/flight or fear responses (Gawronski & Bodenhausen, 2006).

As discussed in several sections throughout this book, this debate regarding affect versus cognition is ongoing (Fiske, 2004). The difference model (see Chapter 5), as well as the two scales that have been developed within the theoretical framework of that model (see Chapter 6), are framed within the latter of these two positions. Although, from a neuropsychological perspective, there may still be considerable room for further research and debate, the application of the *affect first* position to our more practice-oriented focus on employment and PWDs has been supported by early demonstrations of theoretical and psychometric coherence.

4 Models, Theory, and Assumptions

Models and Disability

Within the social sciences, individual constructs such as disability may be described within several different models, each of which is intended to consider a separate dimension of that construct (Lave & March, 1975). Models are, essentially, hypotheses about particular processes and how these processes may characterize, reflect, and produce observed facts.

Models are considered to be simplified pictures of an aspect of interest within the real world (Oliver & Barnes, 2012). Models are distinguished from theories in that the latter are explanatory, while the former are more narrow and descriptive (Oliver, 1990). In addition, models are intended only to illustrate or represent specific features, properties or characteristics of a particular construct (Beckett & Campbell, 2014).

We begin this consideration by providing a brief overview of the concept of models within the social sciences; the relationship between people with disabilities (PWDs) and employment; moving the discourse beyond cognition; bringing into focus the construct of attitudes; and reflecting on attitudes and their influence on PWDs in the workplace. We will then provide a summary of the several cognitively based models of disability, with an emphasis on their relationships to PWDs, before providing a fulsome description of the difference model.

This chapter also includes a detailed description of the several models of disability, particularly as these have been influenced by macro sociological assumptions and the effects of language on perceptions of disability. We will compare and contrast these models, including analyses of their chronological relationships and the purposes for which each has been developed. Finally, we will consider the recently introduced concept of ontological validity and its impact on any determination of legitimacy associated with models and definitions of disability. The overarching purpose of this chapter is to provide a framework, both conceptually and linguistically, for further considerations of disability and the relationships between PWDs and others.

We agree with Oliver and Barnes (2012), who state that models are understood as simplified descriptions of reality that focus on specific

DOI: 10.4324/9781003220695-4

characteristics of that reality. By extension, this argument suggests that none of the several models of disability is necessarily to be considered as *correct* but each may be of value in assisting with understanding particular aspects of disability. In addition, although each of these several models of disability may well demonstrate internal coherence, we extend the position put forward by Beaudry (2016) to argue that the inherent differences found within the several models, and the theoretical frameworks upon which they are based, are so contradictory that any evaluation of relative correctness is impossible.

This notion of incompatibility, or *incommensurability*, as described by Fay (1996) in a consideration of epistemological and ontological relativism, refers to differences that are so deep within different conceptual schemes as to be without common measure. Fay also suggests that an individual conceptual scheme is not susceptible to rational scrutiny from outside of that particular scheme, since any enquiry must be conducted within the terms of the framework that provides the criteria in support of explanations or judgements. To make use of an analogy from mathematics, one need only consider trying to determine the relative correctness of two arithmetic solutions, the first derived through a base ten imaginary and the second through another that relies upon a base eight framework. Each will present an equally coherent internal structure and yet reveal significantly different results.

Various descriptions of the relationship between employment and PWDs have been found, either directly or through implication, within an expanding group of models of disability, including the moral model (Albrecht, 1992; Mackelprang, 2010), medical model (Parsons, 1951), variations of the social model (Thomas, 2007), the embodiment model (Shakespeare, 2004), the minority model (Mitchell & Snyder, 2012), and the Nordic relational model (Goodley, 2013).

As will be apparent within the descriptions provided next, each of these models has generated a number of variations as they have become more nuanced and refined over time by different theorists. However, each shares a single, most basic assumption. They each rely upon a cognitively based set of premises, which have been variously understood as purposeful, negligent, or inadvertent (Bonaccio et al., 2019; Silvers, 2003).

Each of these models argues that life could, and should, be better for PWDs. However, the location of the responsibility, the methods, and the forces required to create that change – especially, whether it resides internally within the individual, externally within society, or in a relationship created by the interaction of these two locations – separates these approaches.

With a focus specifically on employment, it is clear that the application of these models has not resulted in increased rates of employment for PWDs (Breen 2018a; Breen & Forwell, 2020). This failure is particularly evident when considering that the employment rates of PWDs have not changed significantly since these data were first gathered in the 1980s (Rioux & Patton, 2014).

Prior to describing each of these models in some detail, we will first consider an anticipated response to the above critique. It has been suggested that the difficulty is not with the models themselves, at least as this applies to the social model, but to a lack of appropriate application (Oliver, 2013). This sentiment is echoed by Barnes (2019), although that author acknowledges that the various legislative measures and policy initiatives that have been developed within a social model framework have been largely ineffective in improving the economic and social lives of PWDs. Barnes also leaves open an opportunity for further enquiry into determining the reasons why these measures have been unsuccessful.

We suggest that these explanatory determinations of the ongoing improper application of social model tenets may be illustrative of a larger and more challenging critique of the social model in particular and to model generation and application in general. As is generally acknowledged, the social model of disability was first clearly framed in the United Kingdom by the Union of the Physically Impaired Against Segregation (UPIAS, 1976). During the intervening period, which at the time of this writing is more than 45 years, a lack of appropriate application speaks to a larger challenge that cannot easily be explained away as a continuous failure on the part of employers, legislators, and others to "get it right." Instead, the model itself may well be instrumentally insufficient to serve as an effective framework for addressing issues of employment.

More generally, the cognitively based arguments put forward by these models, which premise workplace solutions principally within the procedural and built environments, have not led to any improvements in the employment rates of PWDs.

Any determination of the value of any or all of these models should be based on their predictive ability, be testable, and address real-world empirical problems (Altman, 2001). These determinants, and their associated analyses, provide evidence for the validity of their underlying premises. According to Oliver (2009):

> All social theory must be judged on three interrelated elements: its adequacy in describing experience; its ability to explain experience; and, finally, its potential to transform experience (p. 89).

We suggest that the models of disability described next do not adequately resolve the social-relational challenges that continue to exist in the workplace between IWODs and PWDs. They have failed to consider the relationship between the ontological drivers of these social relations and the epistemologically driven solutions that have been put forward. They have most commonly been focused on ameliorating symptoms rather than considering causes.

It is our contention that workplace-related relationships between PWDs and others are driven at a most basic level by emotion. Applying the affect-based difference model of disability provides a new theoretical framework to serve as a guide and support for the development of organizational strategies to enhance these workplace relationships. As will be noted next, we discuss several characteristics of the difference model itself that distinguish it from other models; however, we argue that it is this single differentiating premise of affect rather than cognition as the driver of workplace relationships that is key to addressing this obdurate challenge of employment.

Prior to describing the development and real-world applications of the difference model, we provide a preliminary sketch of the environment, both theoretical and practical, within which it has been developed. Our purpose in presenting a relatively extensive foregrounding framework within which the difference model is described is twofold.

First, the difference model, similar to other models within the social sciences, is contextual. That context speaks to its purpose and potential value. Second, a description of that same context provides a more ready opportunity for critique.

As noted above, it is possible to create several models of the same construct, each of which has been intended to consider a different structural or procedural aspect of that particular construct (Lave & March, 1975). However, if the selection of that specific aspect as a focal point for a particular model is based upon a pre-existing sociological or politico-ideological position, the model itself risks being inherently biased or *perspectivized* (Schatzman, 1991). That perspectivized model is less likely to objectively describe a construct and more likely only to serve as a support for the validity of its premises. Such bias can be avoided through the prior consideration of other options in order to determine which provides the most useful analysis (Kools et al., 1996).

Disability theorists have frequently acknowledged this biasing influence of pre-existing ideologies on the development of models of disability. Shakespeare (1994) states that the social model of disability has been developed within an anti-capitalist ideology. This challenge is elaborated upon by Corker (1999a), who notes that the development of models of disability has "often [been] designed from within particular perspectives conceived at particular times in history which do not reflect 'disability' and 'society' as we understand it today" (p. 628). Thomas (1999a) acknowledges that any attempts to explain disability-related questions are driven by the previously developed theoretical framework one applies to the social world. Priestley (1998) creates a four-quadrant matrix of models of disability – individual versus social and materialist versus idealist – representing the four main approaches to considerations of disability theory. Priestley then argues that each of these has been based on premises that support their particular models but that none meet the criterion of being testable.

Other writers recognize and acknowledge their reliance on prior personal experiences to inform model development. Rioux (1997) addresses this consideration by stating that researchers have a moral obligation to consider and to acknowledge their worldviews, in recognition of the fact that these will influence any subsequent interpretations of disability. Albrecht (1992) notes that Talcott Parsons, an influential proponent of the medical model of disability, developed the *sick role* mantle for PWDs following his personal experiences in seeking help for his own illness. Hughes (2019), in what he describes as a "confessional desire", characterizes his identity as a "white, able-bodied, heterosexual, Anglo-Saxon male" (p. 25) with neither personal experience of either impairment or disability. Hughes adds to this description by providing an account of his developing relationship to disability and PWDs. Each of these examples illustrates the challenges associated with disentangling the premises driven by personal experience from Priestley's testability.

A further challenge to the interpretation of models of disability is the impact of changing social relationships and language usage. Abberley (1987) states that the premise of *oppression*, as contained within the social model of disability, was first used as an equivalent to *exploitation* (citing Oliver, 1986) but later was interpreted more structurally, as an obvious characteristic of social relations that had been informed by capitalism. Abberley also maintains, to be considered oppression, activities must contain a degree of purposefulness. However, Barnes and Mercer (2003) argue that various social activities may generate oppression through inadvertence. This theme is expanded by Shakespeare (2014), who describes disability-related oppression as including unwitting prejudice, thoughtlessness, and ignorance.

A number of safeguards have been proposed to address these linguistic and ontological challenges to the premises supporting various models of disability. Kools et al. (1996) argue for a comparative analysis to safeguard against the incorporation of premises that influence analyses of models toward a specific goal, whether purposeful or inadvertent. Another safeguarding approach is to consider how best to evaluate a particular model. Altman (2001) states that the value of a model is determined by its ability to correctly predict new facts. Specifically, this determination of value requires that a model must be testable and should be evaluated based on its ability to consider empirical problems. This relationship of a model to the real world can only be determined by evaluating the truth of that model's derivations or predictions (Lave & March, 1975).

As described next in more detail (see Chapter 5), we have attempted to meet this challenge by generating validity evidence for the difference model through a reflexive analysis, including a consideration of ontological validity. In addition, we have generated quantifiable analyses based on two workplace attitude measures developed subsequent to, and based upon, that model.

Current Models of Disability

At the outset, we wish to state that we have selected the following models of disability (see Table 4.1) as representative of the broad spectrum of

Table 4.1 Sample of models of disability and location of social responsibility

Model of Disability	*Individual Context*	*Social Context*	*Location of Responsibility*
Moral	Cognitive/Personal	Ethical/Religious	Individual
Medical	Cognitive/Personal	Political	Individual
Social	Cognitive/Political	Political	Society
Embodiment	Cognitive/Relational	Relational	Individual & Society
Nordic	Cognitive/Relational	Relational	Individual & Society
Difference	Affective/Social Notice	Social Notice	None (relational only)

Source: Adapted from Breen (2018a).
Note: The relationship between models of disability, their social context, and implications for the individual.

positionings put forward along the dimension of social responsibility and in terms of their considerations of PWDs relative to the larger community and to employment. In addition, the following summaries should not be understood as complete in either breadth or depth, or in terms of the many subtleties that have been debated to address critiques and to remain contemporary.

Others have explored models of disability from quite different perspectives. To illustrate, Altman (2001) describes eight different models of disability, without mentioning the medical or embodiment models. Within a different representation, Mitra (2006) subdivided the social model into nine distinct categories. Disabled World, an internationally known website that presents a range of disability-related information, describes 19 models of disability (Disabled World, 2021).

Finally, the models that we describe are also representative of what has not been debated; that is, any consideration of options other than a cognitively based framing of the construct of disability. Our intention is to describe and juxtapose these several models and associated representations of PWDs with our current project – the development of an affective model of disability and its application to supporting employment opportunities for PWDs.

We would also like to acknowledge that each of these other models described next has had significant value. The moral model has served as a means to provide spiritual coherence in the face of a lack, or lack of acceptance, of scientific evidence. The medical model has offered various methods of prolonging and optimizing life for those incurring traumatic injury and other impairments. The social model has served as a political rallying point for millions of PWDs. The embodiment model has offered meaning to many whose impairments are neither credibilized nor ameliorated through external manipulations or accommodations.

Keeping in mind the various challenges that may beset the creation and application of models of disability, we now describe the first five of these models (as illustrated in Table 4.1). The first of these, the moral model of disability, is most typically referred to within a historical context in current academic considerations. However, as we describe next, it remains a viable worldview for many who may be in contact with, and have influence over, PWDs. As such, its magico-religious construction cannot be easily discounted.

The next three models of disability – the medical, social, and embodiment models – are most commonly considered within current Western discussions of disability theory. Each of these provides a description of disability that is intended to address discriminatory social challenges. Each of these models contains assumptions that change is both possible and necessary. As described in more detail next, these models are separated by their positioning along a common dimension of political and social responsibility. Then the lesser-known Nordic model is described with its unique appreciation of disability, based on premises common to the embodiment model. These models and varied understandings, whether focused on the individual PWD (medical model), society (social model), or a combination of the two (embodiment model), inform correspondingly different methodologies for resolving these agreed-upon social challenges. The last model discussed in Table 4.1, the difference model, will then be described in detail in the subsequent chapter.

The Moral Model

The moral model of disability is clearly distinguished from the three models that follow. Its principal assumption is that disability is a punishment appropriately inflicted by a higher power upon individuals for personal or historical moral transgressions. Although the moral model may no longer be a pervasive worldview, and be given little consideration within much of Western writing, it remains as a summative analysis of a magico-religious explanation for disability across wide swathes of the world population. This explanation has generally followed one of two paths. Most commonly, disability is understood as punishment; however, disability has also been understood as a test of faith (Retief & Letsosa, 2018). These same authors also indicate that most, but not all, theologians and biblical scholars reject this model of disability. Elsewhere, research conducted in 2008 discovered that 50% of Indian families surveyed maintained this outlook on disability (Goodley, 2013). In a Western context, Wendell (1997), a well-known disability theorist, describes her personal circumstance of living with chronic fatigue syndrome (also known as myalgic encephalomyelitis) as being reported by the media in the mid-1980s as "a punishment of nature visited upon the ambitious, especially ambitious women" (p. 62).

Some researchers suggest that only the medical and social models of disability are of current significance (Cluley et al., 2020). Others mention the moral model as present but only occasionally invoked to elicit pity (Andrews, 2017). However, writing within a context of disability theology,

Creamer (2012) acknowledges that the moral model, along with the medical model, are so ingrained in American culture that they are often not recognized as interpretations. Instead, they are treated as accurate depictions of disability.

Creamer (2012) also notes that Christian moral model interpretations of disability "still linger in hymns (such as Amazing Grace), sermons (and) bible studies" (p. 342) and motivate resistance to inclusive hiring practices and modifications to the built environment. As recently as 1986, individuals with what were termed "significant" physical, mental, or physical disabilities were determined by the General Convention of the American Lutheran Church to be unfit for the ordained ministry (Eiesland, 2005).

These examples illustrate that, although recent academic debate has largely chosen to frame the moral model of disability as antiquated and no longer relevant, such is not necessarily the case within public perception. For this reason, the moral model cannot be ignored when considering employment, PWDs, and the attendant attitudes of some IWODs within the workplace.

The moral model most typically indicates that disability itself is a punishment for some form of prior morally reprehensible action. As such, it categorizes disability as unavoidably negative. This model is driven by an acceptance of justifiable punishment as meted out by an external, or externalized, entity. The moral model of disability assigns responsibility and blame to the individual, whether for personal or ancestral moral transgressions. As a core characteristic of the individual perceived as a PWD, this burden of psychical responsibility cannot help but weigh heavily on subsequent decisions regarding any potential selection for or maintenance of employment.

As noted, the moral model of disability no longer serves as the only image of disability. However, its premise of personal responsibility lingers within the medical model. As described next, Parsons (1951) argued that individuals were not necessarily responsible for acquiring their impairments. Instead, that moral responsibility was shifted. No longer understood as a causal link to the acquisition of an impairment, Parsons argued that there was a moral responsibility to eliminate that same impairment.

The Medical Model

The medical model of disability emerged in the late 19th century. Based on a humanist interpretation of the social environment, the medical model replaced the magico-religious notion of universal imperfection with defined boundaries between the acceptable and the unacceptable (Foucault, 1988; Stainton, 2004). In addition, it rejected the punishment-oriented aspects of the moral model.

Each of the several iterations of the medical model was a response to moral or religious explanations of disability. Whether premised upon modernist ideology (Barnes, Mercer, & Shakespeare, 1999), the industrial revolution (Oliver, 1990), language (Goffman, 1963), or a rift between reason and unreason (Stainton, 2004), new scientific methods and the medicalization of disability were understood to be the most progressive way to understand and treat illness (Oliver, 1990). The emerging medical model described the application of what was then considered to be leading-edge technology and newly discovered scientific understandings of individual impairments (Shakespeare, 2006).

The developing interventionist nature of medical science (Barnes, Mercer, & Shakespeare, 1999) coupled with the ethical support provided by the application of newly developed statistical tools to the social sciences, in which the *norm* became associated with the *good,* were combined to support the repair or transformation of those considered to be *deviant* (Rogers, 1995). It was argued that, thanks to medical science, this deviance could now be overcome. Medical science became the recognized, and accepted, corrective instrument for resolving the *deviance* generated by disability.

Regardless of the efforts to relieve suffering and to repair what were seen as physical, emotional, and mental aberrations, the medical model was premised on incapacity, illness, and an authoritarian relationship between care providers and recipients. In addition, the perception of disability as an individualized personal tragedy and incapacity was well entrenched within the medical community (Barnes, Mercer, & Shakespeare, 1999) and accepted as such by various policy-making bodies (Birch & Longmore, 2009).

The medical model has been criticized for its lack of consideration of the subjective experience of impairment, including the social causes of at least some illnesses (Oliver, 1990). However, the medical model cannot easily be dismissed. Although often portrayed within archaic, 19th-century imagery associated with medical misconceptions and gruesome procedures inflicted upon PWDs (Barnes, Mercer, & Shakespeare, 1999), the medical model developed within a period of ontological reconstruction. Modernism, with its emphasis on the individual and a positivist worldview, was replacing long-held religious dogma that stifled scientific exploration and precluded experimentation as a basis for knowledge.

This transition allowed for scientific solutions to be applied to individual impairments (Shakespeare, 2006). The development of the medical model was the embodiment of this transition. Although current proponents of other models of disability, particularly the social model, argue against the continued acceptance of the medical model, that model continues to be acknowledged for its transitional value (Oliver, 1990). The medical model introduced the notion that disability was not purposefully imposed by an external force and, as such, was capable of remediation. The way to that remediation included the application of technological discoveries, newly developed surgical techniques, and pharmaceutical interventions (Aptowicz, 2014). It was thought that, by remediating those with disabilities, they would be transformed from social *deviants* (Parsons, 1951) into what Goffman (1963) would later refer to as *normals.*

Parsons (1951) developed a comprehensive medical model analysis of the relationship between PWDs; that is, the *deviants*, and society. Illness itself was considered to be *deviant behaviour*. This author described those with living with an impairment or illness as adopting a *sick role*, which was a failure to meet the expectations of an individual's participation and contribution within society. Parsons maintained that those who were ill were not at fault for their illness but that they had a moral responsibility and corresponding duty to make every effort to return to a state of what was considered to be normal functioning. This requirement of recovery included the seeking and accepting of appropriate medical advice (Shilling, 2002). Within this description, the behavioural requirements of PWDs included their active support for technological interventions.

More current descriptions of the medical model of disability include those which focus on the absence of disease and the ability to carry out typical bodily activities and functions (Boorse, 1977). However, the concept of disability continues to be defined as a deviation from structural or functional norms, caused by trauma, disease or other health conditions (Bickenbach et al., 1999).

The medical model, at its core, focuses on illness and the body in which it is seen to be situated. The intent is to intervene in a manner that will reduce functional limitations based on biological impairments. This focus is still seen as predominant, although many current proponents and practitioners of the medical model acknowledge the environmental impact on both the cause and consequences of disease (Williams, 2001).

Proponents of the medical model argue that it is being misrepresented (Shah & Mountain, 2007). Scientific rigour, characterized by "observation, description and differentiation, which moves from recognizing and treating symptoms to identifying disease aetiologies and developing specific treatments" (p. 375) is, according to these authors, inaccurately portrayed as relegating people with disabilities to the status of *the problem*. It is also argued by these same authors that critics of the medical model present a reductionist caricature of the medical model in an effort to bolster their own opposing positions. Other supporters of the medical model maintain, somewhat more pointedly, that it continues to be invoked as a theoretical scapegoat by a variety of writers in need of a construct to oppose (McKee & Chappel, 1992).

Although the medical model is generally accepted as a curative model that has demonstrated success when intervening in the acute stages of impairment, its most significant criticism is that it does not adequately address the realities of life of those with stable, functional limitations (Fougeyrollas & Beauregard, 2001).

Regardless of the limitations associated with the medical model, it has been widely acknowledged as having increased survival rates and life expectancy for many PWDs (French & Swain, 2001; Williams, 1999). To illustrate this point, prior to the 1940s, 80–90% of those who acquired a spinal cord injury died within a few weeks. The numbers of these survivors grew exponentially as antibiotics and other medications improved during and after World War II. Over the next 30 years, significant numbers of survivors of spinal cord injuries were able to return to their homes (Zola, 2005). However, many of these individuals encountered a new challenge, that of interacting with a community that had little experience with PWDs (Trieschmann, 1988). This lack of experience serves to foreshadow the development of the social model described next.

The Social Model

The social model of disability arose as a response to the medical model, rejecting what it described as the latter's authoritarian relationship to those with impairments. The social model also rejected the medical model for its assumption that those with impairments live lives of personal tragedy (Oliver, 1990) and for its inability to differentiate between chronic illness and impairment. However, the social model reserves its most pointed criticism of the medical model for failing to distinguish the socially created construct of disability from individually experienced impairments (Oliver & Barnes, 2012; Shakespeare, 2006).

By introducing a conceptual dichotomy between impairment and disability, the social model shifts the blame and responsibility (Siminski, 2003), and what Goffman (1963) called the *stigma* of disability, from the individual to society. This reformulation allowed for the notion of personal tragedy, as imputed to the medical model, to be decoupled from impairment (Barnes, Mercer, & Shakespeare, 1999; Oliver, 1990). However, the separation and clarification of each of these terms did not spring fully formed into existence.

Early theoretical differentiations between the concepts of impairment, functional limitation, and disability were put forward by Nagi (1976) who suggested that one's gaze must extend beyond individual limitations to understand disability. Nagi considered disability to be a combination of individual characteristics and social requirements. In that same period, the Union of the Physically Impaired Against Segregation (UPIAS, 1976) put forward a proposal that clearly distinguished between the constructs of *impairment* and *disability*. The former was described as the functional limitation within the individual; the latter was described as the limitations imposed on those with impairments by social and physical barriers.

This theoretical shift put forward an acceptable option to the medical model that was politically accessible to PWDs. Within this new model, the *personal tragedy* of PWDs within the medical model was transformed into one of *oppression* on the part of others (Oliver, 1990). This shift to a social oppression theory of disability presented PWDs "as the collective victims of an uncaring or unknowing society rather than as individual victims for the tragedies that have befallen them" (p. 2).

This new relationship was also articulated by the World Health Organization in its International Classification of Functioning, Disability and Health (ICF). That model asserts that "disability is not an attribute of an individual, but rather a complex collection of conditions, many of which are created by the social environment" (WHO, 2001, p. 28). These concepts were also being considered by a number of researchers who argued that the social environment is more of a barrier than individual impairments (Shakespeare, 2004).

The strategic value that this overall shift of perspective from that of the medical model to one of a social model was significant for many PWDs. Disability, if interpreted as a socially constructed barrier, justified PWDs in actively seeking remediation from the injustices and oppression created by that barrier (Oliver, 2004). The social model shifted the onus from that of Parsons' (1951) requirement for the repair or correction of individuals to that of social change (Shakespeare, 2004). The responsibility for remediation was repositioned from resting upon the individual to that of the encompassing social environment. In addition, the social model provided a location for individuals who lived with stable, functional limitations but were disabled by environmental impediments.

The social model of disability was further parsed into the strong and weak models (Shakespeare & Watson, 2001). The former, also called the UK model, included three key elements. These were: disabled people are an oppressed group, impairment is distinguished from oppression, and disability is defined as social oppression.

The weak social models of disability do not define disability as resulting from social oppression. These include the American minority rights model and the Nordic or relational model (Gustavsson, 2004). The American model, beginning in the late 1960s, was developed by those involved in the Independent Living Movement and by the growing number of injured veterans who had returned to that country from the Vietnam War (Barnes, 2012; Braddock & Parish, 2001). Members of both of these groups rejected the then-current social expectations of their ongoing dependency on a range of medical and rehabilitation professionals. Both groups also became involved in the burgeoning social protest movements of the time that were advocating for civil rights (Stark, 2001).

This changing social climate in the period following the Vietnam War included a shift in relationship between the disability community and the majority population in North America. A new self-assertiveness was fostered, in part, by disabled war veterans who had not lived through a childhood and adolescence as PWDs. Consequently, they had not been exposed to a medical model assertion of disability as being equated with illness (Oliver, 1990), and had not been habituated into believing that they were "exceeding their place" when demanding increased services and independence.

The American model defined disability as the relationship between impairments, functional limitations, and the social environment (Chan et al., 2009). Without assuming a necessary connection between disability and oppression, this growing understanding of the interaction between impairment and the environment as a source of disability provided the impetus for the North American disability community's rights-based advocacy for self-determination.

The American social model of disability, unlike the UK model, adopted the political position of a social minority in search of its rights of citizenship. Within a *minority paradigm*, disability became a suitable subject of legislative reform in a manner similar to what had been demanded by African-Americans and other minority groups (Safilios-Rothschild, 1976, as cited in Barnes, Mercer, & Shakespeare, 1999). An attempt to address this demand was made by the American federal government with the passage of the Americans with Disabilities Act (ADA) in 1990 (Danermark & Gellerstedt, 2004). This process of American legislative reform has served as the single, most comprehensive example of a legislative solution to establishing disability rights (Bickenbach et al., 1999). However, ongoing concerns have been raised regarding the lack of improved employment statistics in the years following the implementation of the ADA (Burkhauser & Stapleton, 2004; Donoghue, 2003).

The American civil rights model has most often been critiqued by those supporting the strong social model. Barnes (1999) castigates American and Canadian writers for using the terms "disabled people" and "people with disabilities" interchangeably. According to Barnes and many other UK writers, the "people first" language of the North American model does not sufficiently acknowledge that disability has been imposed on those with impairments through social oppressions (see, for example, Barnes, 1999; Shakespeare & Watson, 2001). However, Titchkosky (2001) argues that, in keeping with its rights-based approach, the North American model approaches disability as an attribute of the person, with the "person first" language signifying that relationship. This debate over the appropriate use of people-first language (PFL) versus identity-first language (IFL) continues. More current considerations include a recognition that this debate extends beyond geographical boundaries and that various groups of PWDs have a preference for either PFL or IFL designations.

Researchers have also provided analyses and interpretations of specific aspects of the social model from a variety of perspectives. Thomas (1999b, 2007) describes the recognition of what that author has termed *impairment effects* as a means to resolve the binary of disability and impairment. Although maintaining a position in support of the social model, Thomas argues that it is necessary to distinguish the results of impairments that are socially caused and, therefore, considered to be disabilities, from those that are inherent to particular individual limitations, considered to be impairment effects.

Several other writers see value in exploring the social model within a social constructionist context. Concerns are raised that individual factors, which can limit activity regardless of available accommodations, are not well considered within the social model. Crow (1996) states that impairments themselves can be restraining and that a general rejection of impairment as a possible disadvantage weakens the legitimacy of the social model. In addition, the individual experience of various persistent limitations is not explained by disability as oppression (French, 1996, as cited in Shakespeare & Watson, 2001).

As Oliver (1990, 1992) was delineating the boundaries of the social model within which social change could occur, others were offering more broadly based options. Zola (1989) posited a universalism of disability. In support of a civil rights framework, Zola argued that only through a "universalist" approach can disability be demystified and the notions of *different* and *special* be eliminated. Zola further claimed that chronic illness and disability await the entire population. Therefore, policies and processes are needed that recognize this population, and which eliminate the separation of those with disabilities from the general population.

Shakespeare (2004) notes that several aspects of the strong social model have been counterproductive and unnecessarily alienating of others. These include the anti-capitalist thought that has influenced the strong social model, the counterproductive rift between the strong and weak social models, and the rejection of social model variants proposed by non-disabled researchers. Shakespeare also notes that the social model movement has been dominated by those with physical impairments and has been much less successful in appealing to members of the Deaf community, those with mental health issues, seniors with age-related impairments, and others.

Oliver (2013) responds to claims regarding the theoretical inadequacy of the social model by stating that it was never intended to fill this role. Oliver indicated that it had always been intended as a practical tool to support *practice* and to produce political and social change, including a recognition of the essential and causal nature of the relationship between society and disability.

Barnes (2019) takes a different tack and suggests that the social model of disability is "an 'heuristic device', or aid to understanding" (p. 20). However, this reconsideration of the social model as somewhat explanatory appears to be a teleologically motivated redefinition of the concept of model.

Finally, Oliver (2013) acknowledges that the widespread adoption of the social model of disability "has barely made a dent in the employment system" (p. 1025). Oliver also notes that "it is time to either re-invigorate the social model or replace it" (p. 1026). Finally, Shakespeare (2004) argues that the time has come to reject the strong social model. "Rather than a social theory of disability, we need a social theory of embodiment" (p. 20).

The Embodiment Model

The embodiment model of disability has provided a response to the social model, with a more broadly based grounding to disability. Disability researchers are now engaged with new theories of the body and considering how the body has become key to understanding identity (Barnes & Mercer, 2010). Garland-Thomson (2006) points out that the social model is insufficient to address bodily issues associated with disability. As Hughes and Paterson (1997) argue, the exclusion by the social model of impairment as a conceptual component of disability creates an "untenable separation between body and culture" (p. 326). Furthermore, this separation limits disability by requiring it to be dependent on oppression for its existence (Shakespeare, 2006). The embodiment model of disability attempts to consider and place the subjectivity of the lived, bodily experience within the life world (Turner, 2001).

Within this model, disability is understood as containing some degree of impairment, implying bodily limitations and activity restrictions (Shakespeare & Watson, 2001; Thomas, 2004). Bringing the body, with its concomitant impairments, back into the discussion of disability allows for identity, and identity politics, without requiring the construct of disability as oppression. Identity politics offer a positive representation to its members and to others, with difference from the norm as the common theme (Darling, 2013).

Although identity theory, as extracted from Symbolic Interactionism, is capable of encompassing a range of self-perceptions, disability politics represents these differences as affirmative identities rather than as a tragedy model of disability (Swain & French, 2000). Paradoxically, these various identities of disability require the maintenance of the challenged division for their own existence, even if only as the attitudes directed toward those acknowledged differences (Barnes & Mercer, 2001).

Particularly in the United States, disability scholars and activists have argued for the inclusion of disability into what Davis (2001) refers to as the "race-class-gender triad" (p. 535). The intent of each of these identities is to win full rights of citizenship.

However, this model of disability is critiqued as being distinguished from other identities in several ways. First, its membership is not clearly defined. Individuals can and do leap that divide, in either direction, for a number of reasons including age, accident, recovery or definitional change (Breen, 2015). Unlike identities such as ethnicity and cultural background, the identity of disability is heterogeneous and somewhat arbitrary (Davis, 2013; Ginsberg & Rapp, 2013; Shakespeare & Watson, 2001).

A further distinction from other identities is that disability is seen as inherently containing some degree of impairment and can only be understood if it includes limitations to the body and activity restrictions (Shakespeare & Watson, 2001; Thomas, 2004). Crow (1996) states that impairment cannot be ignored "when pain, fatigue, depression and chronic illness are constant facts of life for many of us" (p. 209). Although these limitations may be caused by environmental or social influences, "it is the individual body within which illness is situated" (Williams, 2001, p. 125).

Identity politics also draws additional critiques. Sherry (2004) categorizes these principally as the debates between constructionism and essentialism.

The constructionist perspective describes identity as resulting from cultural and social conditioning and is, therefore, capable of adjustment. The essentialist understanding of identity is one that is inherent, permanent, and natural. However, according to Galvin (2003), identity politics is unavoidably essentialist, regardless of whether construed as irreducible due to biological or humanistic causes, leaving the construct with little value. This position is contrasted with that of Oliver (1992), who supports an essentialist perspective, criticizing social constructionists and social idealists alike for "denying the essential nature of disability and this existence of disablism throughout society" (p. 22).

This challenge has also been addressed by Imrie (2004), who attempts to bring these opposing viewpoints together. Imrie argues that the impaired body can be viewed as being constructed of physiological, social, and discursive components that exist at the intersection of the social, biological, and psychological. This position is closely aligned with that put forward by the ICF (World Health Organization, 2001), which considers disability to be a variation of functioning caused by any combination of individual impairment, activity limitations, or participation restrictions (Imrie, 2004).

This debate has also been considered by Davis (2006), with a description of the challenge facing disability identity politics if it is included within the collective of oppressed minorities. Davis anticipates a first-level critique of reductionist essentialism, countered by rejoinders demonstrating that identities are socially constructed. But this argument for a social construction of identity is actually what Davis uses to raise a more basic concern. That is, whether a social construction of identity leaves space for any core identity. Davis (2006) refers to this as merely a politically motivated position of "strategic essentialism" (p. 236). This same objection is raised by Hacking (1999) who claims that without a biological basis for disability, a social construction of that identity may not be possible, leading to the retention of a construct of identity simply for strategic purposes, without evidence of a theoretical or biological underpinning.

Others have suggested that, rather than abandoning identity politics altogether, a "universalist" approach to impairment is most appropriate, whether that approach is based on the temporary nature of able-bodiedness (Shakespeare & Watson, 2001; Zola, 1989), a common morality based on a universal ontological identity (Timpanaro, 1975, as cited by Hughes, 2009), or a universalism of injustice and bodily limitations (Davis, 2006). Finally, as noted by Hughes (2009), each of these raises another concern. Universal impairment allows for the re-emergence of a biological essentialism and reductionism akin to that disparaged by critics of the medical model.

Shakespeare and Watson (2001) attempt to avoid the critique of biological essentialism by distinguishing those with impairments who can claim oppression from those who cannot. The ICF (World Health Organization, 2001), has also attempted to avoid this pitfall by presenting disability as falling somewhere between the social model and the medical model, allowing for the joint creation of disability by bodily and social means (Bickenbach et al., 1999; Imrie, 2004). However, this debate is discounted by Russell (2002) who notes that the low rates of employment of PWDs are rooted in purposefully discriminatory attitudes of employers, which are not significantly affected by arguments related to identity politics. Russell states that a "traditional civil rights model would not serve to provide equal [employment] opportunities for disabled people in the labour force" (p. 127).

Russell (2002) further argues that the premise of discriminatory employer attitudes being driven by irrational factors capable of remediation is incorrect. It is the rational, albeit incorrect, decisions made in the name of pre-existing financial goals that discriminate against PWDs. Russell maintains that it is irrelevant whether disability is conceptualized within an essentialist or constructionist framework. It is employers' perceptions of PWDs as both incapable and expensive, each of which raises concerns over profit, that perpetuate low employment rates.

The Nordic Model

The Nordic model of disability, while often described as a separate and unique understanding of disability, is established on premises similar to those found within the several versions of the embodiment model described above. Developed from the self-advocacy movement of the 1970s within which PWDs began to demand more autonomy and control over their daily lives (Barnes, Mercer, & Shakespeare, 1999), the Nordic model argues for a recognition of the interrelationship between the individual and society in the creation of disability. This approach positions disability within a multi-layered, critical realist ontology (Bhaskar & Danermark, 2006), suggesting that "people are disabled by society *and* by their bodies and minds" (Shakespeare 2014, p. 5).

The Nordic model includes three principal considerations: that disability is a person–environment mismatch; that disability is situational; and that disability is relative (Goodley, 2013). These have included arguments against the necessity of oppression as a component of disability (Shakespeare, 2014; Shakespeare & Watson, 2001); the problem of conceding that the impaired body "belongs" to medicine by abandoning impairment as a component of disability; viewing it only through a medical lens (Hughes & Paterson, 1997); and a consideration of the individuality of disability through an analysis of subjective phenomena such as pain (Siebers, 2008).

This model maintains that a deep understanding of these person–environment relationships is necessary if PWDs are to attain a "normal" level of social inclusion (Lid, 2016). According to Owens (2015), the Nordic model does not politically separate impairment from disability. Rather, these two constructs are seen as interacting with each other along a continuum that travels along an individual/social dimension. Similar to the embodiment model described above within which it is located, the Nordic model considers issues of disability from the perspective of the individual and their relationship to the social world.

Common Themes

Disability studies can be characterized as an amalgam of efforts to examine, conceptualize, interpret, and locate those individuals whose physical, cognitive, or affective differences are sufficiently apparent to be of negative social notice (see, for example, Altman, 2001; Shakespeare, 2014; Siebers, 2008; Williams, 2001).

In a review of the medical, social, and embodiment models of disability, each is identified as being cognitively based and located along a dimension of responsibility (Breen, 2018a). The medical model assigns responsibility to the individual PWD (Bickenbach et al., 1999; Parsons, 1951); the social model to society (Oliver, 1990; Oliver & Barnes, 2012); and the embodiment model to a combination of the two (Garland-Thomson, 2006; Hughes & Paterson, 1997).

As the several models of disability described above reveal, the construct of disability has been viewed by scholars and the larger community from a number of perspectives. As within other areas of the social sciences, it is not uncommon for a number of models of disability to co-exist (Owens, 2015). However, if viewed chronologically, a reactionary pattern within the formulation process of these models begins to appear. The medical model can be seen as a science-based reaction to various religious/moral explanations of disability (Parsons, 1951). The social model came into being as a reaction to what it described as an inability on the part of the medical model to separate socially imposed disability from individuals living with impairments (Oliver, 1990). The embodiment model was developed as a response to the social model with a focus on that latter model's abandonment of the lived experience of many PWDs (Shakespeare & Watson, 2001; Thomas, 2004). The Nordic model came about as a means to further consider the complexity of the relationships between PWDs and the societies within which they live.

It is clear that these various efforts have allowed for a broad range of conceptualizations of disability along the common dimensions of cognition and responsibility. There are also several more narrowly framed constants that have emerged within each of these models. We examine each of these next.

Disability Is Not Normal

The first of these constants is that disability is understood as antithetical to what Goffman (1963) described as *normal.* It is, by definition, that which is both noticeably and negatively different from a particular cultural norm (Vehmas & Watson, 2014; Winance, 2007). In this context, *noticeably different* implies a social awareness of that difference; *negatively different* implies a social awareness of a difference of concern.

To illustrate, the average Canadian man is 5' 9" (176 cm) tall and the average Canadian woman is 5' 4" (162 cm) tall (Statistics Canada, 2006). The implications associated with the degree of difference from these means are significant and substantially dissimilar in either direction. For example, individuals who exceed the average height may find themselves able to excel at various endeavours, such as professional sports. These endeavours may result in prestige, financial reward, and enhanced social status. The height of a star basketball player, although significantly beyond what is typically considered to be normal, may be viewed positively. The very successful, 1992 "Be Like Mike" advertising campaign featuring Michael Jordan (6' 5" or 198 cm), a superstar of the American National Basketball Association, illustrates this point.

Within a workplace context, many employers have been found to link above average height with a likelihood of success for salespersons, police officers, business leaders, and others (Judge & Cable, 2004). However beyond a certain point, human height becomes increasingly perceived as both *different* and *negative*. Robert Pershing Ludlow, an American born in 1918, is generally considered to be the tallest person who ever lived. When he died, he was 8' 11.1" (272 cm) tall (Taura, 2011). However, his *difference*, became a disability when it became perceived as *negative*. This negative difference became increasingly noticeable as he was unable to enter many buildings; obtain suitable clothing and shoes; and make use of standard equipment, tools, and modes of transportation.

Of note is that this atypicality with regard to height is generally perceived quite differently when considering statures that are below average. There is no "different but good" area on that side of this bell curve. This difference, beyond a relatively arbitrary point, becomes a disability immediately upon notice. These perceptions of negative difference, at a socially determined point along a particular continuum, continue to inform current models of disability (Nagi, 1976) and determine the degree to which PWDs are integrated or excluded (Priestley, 1998) in various cultures and societies.

The factors that lead to these perspectives have been described within two distinct frameworks. The first, as mentioned earlier, is based on the specific nature of the impairment, the associated personal characteristics of the individual PWD, and the expectancies of the observer (Stone & Colella, 1996). However, this determination does not adequately account for the discrepant and dichotomous characterization of the same individuals as either PWDs or merely individuals with noticeably different but not negative attributes (Ginsberg & Rapp, 2013).

Instead, we agree with Goffman's (1963) analysis of perceived difference as one of relationship rather than attribute. These perceived differences have included, at different times and locations, a variety of particular characteristics and impairments that have been viewed as more or less significant depending upon a particular social structure. The literature abounds with examples of personal characteristics that have vacillated between statuses as disabilities or merely personal attributes. These have included hair colour, left-handedness, incontinence, cancer, and various congenital or acquired impairments (Link & Phelan, 2001). It is only when these particular characteristics are perceived by others as an insufficiency (Galvin, 2003) that they take on the mantle of disability. Each of these determinations has been subject to a kind of filter, whether by degree or kind, based on whether the particular impairment *matters* within a specific social context.

These examples also illustrate a second commonality within the relationship that exists between society and difference. That commonality of negative difference, or disability, is understood to exist within a particular individual or group only when, within a particular social environment, that individual or group has risen above the "*horizon of social notice* (italics in original)" (Breen, 2017, p. 2723). Within the context of disability, this tipping point is determined by whether a particular difference, within a particular culture, is perceived as being sufficiently *different* and *negative* to be of social notice (Breen, 2017). Although considered in more detail in Chapter 7, it is useful to state at this point that this perception of a negative difference can only start with the observer, not the observed. This measure of difference may also be situational, in that its determination by an individual or group may be dependent on a social time or location. For example, an individual PWD's perceived status as impaired may diminish over time (see Text Box 11). Additionally, PWDs may be generally accepted within a variety of social circumstances but not within a general context of employment (Domzal, Houtenville, & Sharma, 2008). Even the circumstance of employment itself may be subject to variations in perceived difference. In a study designed to measure attitudes toward PWDs functioning as restaurant servers, it was determined that there was a greater acceptance of these individuals when customers were attending for social gatherings rather than when attending for either business purposes or romantic assignations (Kuo & Kalargyrou, 2014).

The Fluidity of Disability

Another constant within these several models is that disability itself is perceived as a fluid social construct (Shildrick, 2012), particularly with regard to various skills or behaviours that inform this difference. For example, in today's age of electronic textual communications, various forms of dysgraphia may be perceived by some as sufficiently negative to be considered as disabilities. However, in more traditional, agrarian societies this particular challenge may have been of little notice or concern (Oliver, 1990).

Unlike skill-based differences, differences determined to be based upon behaviours are informed by perceptions of a characteristic as being at odds with prevailing political or religious mores. Possibly the most extreme example of the assignment of disability to a behaviour considered to be antithetical to prevailing social mores would be that of drapetomania, first conjectured by Dr Samuel Cartwright to be a mental illness that caused slaves in the southern American states to flee captivity (White, 2002).

A Reductionist Outlook

The development of the several cognitively driven models of disability has followed a relatively linear path, albeit with significant cultural and chronological imbrications. A meta-analysis of the several models of disability indicates that, to various degrees, each makes use of a similar Socratic *reductio* technique to reduce a prior articulation of a complex social relationship to one with a single, dominant, and ontologically purposeful explanation which is not readily susceptible to refutation or critique. Each of these is framed within a political environment that relies upon its own pre-existing ontological position (Oliver, 1990) and which, consequently, risks generating what Schatzman (1991) refers to as a perspectivized position. That position, when based upon prior sociological or ideological premises, is considered to be inherently biased and serves a teleological purpose rather than describing an exploration of meaning (Blumer, 1969). This concern, in a reference to grounded theory, is raised by Glaser (1992), who cautions against forcing data through predetermined categories.

This biasing, teleologically focused influence of pre-existing social and political preconceptions is acknowledged by many disability theorists. Shakespeare (1994) argues that the social model of disability has its roots in a pre-existing, anti-capitalist ideology. Priestley (1998) goes further and indicates that the various models of disability are based on self-supporting, political premises. Oliver (2013), perhaps more cynically, acknowledges the political roots of the social model of disability and suggests that any critique would be detrimental to that political purpose.

The Causal Nature of Disability

Each of these several models of disability assumes that individual PWDs, or categories of PWDs, generate specific attitudes on the part of IWODs. Although the nature of the particular disabilities that create these attitudes vary by culture, location, and historical timeframe, it is assumed that once specific disabilities rise above the horizon of social notice, these become objects that generate a negatively valenced response. Disability is perceived as the causal factor, the creator of a social anomaly in need of identification, response, and, potentially, remediation. IWODs are understood as subjective participants, responding negatively to disability (Pruett & Chan, 2006) with an ontological anxiety (Shildrick, 2009) that is based on a perceived threat, aberration, or a reminder of their own vulnerability (Shakespeare, 1994).

Each of these models understands disability as a form of difference viewed from within an overarching and pre-established worldview. The moral model sees PWDs as being morally inferior, whether personally bereft or as a consequence of historical transgression. The medical model sees PWDs as being sufficiently medically different from an accepted norm as to be in need of physical, psychological, or emotional remediation. The social model understands disability as being a sociological artefact of an ableist IWOD culture, within which difference is generated through membership in an oppressed group (Oliver, 1990) or as a minority political outlier (Gustavsson, 2004).

Each of these models assumes that PWDs, or at least those who are recognized as such, create a mental state in IWODs that is in need of resolution. This state is understood as being created through a categorical analysis of difference – morally bereft, sick, oppressed – as framed by a particular pre-existing political position (i.e. medical model, social model, etc.). It is the presentation of particular PWDs themselves that is foundational in determining that recognition and valenced response. These presentations and responses are quite clearly dependent upon specific times, cultures, and locations for specific disabilities to appear above that horizon of social notice. Socially pertinent categorizations of disability are understood as the cause of attitudes generated by IWODs toward PWDs. Disability is the object against which IWODs are compelled to determine a response.

Each of these models maintains that, with the implementation of appropriate changes to PWDs themselves or to the environment, the difference associated with disability, or at least the negative aspects of that difference, should sink back below that horizon and, essentially, disappear. However, as demonstrated by the widespread and continued low employment rates for PWDs (Burke et al., 2013; Statistics Canada, 2017c; Turcotte, 2014), none of these three models has been successfully applied in reducing that particular *differencing* aspect of disability.

A Cognitive Analysis

Each of the above models contains an element of responsibility and blame associated with disability, variously directed toward those with disabilities themselves, the community at large, or a combination of these (Breen, 2018b, 2019). The assignment of blame for an action, or in this case a state of being, is only possible through a cognitively framed analysis. As we describe in detail in Chapter 5, the difference model rejects both that methodology and its implication of blame.

The Purpose of Models

In this postmodern environment, it is surprising to note that debate within cognitively focused disability politics appears to be teleologically driven by theorists and apologists, particularly as this applies to demonstrations of the overall efficacy of specific models. Disability politics appears to have wandered from its generally agreed-upon emancipatory purpose of benefitting PWDs (Barnes, 2014) to one which has become absorbed in increasingly turgid positional defenses. It is difficult not to observe the incongruity between a theoretical rejection of a modernist perspective and the various arguments put forward in support of particular cognitively based notions of disability – particularly as these arguments appear to be intended to demonstrate the *correctness* of each of these models through a process of refutation of alternatives. We agree with Shakespeare and Watson (2001), who note that such a modernist understanding of disability "is not a useful or attainable goal" (p. 19).

To foreground the landscape within which the difference model of disability will be described and positioned, we suggest a return to a consideration of models as multiple, simplified, and hypothetical. Multiple, in that models are intended to consider separate aspects of a more complex phenomenon (Owens, 2015). Simplified, in that models are purposefully limited images intended to bring focus to a particular aspect of a complex construct (Schatzman, 1991). Hypothetical, in that models are hypotheses about particular processes and how these processes may reflect and produce observed facts. Although considerations of the latter two characteristics appear to be relatively nuanced within the disability literature, the notion that models may co-exist appears to be rejected out of hand. As illustrated above in the several descriptions of current models of disability, each argues for its own worldview at the expense of all others.

The difference model is presented within a worldview that acknowledges and accepts that these several models are each of value in providing a description, if not an adequate explanation, of a particular aspect of a vexing social circumstance. However, none of these is considered to be *correct*, or even comparable to various theories within the physical sciences which may arguably be understood as the best *explanations* of physical phenomena currently available. Instead, models of disability, including the difference model, are understood as *descriptions* of particular social phenomena associated with disability. Each of these models has been enunciated to provide a framework or a roadmap that connects a particular social goal with a pre-existing worldview.

Multiple Models, Multiple Challenges

The several models described above each answer an existential question generated within their particular social context.

Order versus Chaos

Within a pre-scientific or a theologically driven environment, the moral model of disability has provided some degree of coherence to an otherwise random assignment of impairment to individuals who would otherwise be understood as undeserving of such challenges.

Active versus Passive

Within a period of fledgeling scientific development, during which early methods of medical interventions began to save lives that had hitherto been lost to accident and illness, a medical model of disability has offered a new perspective that allows for human intervention in response to those same individual challenges.

Inclusion versus Exclusion

The social model, which sprang into life early in the latter half of the past century, began with a recognition that PWDs were entitled to become active participants within their communities. This model has focused on what had been determined to be the socially generated barriers to inclusion. Initially, emphasis was placed on the physical barriers that were particularly challenging for wheelchair users, the removal of which would allow for PWDs to attain full citizenship. This emphasis has expanded in an effort to include a more broad cross-section of PWDs.

Internal versus External

The embodiment models, including the Nordic model, step beyond the social model to incorporate the individual circumstances of PWDs, including impairments that are not particularly subject to externally generated influences, into the analysis of factors that influence social participation and associated limitations. This complex matrix of personal and social factors has allowed for a more individualized analysis of the relationship between PWDs and the community.

Simplified

Models are purposefully limited images intended to bring focus to a particular aspect of a complex construct (Schatzman, 1991). They are intended to illustrate only specific properties or characteristics of that construct (Beckett & Campbell, 2014). The advantage of this simplification is that it provides an image of a linear, easily discernable, and uncluttered path from a relevant challenge to a solution within a socially acceptable framework. Each of these may be based on disparate, and unrelated, procedural or structural dimensions from within a particular construct (Lave & March, 1975).

However, models within the social sciences are subject to two disadvantages. First, as described earlier, models are susceptible to politically motivated bias (Schatzman, 1991). Second, if applied beyond their original boundaries, the premises upon which they have been developed become more logically distant. For example, the medical model was generated to describe what was originally understood as a more scientifically oriented relationship between PWDs and society; this in an effort to account for a newly emerging modernist perspective that was beginning to replace a magico-religious understanding of disability.

To illustrate, a basic premise of the medical model includes a responsibility on the part of the PWD to regain an active role in society (Parsons, 1951). However, the medical model does not speak directly to employment. Neither this early iteration nor later versions of the medical model are well suited for considerations of employment beyond a determination of its imminence. Its subject matter has not been developed for application to the social, attitudinal, or procedural aspects of the workplace.

Hypothetical

Models themselves, including the difference model, are hypothetical algorithmic images designed to illustrate processes of interest. The credibility of these images, including the internal building blocks, is supported by real-world demonstrations. The value of models, therefore, is to be found within their abilities to predict and accommodate the social circumstances to which they are applied (Lave & March, 1975). As described in the next chapter, the difference model of disability has been developed specifically to serve as a framework within which the relationship between employment and PWDs may be examined, tested, and enhanced.

Each of the above models posits a separation between PWDs and the larger community. Based upon the several understandings of difference described above, this separation that exists within these several cognitively based models of disability is one associated with the location of error. That location is based on various determinations of *inter-individual* social forces. However, as we describe in the case of the difference model, that relational connection is found to originate from an internal location within each IWOD. In the former instances, that separation can only be obscured, to a greater or lesser degree, through manipulations of those inter-individual social forces. Through applications of the difference model, we suggest that this separation can be removed.

5 The Difference Model

Recent political developments within the world of PWDs have opened up opportunities for new stories to be constructed (Shakespeare, 1996). These nexus, labelled *turning points* by Charmaz (1991), allow for the possibility of changes in identity on the part of PWDs. We argue that the difference model provides a new social relational identity for PWDs that relocates disability from residing within particular individuals with impairments to one that is created and superimposed on those individuals through a collective process initiated by various IWODs. Understandings of disability are reconstructed, moving from an attribute associated with an individual PWD to a symbolic representation of perceived negative difference. The individual PWD, once perceived as an exemplar or locus of this negative difference, becomes a placeholder that is only tangentially related to a particular category or complexity of impairment. Within this model, disability can be created and extinguished through the evolving perceptions of others.

This potential for change in perspective is supported by Barnes (2003), who recognizes a difference between the *natural* world and the *social* world, in that the rules that govern the former are regarded as universal while those that govern the latter may vary depending upon location, time, and cultural context. Hacking (1999) also considers this separation, describing how the iterative nature of the social sciences, and the awareness of the participants within this process, distinguish the social from the natural sciences. The recognition and naming of new categorizations, models, and, consequently, new options for intervention, provide opportunities for the creation of new identities and theoretical constructs.

Although this transition of responsibility from the individual PWD to others is similar to a basic tenet of the social model, the difference model is clearly separated from that earlier model, not through its point of departure, but through its positioning of societal attitude in a role of primary responsibility. We recognize that current descriptions of the social model have included attitude, along with more historical analyses of the primacy of the built environment, as a contributor to a disabling society (Oliver & Barnes, 2012). However, the difference model argues that there is a

DOI: 10.4324/9781003220695-5

hierarchical relationship to these contributing factors, with attitude serving a foundational role.

The difference model understands the concept of disability as a construct that has been created through a reification of the social relationships that exist between IWODs and those individuals who are perceived as negatively different by virtue of an impairment. This process, referred to as hypostatization, is described as a circumstance wherein an abstract or hypothetical construct is treated as if it were a concrete event or a physical entity. Within the social sciences, this process has been described by many as the method through which various social relations are converted into attributes considered to be inherent to the actors within those relationships (see, for example, Lukács, 1923, 1971; Marx, 1867, 1996).

These representations extend the Theory of Planned Behavior [*sic*] (Azjen, 1991), which posits a three-part structure as the predictive matrix in determining future intentions and behaviours. That author argues that the relative importance of each of these – individual or combinations of attitudes, subjective norms, and perceived behavioural control – will vary in the prediction of actions across various behaviours and situations. The difference model posits a more hierarchical relationship among these three factors, with *attitude* as a supervening influence on any intention for action (see Figure 5.1). Assuming an appropriate combination of perceived behavioural control and a perception of adequately approving subjective norms, an appropriate attitude is required to overcome any behavioural inertia such as is exemplified by the historically stagnant employment rates of PWDs.

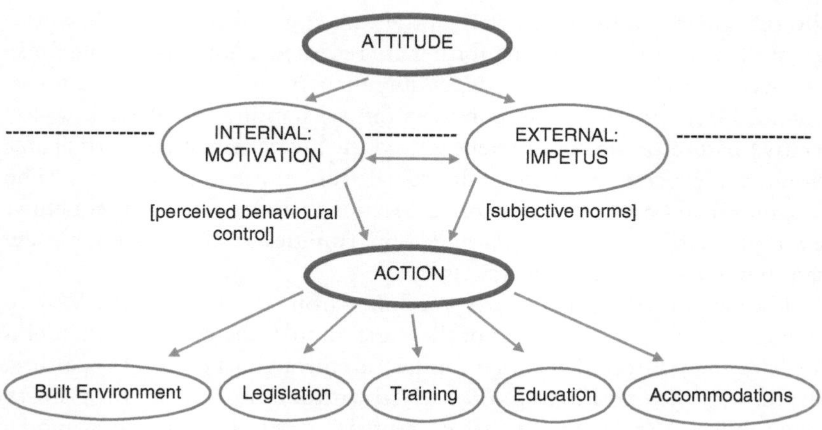

Figure 5.1 The supervening influence of attitude.

Source: A visual construction of the hierarchical relationship that exists between attitudes, subjective norms, and perceived behavioural control.

Overview

A detailed description of the difference model of disability is best served by foregrounding the context within which it has been created, the process through which it has been developed, and a delimitation of its purpose and applicability. Following these descriptions, we will consider several core elements of the difference model itself. These include its ontological position as an affect-driven relational model of disability and the creation of the construct of disability as a consequence of this relationship. Finally, we will describe the changes that the difference model brings to the understanding of the social relationships that exist between IWODs and PWDs, and a brief description of two new tools designed to measure workplace attitudes.

Although we will compare and contrast the difference model with other models of disability, we wish to state at the outset that we are not advocating that any of these, including the difference model, is to be understood as the *singular* or *correct* model of disability. The difference model is not intended to replace any or all of these other models. It is less likely to save lives than has the medical model (Shah & Mountain, 2007); it is less likely to serve as a political rallying point for PWDs than has the social model (Oliver, 1990); and it is less likely to provide a place for pain and other personal challenges than has the embodiment model (Shakespeare, 2014). The goal of the difference model is more narrow. It is focused specifically on employment.

Context

Although earlier described as a *next step* in a line of models of disability (Breen & Forwell, 2020, 2021), our most current analysis suggests that the location of the difference model is better described as somewhat less linear. Instead, it is framed as a meta-analytical response to two common tropes that have been found within these earlier models. These two core themes – a cognitively framed concept of disability and the presentation of disability as an object that demands a response from IWODs – are both rejected by the difference model.

Based on this disjunctive location of the difference model, its position relative to that line of models may be better described as a *step aside*. The difference model steps aside of the internecine debate that has engaged disability theorists for the past half-century, by following a pragmatist theoretical perspective. Charles Sanders Peirce, considered to be the father of pragmatism, proposed that the meaning of an idea or a proposition lies in its observable, practical consequences (Rorty, 1966). Applied specifically to models, a pragmatic approach indicates that their value should be determined by their effects (Reindel, 2008) and by the credibility of their predictions, not by debating the truth of their assumptions (Lave & March, 1975). This pragmatist perspective understands that the meaning of a concept is determined by the practical consequences, or results, of its application (Albrecht, 2002). The difference model of disability, following this pragmatist approach, has been developed as a problem-solving vehicle; its value will ultimately be determined by whether it is able to meet its stated goal – that of improving employment opportunities for PWDs.

Unlike each of the earlier models of disability, the difference model is framed within a set of affect-based premises. Aligned with researchers who indicate that attitudes are created through affect-based processes and then explained through subsequent cognitive efforts (Gawronski & Bodenhausen, 2006), the difference model understands others' perceptions of disability-related difference as primitive (Davis, 2000), spontaneous, and not subject to cognitive control (Guidano, 1995). Dovidio et al. (2000) suggest that these "affective negative reactions ... may have a genetic, evolutionary basis" (p. 14).

The conceptual development of the difference model followed a path that was analogous to a constructivist grounded theory framework (Charmaz, 2000) in its consideration of the social relationships that exist between PWDs and others. In keeping with grounded theory language, the difference model is better understood as a theoretical, second-level coding rather than as the most current in a line of models generated through several distinct first-level codings of those same data.

To explain in more detail, constructivist grounded theory encourages researchers to engage in a non-linear analysis, to code and recode data several times and to build upon initially observed relationships among data by forming more subtle and sophisticated categories of experience (Geertz, 1973). The intent is to continue with the analysis of these initially observed relationships through a meta-analysis in order to arrive at a deeper understanding of the relationships under consideration. Glaser (1992) summarizes the logic that drives grounded theory by offering two questions for consideration. The first asks "What is the chief concern or problem ... and what accounts for most of the variation in responses?" The second asks "What category or what property of what category ... " (p. 4) of this concern or problem is indicated? These questions indicate to the researcher that they must gather data that address a particular problem, consider and categorize this information within a structure that is conceptually analogous to a bell curve, and then extract the most salient commonalities from these data clusters. The next step, as we describe later in this chapter, is the evaluation and application of these learnings in a manner which addresses the original problem – that of the employment of PWDs.

Development Process

The difference model has reached its current state of development through a two-step process as delineated by Glaser (1992). The first of these was the creation of the model itself through a qualitative analysis of a broad array of disability-related data. These included personal reflections on the part of both Breen and Forwell, interactions with hundreds of participants in various disability awareness training sessions delivered by Breen across Canada, and many years of related interactions with PWDs and IWODs within the workplace. This analysis, informed by the interrogative process as suggested above by Glaser (1992), generated two separate data streams associated with the employment challenges that face PWDs. These are:

- Employers most frequently offer cognitively based, *business case*, explanations for any reluctance to recruit or hire PWDs;
- Employers typically demonstrate more negative attitudes toward PWDs within the context of the workplace than in other social environments.

These two sets of responses on the part of employers (see, for example, Domzal, Houtenville, & Sharma, 2008) suggest that *business case* arguments, although most frequently offered as explanations, may well mask overall discomfort with PWDs within a workplace environment (Copeland et al., 2010; Hernandez et al., 2000). As noted by Pettigrew & Tropp (2008), "simply knowing more about the outgroup typically does not have a major effect on reducing prejudice" (p. 927).

The difference model asserts that these employer decisions are not based on errors of knowledge but on prior negative attitudes toward PWDs (Russell, 2002), who are often perceived as deficient or inferior (Gething & Wheeler, 1991). Each of these considerations is described in more detail throughout this chapter.

The second step in this process has been the creation of quantitative means to test the difference model within workplace environments. The development and application of two self-report scales, based on the difference model, have demonstrated that attitudes toward PWDs within the workplace can be accurately measured and analyzed to provide support for effective workplace training and education.

Step One

As noted by Albrecht (1992), to understand PWDs, we must also understand the political, cultural, and economic context within which PWDs live and within which they are defined. This iterative process is counter to a more positivist perspective that perceives qualitative research, including grounded theory, as a process of discovering a pre-existing truth (Strauss & Corbin, 1990).

Several points of separation exist between that typical constructivist grounded theory process and the development of the difference model. First, the iterative process that has been employed with regard to the difference model has been informed by a complex matrix of data that has reached beyond the more typical structure of informant interviews, observations, note-taking, and analysis (Charmaz, 2000). Rather, it has been informed by ongoing and extended personal and professional interactions with PWDs and others, and considerations of these interactions over an extremely extended period of time. It has also been significantly influenced by Breen's personal experiences as a PWD, childhood recollections of which reach back to the mid-1950s. These latter experiences are summarized as an analytically framed, autoethnographic account of Breen's experiences with disability (see Chapter 8). This extended period of data generation is quite distinct within a framework of qualitative research of this type.

A second point of departure from constructivist grounded theory is that the data which have served as the material for analysis were not generated and collected with a research project in mind. Proponents of grounded theory advise that research should be entered into without a clearly defined project or purpose (Glaser, 1992). However, an interest in a more general, and related, research topic is necessary to provide direction. In contrast, the development of the difference model relied upon a reflexive analysis of historical data that had been generated through a broad range of observations, relationships, and interactions, none of which had included a consideration of research topics such as a comparative analysis of models of disability. Instead, these data were gathered within a practice environment. Two examples illustrate this process.

The first of these, as described above in Chapter 4, is our review and categorization of the several current models of disability as being cognitively based that followed subsequent to the original data gathering and analysis that was conducted prior to the initiation of the development of the difference model. This model resulted from an abductive consideration of whether the commonly held cognitive aspects of these other models could be contributing to their inability to support enhanced employment opportunities for PWDs.

Second, one of us (Breen) and colleagues (Michael Hanson and Dr Stephen Jull) had developed and delivered a series of disability awareness training interventions to a total of 337 employees of the Government of the Northwest Territories (GNWT) in Canada between 2011 and 2014. The presentation topics and training materials had been modified from within the START Model (skills training, awareness, resources, theory) framework, previously developed by Breen, to explore and provide opportunities for participants to consider their own knowledge of and feelings toward PWDs in the workplace.

These GNWT training sessions included two unique features. First, they were framed within the affect-based perspective that serves as the theoretical basis of the difference model. Second, participants' workplace attitudes toward PWDs were measured on a pre- and post-basis, making use of an early iteration of what was subsequently developed into the most current version of the CADE Scale (see Chapter 6).

Critically, although a range of disability awareness training programs continue to be delivered to business and government, there has been very little analysis of their efficacy (Brostrand, 2006). Additionally, although at least 40 scales are available to measure attitudes toward PWDs within various social environments (Antonak & Livneh, 2000; Vornholt, Uitdewilligen, & Nijhuis, 2013), very few of these focus on attitudes in employment environments and only a fraction of this smaller group examines co-worker attributes that correlate specifically with levels of acceptance in the workplace (DeWall & Bushman, 2011; Vornholt, Uitdewilligen, & Nijhuis, 2013). To our knowledge, none of these have been systematically applied on a pre- and post-basis to determine the effect of disability-related training on workplace attitudes toward PWDs. This early measure of change to GNWT employees' attitudes was intended to address this gap in workplace training associated with PWDs.

In 2011, the Six Steps to Success Conference was held in Whitehorse, Yukon. One of us (Breen) was then the manager of the Workplace Diversity Employment Office for the Yukon government and served as the Conference Chair. In partnership with the Yukon Council on Disability and the Yukon Workers' Compensation, Health and Safety Board, Breen's office hosted this international conference that focused on the employment challenges faced by PWDs. The conference was attended by over 300 delegates and 30 speakers from Canada, the United States, and elsewhere. Attendees and speakers included several well-respected disability awareness trainers from both Canada and the United States. Breen, who was in the early stages of developing the scale that was to be administered within the GNWT training program, was advised by each of these trainers that there was not a formal protocol in place, such as a pre- and post-measure, to determine the effect of various training sessions. *(For further information on the Six Steps to Success Conference, see, for example, the Yukon News article at* https://www.yukon-news.com/business/making-disability-work-in-whitehorse/)

It must be noted that the scale administered within the GNWT program was a very early version of the CADE Scale and was potentially subject to a number of biases that have subsequently been addressed in later iterations of the scale (see Chapter 6). However, the most striking result of the data analysis indicated that participants shifted their perception of employees with disabilities along a continuum of *difference*. Items associated with knowledge and knowing, which clustered within the first factor in the pre-test were generally replaced by items associated with emotions and attitudes in the post-test. Further to these data analyses, we hypothesized that those items that were more directly related to affective experiences accrued more importance to participants following our training intervention; and, that these changes correlated with a reduction in the difference relationship that had previously existed between co-workers and PWDs. These findings were analogous to those discovered within a meta-analysis of 515 studies that determined the effect size between contact and prejudice (Pettigrew & Tropp, 2008). In that study, contact with outgroups facilitated individuals to "extend their sense of self to include the outgroup" (p. 923). Importantly, that study found that affective indices were significantly more positively mediated by contact than were those that were cognitively based.

We further hypothesized that by creating an environment of what we termed *affective dissonance*, which resulted from our presentation of novel ways of experiencing disability, we were able to influence participant attitudes within a very short training timeframe. This dissonance was demonstrated by a significantly positive increase in the mean scores of each of the scale items, a reduction in the standard deviations of those scores, and the above-mentioned changes in factor loadings. These data, coupled with the hundreds of participant comments subsequently gathered by the employer, provided a strong incentive to continue further development of the CADE Scale within the framework of the difference model.

Step Two

Following Charmaz (2000), the difference model "celebrates firsthand knowledge of empirical worlds, (and) takes a middle ground between postmodernism and positivism" (p. 510). Referring to grounded theory as originally developed by Glaser and Strauss (1967), Charmaz (2000) states that "a grounded theory must work; it must provide a useful conceptual rendering and ordering of the data that explains the studied phenomena" (p. 511). Grounded theory, as argued by Glaser (1992), is intended to generate theory rather than to verify it. However, this creative process "do (es) not approach some level of generalizable truth" (Charmaz, 2000, p. 524). That is left to next steps. In this case, to empirical tests of these observations and analyses.

Specifically, the development of the difference model first applied a qualitative methodology of meaning generation from a broad range of data and then next applied empirical methods as a means of further validating that meaning. This technique of employing both qualitative and quantitative research methods and measures of validity provides a degree of support for the difference model that allows for a measurable analysis of practical benefits to PWDs. By joining the "intimate familiarity" (Blumer, 1969) of the qualitative method of data generation with hypothesis testing procedures supported by analyses based upon quantitatively driven validity theory (Messick, 1990), the difference model provides a more fulsome approach to resolving the longstanding employment challenges that face PWDs.

This second, empirically driven step in the development of the difference model has included initial verifications of the observed social relationships that exist between PWDs and others in the workplace. These have been generated through the development and application of quantifiable, workplace-oriented measures of attitudes toward PWDs. These measures, based on a social relational perspective, include the above-mentioned Co-worker Acceptance of Disabled Employees (CADE) Scale (Breen, 2019) and the Perceived Barriers to Employing Persons with Disabilities (PBED) Scale (Breen, Havaei, & Pitassi, 2019). As described in detail below in Chapter 6, the development process and early applications of these two scales have begun to lay a foundation for measuring workplace attitudes toward PWDs and to provide quantifiable evidence in support of engaging these scales within strategic interventions to create more positive workplace environments for PWDs.

Boundaries and Delimitations

As has been indicated throughout this book, we are engaged in a project with one principal objective – to develop and make available a set of tools that will support PWDs in reaching their employment goals. To this end, all applications of the difference model have been specific to the employment of PWDs. All data have been generated principally from workplaces across Canada, as well as from the United States and Armenia.

Although we would be remiss not to acknowledge our critiques of various other models of disability and particular strategies that have been employed to address the generally accepted employment barriers facing PWDs, our intent has been to demonstrate that, overall, these have been ineffective in supporting initiatives required to meet this very difficult challenge.

The difference model brings a new focus to the workplace itself – to employers, supervisors, and co-workers – that, in these early days, appears to make a difference for PWDs.

Core Elements of the Difference Model

The core elements of the difference model are presented within the following sections to provide readers with a detailed account of the model itself, partly to describe its conceptual building blocks and partly to offer a framework for consideration during any efforts to apply the tools that have been developed within this construct. Each of these elements is presented for both consideration and critique. It should be noted that the difference model is in the early stages of development and may require modifications, testing, and further considerations of its applications in order to generate the most efficacious employment benefits to PWDs.

Beyond Cognition

Wendell (1997), in a consideration of disability through a feminist lens, contends that derogated groups, presented as "the Other," are typically perceived as objects of our experience rather than subjects of their own. In this way, they are understood as symbolic of what non-disabled people fear and reject – "imperfection, failure to control the body, and everyone's vulnerability to weakness, pain, and death" (p. 60). Although we agree with that author's location of these groups, including PWDs, these representational recognitions of disability are at a level of mental sophistication much beyond an initial response state (Buller, 2005). As such, they are a secondary step, in which a cognitive process has categorized and rationalized an initial perception. We suggest that the construct of disability, as contained within the difference model, is more accurately described as an immediate response that occurs at a visceral level and which generates a "fearful and negative reaction … to the different and strange" (Livneh, 1982, p. 341).

Priestley (1998) provides an insightful analysis that is useful in linking the relationship between the more general concept of social models and those specific to disability. That author creates a four-quadrant matrix of individual versus social and materialist versus idealist dualities to demonstrate the four main approaches to considerations of disability theory. Priestley argues that the individual models and social models each offer a range of explanations, some more focused on the material and some more focused on cultural, representational, and psychological conditions.

However, an examination of these options provides an implicitly cognitive framework that follows from a long history of cognition-driven social theories that began in an age where an assumption of our differentiation from other animals, based on our cognitive abilities as a species, was not only a means to differentiate us from them, but was also transitioned into an assumed premise in terms of any sociology.

If we follow this argument along its course, each of the four quadrants described by Priestley (1998) can be seen as addressing a different aspect of this structure, each with its own set of supporting reasons. What is not considered is the logical necessity for a predetermined, underlying notion of difference existing as a prior state and that there is an assumption that each of these variations is based on a cognitively driven explanation.

We are not attempting to ignore the sociologies of disability suggested by UPIAS, Finkelstein, Oliver, Zola, and others. Rather, we are offering a novel approach to understanding disability that we believe will prove fruitful in addressing the seemingly intractable issue of employment. We suggest that there is a need to be exploring different avenues to determine whether they can offer some degree of success.

The issue of concern is not the debate between materialists and idealists or even between individual and social models, but that of the almost singular focus on the cognitive dimension. As indicated by Corker (1999a), theoretical discussions, as they play out within the current debate, "exclude other kinds of experience" (p. 628) that do not fit within currently agreed upon parameters. That author notes that, for example, the social model of disability is only "one strand in an emerging theory of disability ... some of which have not yet been fully developed" (p. 629). Twenty-three years after these comments were offered, we suggest that it may be time to consider other kinds of experience beyond the cognitive, particularly those that foreground affect and attitudes. Bhaskar and Danermark (2006), with a focus specifically on disability, suggest that cognitive mechanisms and "their extra-cognitive causes ... must be viewed as both transient and corrigible" (p. 296).

As noted by Reindal (2008), it is time to abandon arguing over which model of disability may be *true* and focus on what use may be made of any given model. Theoretical consensus should give way to accepting the evidence. Danforth (2001), from a philosophically pragmatist perspective, argues that service providers should ask "What can we ... do with this model? Where will it take us within the social-moral world?" (p. 347). Hughes (2005) offers a more pointed comment; that author states that theoretical contributions must be evaluated by whether and by how much they can "improve the circumstances of disabled people's lives" (p. 79).

The difference model of disability is intended to provide a step forward in framing disability in a manner that enhances opportunities for PWDs, with a particular focus on employment. It also offers a means for the disability community to extricate itself from the increasingly convoluted arguments put forward by the several cognitively based models of disability (Beaudry, 2016).

The difference model has been developed through a "bottom-up" approach rather than through a "top-down" process. By this we mean that the model itself has been based on data generated through hypothesis testing rather than upon an unsubstantiated, albeit internally coherent, description of a path to a desired goal.

The difference model also steps aside of cognitively based theoretical debates, to focus on the affective aspects of the relationship between PWDs and the employment community. In a description of workplace discrimination at the level of the individual, Dovidio and Hebl (2013) state that "cognitive and affective factors operate independently" (p. 12) with affective factors typically being more negative.

The difference model aligns with theorists who argue that attitudes are created through affect-based processes. Specific to disability, Pruett and Chan (2006) suggest that unconscious, negative attitudes are automatically created when individuals encounter new and uncomfortable situations. The difference model postulates that social relations with PWDs are initially generated within the limbic system as acognitive responses to perceived difference (Breen & Forwell, 2020). These responses are considered to be spontaneous, automatic, and not subject to cognitive control (Gawronski &

Bodenhausen, 2006). Considered to be "as primitive as our thought processes can be" (Davis, 2000, p. 53), these perceptions occur without analysis. These affect-based responses can perceive difference itself as potentially dangerous (Guidano, 1987). The cognitive process, which assimilates these data into a coherent worldview and provides clarity to this relationship, is a secondary step (Damasio, 1999, 2010).

New options have recently been developed that allow for a further consideration of the relationship between disability and society. As noted by Shakespeare (1996), new narratives are being created which allow for new interpretations of disability. In addition, recent scientific developments promise further considerations of this relationship. This relationship between PWDs and society can now be altered, at least in some cases, through relatively commonplace technological means (Breen, 2015; Wolbring, 2008). It is within this new context, which contains the potential for a change that goes beyond crafting a new position along the dimension of responsibility, that we describe the difference model of disability.

To illustrate further, Buller (2005) states that initial fear responses to potentially dangerous or unfamiliar phenomena are immediate and cautious but "not very sophisticated" (p. 143). As Buller describes, it is only through a secondary cognitive analysis that a perceived danger is determined to be a snake or a coil of rope. In a more recent study, it was found that infants responded with increased pupillary dilation when shown images of spiders or snakes as compared to flowers and fish. These results indicate an evolved preparedness for the development of a fear response to these ancestral threats (Hoehl et al., 2017). Others have proposed that primates have evolved a preparedness to associate these ancestral threats with fear (Seligman, 1971) and that such evolved fears do not require individual learning in ontogeny (Poulton & Menzies, 2002). As noted by Breen (2018a), "disability, when initially perceived as sufficiently different, evokes (an) affective response similar to a variety of other 'hardwired' fears" (p. 74).

The difference model is not the first to apply this affect-based paradigm to attitudes toward disability. Shildrick (2012) describes how disability formulates a "transhistorical ontological anxiety operating at a psychic level" (p. 52). Within the academic literature of economics, Becker (1957) employs the phrase *taste-based discrimination* to describe an unwillingness on the part of employers to interact with people from an out-group (e.g. PWDs); this was distinguished from what was named *statistical discrimination*. This latter term, which aligns with current cognitive models of disability, referred to discrimination that was based on a lack of information. Taste-based discrimination, considered to be affect-driven, was understood by employers to bear an acceptable financial cost. By conducting a cost/benefit analysis, employers could determine that discriminating against PWDs was worth paying a financial penalty to avoid distasteful contacts with PWDs.

This affect-driven relationship is illustrated much more recently in an American study by Friedman (2020) that compared employment rates of

PWDs with disability prejudice rates on a state-by-state basis. States with higher disability prejudice scores, as determined through a data review of 266,181 responses obtained through Project Implicit (see projectimplicit.net), demonstrated lower rates of employment by PWDs.

To create a community within which PWDs are accepted as members of the *in-group*, the difference model argues for an expansion of the social ground currently held by the *normals*, as these terms were originally described by Goffman (1963). This position is distinguished from the position taken by the cognitive models of disability, each of which argues that PWDs are entitled to enter the *current* in-group after accommodations suitable to each particular model have been made. The difference model argues for an acceptance of difference; the cognitive models argue for adjusting PWDs themselves, the environment, or a combination of both, to allow PWDs to fit within the current in-group (Breen, 2018a).

The difference model *stretches* normal to include PWDs – the atypical becomes part of a larger normal. Winance (2007) describes the resulting relationship as one in which PWDs emerge as "both different and normal" (p. 625). The cognitive models *shrink* PWDs, by masking differences through accommodations, and creating a perception of normalcy within the present conception of normal. Winance, relying on Goffman's (1968) language of *stigma*, states that relationships between the *stigmatized* and the *unstigmatized* occur within the current norm only through the creation of an "as if." This "as if" is "based on a negation of the difference whilst at the same time creating an irreducible distance between the two people" (p. 628).

This difference can be illustrated through a simplified example of a wheelchair user. The medical model argues that the PWD, following suitable rehabilitation or other intervention, will not need the wheelchair. The social model argues that, if suitable ramps and other accommodations were to be made available, the mobility disability would disappear. The embodiment model argues that, although these accommodations would be helpful, they would not necessarily address all of the individual realities of various wheelchair users. The difference model separates the wheelchair user from the wheelchair. Following Shakespeare (2014), the difference model recognizes that a wheelchair is more than a travel option for a paralyzed person. It is a necessary mobility tool. However, we also suggest that it is critical to separate the accommodation from the paralyzed person. The wheelchair is not a part of that person. Acceptance of this PWD by the larger community, based on a difference model of disability, requires that the in-group be expanded to include the paralyzed person, not the accommodated PWD in a wheelchair.

A Relational Model

The difference model is concerned principally with the relationship between PWDs and IWODs (Bogdan & Taylor, 1989) rather than with specific features of particular impairments, or their associated accommodation requirements. Specifically, it is built upon a consideration of the manner and degree to which IWODs, in a Symbolic Interactionism sense (Mead, 1934), view disability as having relevance or importance in determining consequent social responses or actions.

As articulated by Blumer (1969), the individual responds, not to what is observed, but to what is interpreted from that observation. Responses, or actions, are based on an interpreted meaning of what is perceived. It is that affective interpretation of difference by IWODs that drives the difference model. In this context, *interpretation,* although still within the broad category of mental processes, refers to an interpretation of a stimulus at a most basic, precognitive level (de Jonge, 2012; Damasio, 2010). This notion of interpretation may be more accurately described as an immediate response to a stimulus as first *perceived*, consequently falling within one of the primitive relational categories of good/bad, friend/foe, or same/different. The stimulus itself, in this case a perception of difference that is sufficiently negative to be above the horizon of social notice, creates what could be likened to an *early warning system alert* that generates a reaction ranging from a relational guardedness to an immediate active response. As described above in Chapter 3, it is only after this initial perception has been assimilated by the observer into a cognitive matrix designed to provide coherence and support for subsequent action, that self-reflection and justification for that action are possible (Zajonc, 1980, 2000).

This relational aspect of the difference model is procedurally similar to that put forward by the social model in that both argue that disability itself is created by external forces. However, it is the nature of these forces themselves that sets these two models apart. The social model of disability posits that society's lack of accommodation for impairment, whether purposeful, negligent, or inadvertent, *disables* those living with impairments. This lack, most frequently described in terms of the built environment, is described as creating a state of oppression by proponents of the UK version of the social model and as a withholding of minority rights within the American version. However, regardless of where these choices are made along this axis of determination, they are cognitively driven choices.

The difference model argues that the relationship between PWDs and IWODs is neither created nor measured by a determination of the degree or availability of accommodations to various impairments. Instead, these are understood as consequential to a more basic, underlying relationship that is engendered at a relatively autonomic level (Bhaskar & Danermark, 2006). That relationship, generated by a perception of difference, is initiated within the sympathetic nervous system, triggering an acognitive fight-or-flight response. As the perceived triggering object (i.e. the PWD) is more clearly recognized, this response may well be quickly moderated by the parasympathetic nervous system, creating an opportunity for the cognitive processes to engage in "compensatory positive cognitions" (Vilchinsky & Findler, 2010) in an effort to normalize the initial response.

The above description of the difference model is based on the critical realism approach that, as earlier described, applies the reasoning tools of abduction and retroduction in an effort to support explanations of observed phenomena (Craig & Bigby, 2015). The relational aspect of the difference model, as put forward above, has been developed through several ongoing observations and efforts. Our observations have included the general failure of the several other models of disability to improve employment opportunities for PWDs. Our efforts have included the initial successes that have been demonstrated by applications of the difference model. These successes have been attained by rejecting the cognitively based premises that inform these other models and substituting affectively based premises in the development and applications of two self-report measures (see Chapter 6) and through a variety of workplace applications of the difference model.

One of us (Breen) served as the manager of the Workplace Diversity Disability Employment Office (WDEO) within the Yukon government (Canada) from 2004 until 2013. During this period, several projects and programs based on the difference model of disability were implemented throughout that workplace. The WDEO provided disability awareness training modules based on the START Model, which is itself based on the difference model of disability. Other initiatives included an internal email Question and Answer column (i.e. Dear Jon) that addressed various attitudinal issues associated with PWDs and organization-wide communications regarding the availability of accommodations through a centrally held fund within the WDEO.

Over this period, the self-reported rate of disability within this organization increased from 4.4% of those who responded to an internal equity survey in 2000 (response rate unavailable) to 10.5% in 2007 (response rate ~69%), remained stable at that rate until 2009, and then increased to 12% by 2013 (response rate ~64%). These data have been gathered through personal communications by Breen with officials from within the Yukon government Department of Statistics and through that organization's 2009 and 2010 Corporate Employment Equity Reports (both unpublished).

Between 2011 and 2014, Breen had also been contracted by the Government of the Northwest Territories (GNWT) to provide input into the creation of an Equity Office and to deliver a series of 40 disability awareness training sessions, also based on the START Model, over a period of three years. In 2010, when that government had first contacted Breen, he was advised that, other than those few

PWDs engaged with a Return To Work program, the self-declared representation rate of PWDs was essentially zero. Concurrent with various informational materials distributed throughout the organization regarding the creation of this Office and the delivery of the disability awareness training sessions, an internal government census indicated that 15% of respondents self-declared as PWDs (response rate ~45%). These response data have been gathered from the GNWT 2012 Inclusive Public Service Survey (unpublished).

Affect and the Workplace

The difference model frames the workplace-related disability relationship within an affect-based context. This allows for remediative strategies that focus on building more positive affective relationships to disability rather than foregrounding cognitively based *business case* arguments designed to demonstrate to employers and others that they are mistaken in their beliefs regarding PWDs. These latter arguments include demonstrating the low cost of accommodation (workplace adjustment) solutions, describing good or very good productivity levels, no more than average use of sick time, excellent retention rates, and enhanced corporate images that will accrue within the community (see, for example, Bonaccio et al., 2019; Burke et al., 2013; Hernandez et al., 2008; Kaye et al., 2011). We contend that presentations of these business case arguments may actually create a divide between employers and practitioners/academics rather than building alliances. By repeatedly advising employers that they are incorrect in their analyses regarding PWDs, there is a risk of entrenching these positions, regardless of their veracity.

Business case arguments have also been framed within the limitations imposed by various business cycles. Most typically, explanations for past poor employment numbers focus on previous recessions or other periods of low economic activity. These explanations have been followed by arguments that indicate how the current, or next, economic upturn will generate improved employment rates for PWDs (Bonaccio et al., 2019). These arguments are based on a belief that employers will incorporate this new, more positive information into their cognitively based perceptions of PWDs when faced with various workplace challenges, such as a shrinking available workforce; however, historical data suggest the opposite (Burkhauser, Houtenville, & Rovba, 2005).

It is not that the difference model suggests that these business case arguments in favour of employing PWDs are incorrect. Rather, the difference model argues that affect-based perceptions of PWDs by employers are not substantially changed by information designed to correct cognitively based misperceptions about attendance, productivity, costs of accommodations, and other employment characteristics of PWDs.

Eliminates Blame

The difference model eliminates the concept of blame, whether directed at PWDs themselves or at the community (see Table 5.1). This allows for remedial strategies that focus on building more positive affective relationships with PWDs rather than on designing methods to convince employers that they are mistaken in their views or disguising PWDs as members of the current in-group through the camouflage of accommodations.

Framed within this affect-based paradigm, the difference model posits that *blame* has no place as an impetus for creating a useful employment-focused model of disability or in generating strategies to remediate current inequities. Redress is not required because, in a very specific sense, no *wrongs* have been committed (Breen & Forwell, 2020). As positioned within the difference model, disability is more akin to a limbic response to difference than to a purposeful diminution of PWDs generated from within a cognitive process, regardless of whether the latter interpretation is understood as purposeful, negligent, or inadvertent.

As stated by Breen and Forwell (2020), the meaning of the word *wrong* in this context refers specifically to its relationship to the cognitive process. By removing the *wrong* and the notion of responsibility from the relationship between PWDs and the larger community, the difference model is able to offer a new framework for understanding disability. This framework adopts *the perception of difference* as its dominant dimension. For PWDs to be accepted, the difference model argues that disability must be perceived within an expanded *normal* (Goffman, 1963), not as a personal characteristic

Table 5.1 Social locations of blame

Model of Disability	*Relationship to IWOD Community*	*Blame*	*Cause*	*Self-image*
Moral Model	Moral difference	Individual/familial	Personal	Morally bereft
Medical Model	Individual difference	Individual	Personal	Resignation & deficiency
Social Model	Imposed difference	Society	Social/Political	Frustrated & angry
Embodiment Model	Group difference	Individual & society	Social	Acknowledged difference
Difference Model	Affective difference	Not applicable	Perception of difference	Acceptance

Source: (Adapted from Breen, 2018a) The perceived relationships between PWDs and the IWOD community.

that, through various individual or social adjustments, can be made to fit within the current boundaries of normalcy.

Attitude and the Built Environment

The built environment has been presented as the single most important barrier facing PWDs since social modelists began to distinguish between disability and impairment. An overall lack of social attention to issues of accessibility is understood to disable individuals beyond the limitations created by individual impairments (UPIAS, 1976). In addition, from a strategic perspective, a focus on barriers within the built environment has provided a set of images that focused on the mobility and accessibility challenges facing the early proponents of the social model. Although researchers and theorists have moved from these early arguments that focused exclusively on the physical environment to those which include the social context, physical barriers continue to be most frequently considered as of principal concern (Thomas, 2004).

This determination is rejected for two reasons. The first is that it is well-accepted that disability represents a much broader segment of the population than those impacted by barriers to the built environment (Cluley et al., 2020; Statistics Canada, 2017b). The second reason is that although the significant changes that have been made to the built environment since the time of the UPIAS (1976) statement have added significantly to the overall quality of life for many PWDs, they have proven to be ineffective with regard to employment. During this period, there has been no significant change to either employment or unemployment rates for PWDs engendered by the construction of ramps, curb cuts, transportation improvements, and many other improvements to the built environment.

In addition, legislation in support of accessibility and other physical accommodations has been enacted in many countries over the past 30 years. However, none of this, including the Americans with Disabilities Act (ADA, 1990), which is considered by many to be the most comprehensive legislation associated with disability rights (Bickenbach, Jerome, Chatterji, Badley, & Ustun, 1999), has generated improved employment for PWDs (Donoghue, 2003; Burkhauser & Stapleton, 2004). The difference model argues that the attitude of those within the workplace, not the built environment, is the principal impediment to the employment success of PWDs (Antonak, 1982; Breen & Forwell, 2021; Burke et al., 2013; Copeland, Chan, Bezyak, & Fraser, 2010; Vornholt, Uitdewilligen, & Nijhuis, 2013).

Applying the Difference Model

From a practice perspective, the difference model provides a framework from within which to more effectively create positive relationships between

PWDs and the workplace. To illustrate, workplace interventions, such as the START Model of disability awareness training (see Chapter 6), can be structured to offer role-played, *in the moment* experiences with PWDs rather than focusing on statistically based demonstrations of attendance, use of sick time, accommodation costs, and other efforts to "correct" employer misperceptions. The difference model also supports efforts to provide various relationship-building exercises between PWDs and employers, including individual workplace-based mentorship programs.

The difference model provides PWDs, employers, and co-workers a means to view disability through a less adversarial lens, creating opportunities for more collegial and less intimidating workplace relationships. Indirect applications of the difference model, through pre- and post-administrations of tools such as the CADE Scale (see Chapter 6), can benefit both vocational rehabilitation specialists and employers in determining the effectiveness of workplace interventions.

Within the burgeoning digital workplace, organizations are attempting to create environments that provide a positive experience for all employees (Gheidar & ShamiZanjani, 2020). As noted by Plaskoff (2017), "a company must truly understand and empathize with its employees, both as individuals and as part of representative groups" (p. 137). If a workplace is to meet this goal with regard to employees and job seekers with disabilities, it must respond to the relationships that exist between PWDs and others. As we maintain, these relationships are affect-driven. However, to date, this component has received little attention in the scholarly and employment literature or in practice settings (Chordiya, 2022).

The difference model of disability foregrounds an attribute that has otherwise been overlooked but which weighs heavily on workplace decisions regarding the hiring, retention and promotion of employees with disabilities (Sundar et al., 2018). This allows the agile employer to go beyond more limited cognitively driven assumptions and consider the full scope of the employee-focused relationships that exist within the workplace. Many of our current employment environments, particularly those within rapidly changing organizational contexts, workplace designs, processes, and leading-edge technology are understood to be inherently flexible (see, for example, Ferreira, Potgieter, & Coetzee, 2021). A more comprehensive analysis of the workplace relationships that exist between PWDs and others will support a more generally positive employee experience and inform employer strategies to hire members of this trained, skilled, and under-utilized group (Bruyère, VanLooy, von Schrader, & Barrington, 2016; Gillies, 2012).

A Final Comment

As we have described in the above chapters, models within the social sciences are delineated from theories in that the former are descriptive, while the latter are explanatory (Oliver, 1990). Within that dichotomous construction, the difference model may well be understood as a first, albeit very narrow step, in the creation of a theory of disability. We raise this point for future reference as we continue with our consideration of the means by which the difference model has been applied in explaining at least some of the challenges associated with employment and PWDs. Although we acknowledge that these are very early days, initial applications of the difference model within specific workplace environments have positively correlated with increased rates of employment, and rates of self-disclosure, on the part of PWDs.

6 Workplace Attitudes toward PWDs

Introduction

As we have described in previous chapters of this book, PWDs continue to struggle to reach equitable rates of employment in parallel with their IWOD counterparts (Saleh & Bruyère, 2018). We have also described the related contribution of negative attitudes toward PWDs (see Chapters 3–5 of this book) and will not do so again in this section. Instead, we provide a description of two streams of practice designed to support efforts to resolve this societal inequity.

The first of these, the Employment Mentorship Support Project (EMSP), includes the development and implementation of training interventions created to influence a specific aspect of pre-work and workplace-related skills and attitudes, described collectively as the characteristics and attitudes of PWDs and employers (Stone & Colella, 1996). The EMSP supports PWDs who are in pursuit of employment opportunities. It is intended to provide guidance, confidence, and interactional skills to those PWDs who could benefit from a structured exposure to the job seeking process or development of entrepreneurial skills and structures with the assistance of a mentor who has employment experience.

The second is the START Model of disability awareness training. This intervention is designed to provide IWODs with an opportunity for discovery; that is, discovering different ways of knowing PWDs within the workplace. This Model is supported by two recently developed self-report scales designed to measure workplace attitudes toward PWDs. Each of these scales – the Co-Worker Acceptance of Disabled Employees (CADE) Scale and the Perceived Barriers to Employing Persons with Disabilities (PBED) Scale – was created, for somewhat different purposes, within the theoretical framework of the difference model. Each of these is described below (see *Measuring Workplace Attitudes*).

DOI: 10.4324/9781003220695-6

Influencing Workplace Attitudes

The Employment Mentorship Support Project

The EMSP was created by a Canadian not-for-profit organization, CONNECTra, an organization with a singular mandate to support employment among PWDs. The objective of the community-based EMSP was to pair a PWD with a mentor with employment experience (one-to-one mentorship) to work toward employment and/or employment-related goals. Matching was based on a number of criteria, including geographical proximity, ease of transportation, ability to meet regularly, and the compatibility of job interests and experience, each of which was intended to facilitate a positive relationship and rapport. Once a PWD-mentor match was formed, the PWD received assistance from the mentor to set concrete, employment-related goals based on personal abilities and interests. PWDs then met their mentor on a weekly basis for eight months to work toward these goals and assess goal outcomes. These PWD-mentor matches were guided by Connectors, who were adults with physical disabilities with an acumen for facilitating the program and individual goals through thoughtful listening, supportive problem solving, and providing resources to PWDs and mentors throughout the program.

A pilot test of the program was undertaken to work through the logistics of the PWD-mentor matches, determine the types of supports needed, the length of the program necessary to get meaningful outcomes, and to smooth out other logistical matters (reporting, gathering resources, etc.). That first pilot test generated favourable results. In particular, 30 out of the 217 PWDs paired with a mentor, or 14% of participants, were hired or met a self-employment objective.

Before finalizing the program, a second exploratory study was undertaken to understand the experiences of PWDs who were receiving social benefits and to consider the impact of this circumstance on employment options. In this study, which included 23 PWDs, 60% were unemployed but 91% desired to work. Several issues and barriers to employment emerged, including system-level disincentives to employment (such as restrictions on monthly earnings), low and unspecialized employment support (such as employer resistance to flexible work and lack of accommodations), and societal and attitudinal barriers (by employers, potential peer employees, and society in general).

With the knowledge gained from the first two studies, the EMSP program was improved with the development of a resource manual for the PWDs and their mentors and report forms developed to facilitate the recording of events and issues. This third study recorded and focused on the employment goals of the PWDs, the outcome of meeting those goals, and the barriers and supports that presented. Importantly, 31% of 87 PWDs gained employment by the end of the EMSP program.

Some issues did remain however, such that 98% of employed PWDs identified facing at least one type of physical or personal barrier in the workplace and over 50% reported that workplace accommodation solutions related to flexible work hours, breaks, elevator access, and supports were significantly below the identified need. However, after completing the EMSP intervention, PWDs identified that the mentorship they received fostered skill development and greater self-confidence. Additionally, mentors and Connectors described the importance of fostering relationships as key for PWDs to move toward employment and that mentoring relationships appeared to help broaden personal perspectives about living with disabilities.

Also revealed was that PWDs believed that they had limited employment options due, in part, to employer attitudes. This, in turn, led to accepting work (paid or volunteer) that did not match individual skill sets or capabilities. Overall, biases and attitudes of potential employers and co-workers were perceived by PWDs as creating expectations that were either too high or too low. Finally, PWDs described having a continuous burden of demonstrating their competence.

There were several recommendations that emerged from this work for both PWDs and employers. For PWDs, recommendations included a need to familiarize themselves with community and government resources related to employment, and their rights in the workplace. Recommendations for employers were around the need to comply with required modifications and accommodations, as well as to address workplace biases or attitudes that may serve as barriers to inclusive employment. It is this recommendation, addressing attitudes in the workplace, that the next intervention, the START Model, targets in support of enhanced employment opportunities among PWDs.

The START Model

The purpose of the START Model is to expose participants to an environment that is conducive to a shift in perspective from one that perceives PWDs as different to one that encompasses PWDs within an expanded sense of workplace normality. This intervention has been developed over the past several years as a means to apply the difference model of disability within a practice environment.

This training module describes four distinct dimensions of influence that affect the relationships that exist between IWODs and PWDs in the workplace (see Figure 6.1). These four dimensions – skills training, awareness, resources, and theory – are explored within each training session and, with the input of participants, related to how PWDs are most typically perceived within an employment environment. Each of the four components is presented in a manner intended to break down barriers to the acceptance of PWDs required for a transition from membership in an *outgroup* to that of the *ingroup* (Goffman, 1963).

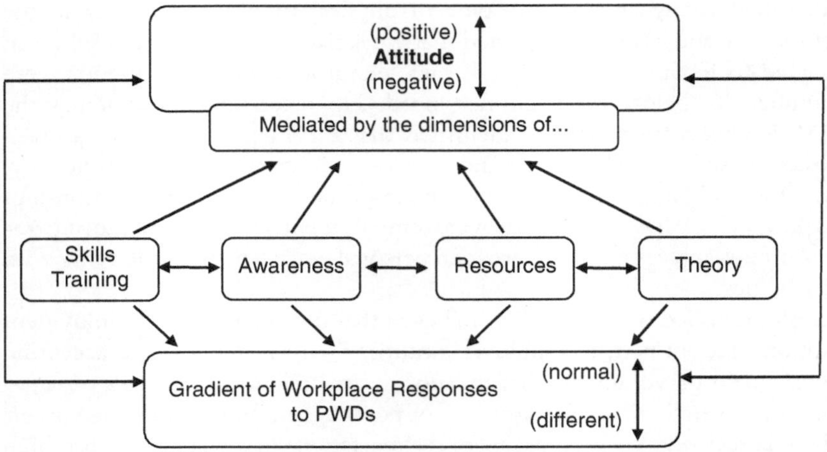

Figure 6.1 The START Model.

The START Model posits that attitudes toward PWDs can be influenced by exposure to four mediating elements.

Procedurally, five points are of note. First, the several specific topics that are considered throughout this training are typically somewhat imbricated and, to a significant degree, the discussion details are influenced by questions and comments provided by participants. Second, participants are encouraged throughout these sessions to voice concerns, describe perceived challenges, and to offer past experiences with PWDs in the workplace. Third, at the beginning of each training module, participants are asked to confidentially submit a question regarding disability that will be addressed either during or at the end of the session. Each of these three efforts is intended to provide participants with a sense of involvement in the structure of the training session and an acknowledgement of prior conflicting or negative experiences with PWDs in the workplace. The fourth point of note is the administration of the CADE Scale to each participant on a pre- and post- basis. As described in detail later in this chapter, the CADE Scale has been developed to measure workplace attitudes, and changes to these attitudes, toward PWDs. Administered one day prior to and two weeks following the START training module, response data are analysed for indications of attitude change (Furr & Bacharach, 2014).

The final procedural point is the disability-related identity of the trainer (s) within deliveries of the START Model. As indicated by Beattie, Anderson, and Antonak (1997), disability awareness training delivered by a PWD has resulted in significantly more positive attitudes by participants. Barr (2012) notes that these positive attitudes toward PWDs are also influenced by the "quality of contact" (p. 11) between PWDs and IWODs, with this *quality* understood as including an equality of status within a personal relationship. Qualitative support for these findings has also been found within the many comments provided by participants through organizational follow-up questionnaires within various START Model training venues. In particular, participants noted that potentially awkward questions regarding disability were more comfortably raised with facilitators who were PWDs.

As of this writing date, the START Model of disability awareness training has been delivered over 50 times since 2010. All of these have been delivered either by Breen or by Breen with a training partner who is also a PWD. Each of these has been in-person. Breen and Forwell are currently engaged in transforming this training model into a digital format that will retain its interactive structure and maintain a similar "quality of contact."

As described above, the START Model considers four separate dimensions within the workplace relationships that exist between IWODs and PWDs. However, of principal significance is the role that each of these play in mediating second-level supervenient attitudes as these have been previously internalized by participants (see Chapter 3). These attitudes, as mediated by these four dimensions, are considered to directly influence practice activities, including the hiring, supervision, discipline, and dismissal of PWDs. This process is illustrated in Figure 6.1.

Each of these four dimensions contained within the START Model, as well as their individual and collective effects on workplace attitudes toward PWDs, are described below.

Skills Training

These materials and presentation segments provide basic knowledge regarding current communication, language, accommodation considerations, and duties and responsibilities on the part of employers, supervisors, and coworkers. Discussion points are based on workplace-related case studies designed to illustrate these several informationally based protocols. To illustrate, the generally accepted language around disability, including *persons with disabilities*, *disabled persons*, or *PWDs*, is considered by participants. The purpose of presenting this topic is not necessarily to arrive at an agreed-upon choice of language but rather to raise this ongoing debate in a manner that generates comfort with that language.

Awareness

This topic includes summaries of several of the realities and myths regarding PWDs, including discussions regarding discrepant understandings of motivations that may be driving various behaviours, demographic analyses of PWDs in the workforce, and descriptions of the effects of relational challenges, whether purposeful or inadvertent, that are experienced by PWDs.

Resources

Demonstrations are provided of current accommodation resources for PWDs as well as those suitable for IWODs within the workplace environment. Examples of the former are included as demonstrations of supports for various limitations on the part of some PWDs. Within these are a variety of what are now considered to be commonplace by many PWDs but which may be unknown to IWODs. Supports for IWODs are also considered. These include local, national, and international solution-focused organizations that provide expertise in topics such as relationship building, interview techniques, approaches to difficult conversations, and other potentially sensitive workplace communications.

Theory

Considerations include a historical review of the several models of disability, with an emphasis on the difference model. These also include a description of the means by which attitudes are formed, how they may be affected, and an account of the effects that IWOD attitudes have on the success of PWDs in the workplace.

START Model Introduction

Each of the training sessions begins with an introduction of the facilitator(s) and a description of the purpose. That purpose is presented as follows:

> As you may be aware, [insert name of organization] has made this training available to you as a part of its efforts to provide a more fair and equitable employment environment for PWDs. I realize that this statement implies that this is not the case right now. Unfortunately, this is demonstrably true across the employment spectrum here in Canada and elsewhere. PWDs have been and continue to be unemployed and underemployed at a rate that is both measurable and considerably below the employment rates for others without disabilities. My research, and that of many others, indicates that this state of affairs is driven principally by the attitudes of employers, supervisors, and co-workers of PWDs, as well as by the attitudes of others who may be involved in the hiring process itself.
>
> Although these may appear to be harsh words, they reflect employment rates that have been very low and virtually constant since this information was first accumulated by Canadian, American, and other national statistics-gathering agencies. However, please keep in mind that these indicators are based on data that are gathered across the employment spectrum and do not apply equally to every individual or every organization. Also, since they are averages, they do not reflect the fact

> that some organizations are doing much better than others. As you may be aware, [insert name of organization] is making efforts to improve the representation rate of PWDs within its workforce and to ensure that those individuals who are already here are able to reach their full potential.
>
> If, as I have indicated, there is a direct correlation between workplace attitudes and the overall employment success of PWDs, it makes sense for us to spend time today looking closely at what we mean by attitudes, how they are created, and how do they actually relate to the employment success of PWDs. And, importantly, do we even recognize our own attitudes and the impact that they may have on seemingly unrelated decisions.
>
> Before we begin to consider these and a number of related issues, I would like to take just a minute and let you know what my goal is for our time together today. I will take each of you on a three-hour journey of *compressed experience*. Framed partly by my own lessons learned as a lifelong PWD, partly by my professional and academic background, and partly by the relationships that each of you may already have with PWDs, we will spend the next few hours examining issues and perspectives that impact PWDs in the workplace.
>
> Although this journey is short, I hope that it proves valuable.
>
> The notion of *how we understand disability* is critical. It is more than an appreciation of various facts concerning PWDs. It also includes the relationships that exist between PWDs and others. We will look at *how* people understand disability, *why* this is so, and what *differences* these various understandings may make regarding topics such as - the entitlement to accommodations in the workplace, supervising PWDs, and even deciding who actually is a PWD and who is not.

The introduction ends with a message of anticipation; that each participant will leave with a greater appreciation of the issues that influence employment and PWDs. And, finally, that PWDs themselves are perceived from a more clearly informed perspective.

Following the introduction, the training module draws upon a variety of teaching modalities designed to draw participants into real-time, real-life interactions with and about PWDs. These include deliberations associated with case studies, practice presentations to work groups, and group problem-solving exercises. Each of these explores one or more of the four principal dimensions described above.

Measuring Workplace Attitudes

The first of these self-reports, the CADE Scale, was developed to be administered as a measure of attitudes toward PWDs across a broad spectrum of workplace environments and locations (Breen, 2018b, 2019). In its current form, response data can be analysed to determine relationships between these attitudes and gender, age, and organizational strata. In addition, the scale structure allows for a comparison between those attitudes toward PWDs perceived by respondents to be of immediate personal effect and those perceived to be of general impact on the organization. The CADE Scale can also be applied over time to determine changes in these attitudes, whether various workplace interventions bring about these changes, and whether such changes are sustained over various periods.

The second, the PBED Scale, was developed by a team led by one of us (Breen) at the behest of the United Nations Industrial Development Organization (Breen, Havaei, & Pitassi, 2019). This scale was created and administered specifically to measure employer attitudes toward PWDs in Armenia. Although similar to the CADE Scale in its overall purpose as a measure of employer attitudes, it was designed in collaboration with a range of Armenian stakeholders to reflect that group's perceptions of local workplace attitudes toward PWDs.

The development processes, psychometric analyses, and initial applications of each of these scales are detailed later in this chapter. However, prior to a consideration of the scales themselves, it is necessary to foreground these descriptions by considering two issues that have precipitated these specific development processes. The first of these issues is, simply, a recognition of the need for such measures. There has been an absence of a scale which has been demonstrated to effectively measure co-workers' acceptance of disabled employees (Breen, 2019). This research gap has been acknowledged regarding the availability of measures specific to attitudes toward PWDs in the workplace (Brostrand, 2006) and, more narrowly, of measures designed to measure changes in these attitudes over time (Wang, 2021).

The second issue to be considered is the degree to which the data obtained through applications of these two new measures generates information based on a meaningful degree of validity evidence in order to meet current psychometric standards.

Other Measures of Workplace Attitudes

As noted elsewhere, several instruments have been designed to measure attitudes toward PWDs (see, for example, Antonak, 1982; Findler, Vilchinsky, & Werner, 2007; Yuker, Block, & Younng, 1970), although few such measures have been developed specifically for the workplace (Breen, 2018b; Popovich, Scherbaum, Scherbaum, & Polinko, 2003). Of these few instruments, each has been demonstrated to face one or both of two distinct sets of challenges; those challenges found within the construction of the instruments themselves and those that fail to apply coherent theoretical frameworks to support determinations of attitudes toward PWDs within the workplace.

Within the first category, these scales have been most frequently developed to measure attitudes toward particular impairments, resulting in a limited degree of generalizability across the broad construct of disability. In addition, these scales have not typically engaged employees or co-workers as respondents, which has led to further concerns over generalizability (Gething & Wheeler, 1992; Loo, 2004) and scale validation (Waltz, Strickland, & Lenz, 2005).

The overall psychometric soundness of these few available instruments has also been questioned by others (see, for example, Antonak, 1988; Findler et al., 2007). These limitations include insufficient descriptions of particular models or frameworks of disability within which these instruments were created to allow for suitable evaluations of individual scale items (Messick, 1995), limited articulations of specific worldviews that would inform particular theoretical constructions (Young, 1990), and a failure to provide descriptions of specific understandings of disability which could inform various data interpretations (Hacking, 1999).

Finally, none of these scales has provided sufficient evidence of theoretical validity in support of subsequent interpretations and uses of test scores (American Educational Research Association et al. [AERA], 2014; Messick, 1995). A systematic review of scales that have been applied as measures of workplace attitudes toward PWDs found significant limitations associated with theoretical validity evidence. None of these measures provided a degree of theoretical coherence suitable for a reasonable determination of theoretical validity (Breen, 2018b). That review also indicates that current measures have typically demonstrated limited psychometric soundness in support of their conclusions. As indicated by Hubley and Zumbo (2013), measurement instruments require sufficient evidence of theoretical validity, in addition to empirical validity, in order to determine their effectiveness. Without a consideration of both empirical and theoretical validity, these authors state, any test inferences are meaningless.

Within the second category, that of applicability within the workplace, these few extant scales have not adequately considered the generally agreed upon differences between overall attitudes toward PWDs and those specific to workplace environments (Araten-Bergman, 2016). Research indicates that what are found to be relatively positive attitudes toward PWDs in various social environments are not similarly reflected within the workplace (Burke et al., 2013). Many employers acknowledge generally positive attitudes toward PWDs. However, these same employers provide comparatively negative responses toward PWDs with regard to their hiring intentions and support for workplace accommodations (Hernandez et al., 2000). Finally, to our knowledge, there has been little prior research directed specifically toward a comparative analysis of these bifurcated attitudes toward PWDs and the subsequent success of these individuals within public or private organizations. This lack of research "has limited our ability to understand and design interventions that address the discriminatory behaviors that affect persons with disabilities in the workplace" (Popovich et al., 2003, p. 164).

An Evidence-Based Approach

Unlike the cognitively based models of disability, which typically have not provided substantial empirical evidence in support of their various claims (Shakespeare, 2014), the difference model was developed within an evidence-based process. This has included the conceptualization of the model, as well as the development, initial applications, and testing programs of these two scales. Each has been designed within the difference model framework to measure workplace attitudes toward employees with disabilities.

The development of the difference model occurred over many years during which one of us (Breen) had delivered over 100 disability awareness training sessions to employees of public and private sector organizations across Canada. These began as information sharing sessions using a psycho-educational framework; that is, an educational approach with the objective of increasing knowledge as a means to affect attitude change. This approach focused on business case arguments, appropriate language use, and procedural issues associated with disability management. During this period, a basic post-workshop questionnaire was developed and administered to participants in an attempt to determine if knowledge was enhanced.

Based on these responses by participants, we tentatively concluded that, while enhanced knowledge was critical, it was also imperative to consider the relationship between knowledge and the attitudes of employers and co-workers. Consequently, these training sessions and the associated questionnaire began to include increased attitude-specific content. This recognition led to a shift in emphasis and the subsequent development of the CADE Scale and the PBED Scale. Each of these scales was developed to measure attitudes toward PWDs, as well as changes to these attitudes over time and/or following workplace interventions.

In both cases, this development process followed generally accepted guidelines to allow for validity testing (Beck & Gable, 2001; Lynn, 1986) and included their initial administrations, subsequent psychometric analyses, and evaluations of response data. These processes are described in detail in the final two sections of this chapter. As noted, it was determined that each of these scales is capable of measuring workplace attitudes toward PWDs within several demographic and organizational categories, including those that are related to the individual respondent's circumstance versus perceptions of corporate challenges, by gender, by age, etc. This data-driven approach supports tailored approaches to training and other interventions. The empirical evidence generated by the application of these scales was also found to support the difference model in its description of the affect-based relationship between PWDs and IWODs within the larger community.

A Brief Review of Validity Theory

Our second foregrounding consideration within the development of the CADE Scale and the PBED Scale is that related specifically to validity. Validity, in an informal sense, represents the degree to which measures, such as these two scales, can be relied upon to provide credible data. More formally, within the context of psychometric analysis, validity is defined as "the degree to which evidence and theory support the interpretations of test scores for proposed uses of tests" (AERA, 2014, p. 9). Within this latter context, a lack of significant evidence of either theoretical or empirical validity renders any hypotheses based on response data generated by the administration of various scales and other tests as relatively worthless (Hubley & Zumbo, 2013).

An understanding of this critical relationship between validity and the CADE Scale and the PBED Scale requires a consideration of this concept as it applies more generally to measurement instruments within the social sciences. Five sources of validity evidence are most typically considered to support those interpretations of test scores. These sources include: evidence based on test content, response processes, internal structures, relations to other variables, and the consequences of testing (AERA, 2014). These sources of validity evidence are summarized as follows:

Test Content

Evidence based on test content is obtained by evaluating the relationship between the content of a test, such as the items within a scale, and the construct it is intended to measure. This analysis typically includes an evaluation of the theoretical and empirical adequacy of a test to effectively represent the construct domain being measured. This form of validity evidence is most often obtained through analysis and input provided by subject matter experts (SMEs).

Response Processes

Evidence based on response processes is gathered through an analysis of those mental processes enlisted by participants in their responses to the items within a test. This evidence is generated through analyses of overall response times, comparisons between various test sections, or between test responses and other variables. Comparative analyses between sub-groups of respondents also contribute to a determination of meaning variance within the test items.

Internal Structure

Evidence based on the internal structure of a test refers to the degree to which the specific items within a test correspond with the construct under consideration. For example, variations in test structure could imply or represent a unidimensional or multidimensional theoretical construct. Each of these would correspond to appropriate levels of homogeneity or heterogeneity amongst various item scores.

Relations to Other Variables

The interpretation of test scores for a particular use may have some degree of correlation to external variables. Therefore, a comparison of test scores with these other variables may add to an overall accumulation of validity evidence. These external variables may include criteria such as performance measures that the test is anticipated to predict or to different tests that have been hypothesized to measure the same or related constructs.

Consequences of Testing

Evidence based on the consequences of testing may include uses that are intended by the test developer or those that are unintended. To illustrate the former, if a particular test is designed to inform more effective workplace training strategies associated with a measure of co-worker attitudes toward PWDs, validation would be supported by evidence of increased rates of hiring PWDs and corresponding employee retention. As an unintended consequence of testing, the specific act of administering that same test could generate either more positive or more negative value judgments toward PWDs on the part of some respondents.

A Unitary Concept

Validity is most generally conceived of as a unitary concept in which the several lines of validity evidence are considered and brought together within an overarching framework of construct validity (see, for example, Hubley & Zumbo, 1996; Messick, 1989, 1995; Sireci, 1998; cf. DeVellis, 2017; Kane, 2001, 2016). In broad terms, validity is "an integrated evaluative judgment of the degree to which empirical evidence and theoretical rationales support the adequacy and appropriateness of interpretations and actions based on test scores" (Messick, 1990, p. 5). Of most critical significance within this description of validity is the central premise that validity does not exist as an objective construct that is capable of being more or less accurately described. It is more accurately considered to be a hypothesis that is supported to various degrees by theoretical and empirical information generated from within several agreed upon sources of evidence (Downing, 2003). It is this overall hypothesis of validity, and its supporting evidence, that must be evaluated in order to determine the credibility of inferences from scores on various tests or measures to unobservable constructs (Sireci, 1998). These unobservable constructs include workplace attitudes toward PWDs.

This concept of validity continues to undergo significant development. The unitary conception of validity has not always represented the manner in which validity has been understood. Historically, this understanding has ranged from a narrow set of measures that were understood to exist as a function of validity within a specific scale (Loevinger, 1957) to more current conceptions of validity that rest on the interpretation of test scores for specific purposes. This process of revision and reconceptualization of validity is recognized and acknowledged as an ongoing and evolving property. Overall validation is considered to be a continuing process (Messick, 1995) and these understandings of validity continue to develop (Hubley & Zumbo, 2011; Loevinger, 1957; Messick, 1980, 1989). These interpretations have only relatively recently been understood to incorporate considerations that include those implications that exist consequent to any data analysis generated from within test scores. These implications from external sources include a range of social and axiological relationships (Hubley & Zumbo, 2011; Messick, 1998).

However, this unitary conception of disability is not universally accepted. DeVellis (2017) presents a more restrictive image of validity that is limited to content, criterion, and construct validity. Kane (2001, 2013) presents what that author refers to as an argument-based approach to validation that is focused on the several inferences and assumptions required to move from test responses to interpretations and uses that are based upon those scores. Validation is based on a consideration of the coherence of this argument in terms of the plausibility of those inferences and assumptions.

We have chosen to follow the unitary concept of validity as it most clearly includes a consideration of "value implications" (Hubley & Zumbo, 2011, p. 222). These are the personal or social values implied by a researcher's interest in a particular topic, and the theoretical underpinnings associated with these interests. Various commentaries acknowledge the broad and pervasive effect of values throughout the testing process (Messick, 1995; Schatzman, 1991). These also include a requirement as put forward by Brennan (2001), who states that researchers have a responsibility to disclose their own "personal politics" (p. 12) as these may influence value-based assumptions.

Value implications have been acknowledged by Hubley & Zumbo (2011) and others as a part of the ongoing reconsideration of validity. Messick (1989) states that "test validity and social values are intertwined and that evaluation of intended and unintended consequences of any testing is integral to the validation of test interpretation and use" (p. 13). Messick (1998) also notes that "value implications both derive from and contribute to score meaning, (therefore) different value perspectives may lead to different score implications" (p. 37). These value implications require that we are "more cognizant of and question how our values may shape our theories, the development and evaluation of our measures, and our interpretations of research findings" (Hubley & Zumbo, 2011, p. 223).

Value implications and social consequences are considered to be intrinsic to the meanings and outcomes of the testing process. These should not be construed as recent additions; instead, they have always been intrinsic, but have only recently been exposed as such (Messick, 1994). The unified theory of validity "makes explicit what has been latent all along, namely, that validity judgments *are* value judgments (italics in original)" (p. 748). Messick (1995) notes that these subjective elements, or personal politics, exist as either precursors to or as consequences of a test development process. Until recently, the principal focus has remained on those personal values associated with the consequences of scale applications. Although the antecedent values and outlooks of scale developers has also been raised as a topic of interest (Hubley & Zumbo, 2011; Messick, 1995), antecedent ontological validity as a distinct category of validity is newly emerging (Breen, 2018a; Breen & Forwell, 2021).

It is of note that the arguments put forward in support of these increasingly prominent considerations of value implications within current analyses of validity (AERA, 2014) are very similar to those associated with the value implications that are acknowledged as influencing the development of various models of disability (Corker, 1999b; Hughes, 2019; Thomas, 1999b). Each of these groups of researchers – those involved in validity theory and those working within disability theory – suggest that a failure to consider these value implications may skew any resulting interpretations. However, we are unaware of further analysis within the literature in either of these domains regarding the particular effects that may be engendered through influences of these unconsidered personal politics. Similarly, there is little discussion regarding any concrete steps that can be taken to ameliorate these concerns. The one exception is what is described as the unintended consequences of various test scores generated by a failure to consider associated value implications (Hubley & Zumbo, 2011). The introduction of ontological validity (Breen, 2018a), the most recently developed line of validity evidence, addresses this research gap by providing a framework for a consideration of the political and cultural influences that motivate the direction of research and subsequent data interpretation.

Ontological Validity Evidence

We present the concept of ontological validity as a means to explicate and categorize the relationships between antecedent value judgments and their influence over subsequent determinations of overall validity evidence. We consider the meaning of ontological validity, its location, and its effect on subsequent hypotheses drawn from data generated through the administration of various tests. Finally, we move from a theoretical consideration to one that is practice oriented by examining these attributes within the context of the CADE Scale and the PBED Scale, each of which has been designed specifically to measure workplace attitudes toward PWDs.

Many scholars within the field of validity studies acknowledge the relationship, significance, and impact of the worldview of researchers and their subsequent interpretations of research data. Kane (2001) notes that the "interpretations of observations always rely on prior assumptions" (p. 334). Messick (1995) states that the unified theory of validity allows for both objective and subjective elements. In addition, that author indicates that these latter elements, including self-knowledge, may exist antecedently to scale development. Schatzman (1991) suggests that data interpretation will be enhanced through a prior consideration of researchers' "commitments to received conception, sociological or political-ideological" (p. 311) positions. Kools et al. (1996) make a similar recommendation, stating that research perspectives require explanation because each "provides a different configuration to the data and results in a different interpretation of meaning" (p. 319). This perspective is supported by Vehmas and Watson (2016), who state that "without clearly articulated normative judgments" (p. 5) the guidelines necessary to interpret data generated by respondent scores are not available. Others refer specifically to the relationship between pre-existing ontological perspectives and test construction. DeVellis (2017) indicates that it is possible that individual items within a single measure could relate positively or negatively to a particular construct. Without an articulation of the particular construct upon which a scale has been developed, that author notes that it is difficult to know how to determine the intended valence of these items.

These normative judgments have been referred to variously as *value implications* (Hubley & Zumbo, 2011; Messick, 1998), *personal politics* (Brennan, 2001) and *ontological bias* (Breen, 2018a). These several descriptors share an understanding that disclosure is a critical component of any validation of test measures (Breen, 2018b). Rioux (1997) argues that the acknowledgment of the relationship between pre-existing normative judgments and consequent score meanings, particularly within disability-related research, should be considered to be a moral imperative.

These considerations of values, and their influence on research findings, occupy considerable space within current validity discussions. However, there has been little exploration beyond these variously stated acknowledgements. Although, as noted by Connolly (2002), "no affirmative theory can proceed without invoking ontological assumptions" (p. 67), few efforts appear to have been made to determine the relationships that exist between these antecedent ontological positions, the subsequent test development processes, and final determinations of validity.

This procedural gap undermines any resultant determinations of validity evidence within the process of scale development, administration, and analysis. This omission within that process also allows for a skewed interpretation of that validity evidence that may be considered in support of inferences based on test scores. This failure to acknowledge and describe a researcher's specific antecedent ontological underpinning vitiates a significant and required component of the unitary validity matrix when considering "the degree to which evidence and theory support the interpretations of test scores for proposed uses of tests" (AERA, 2014, p. 9). We suggest that a solution to this particular analytical lacuna may be found by including ontological validity evidence in that evaluative matrix in future determinations of validity.

The process involved in scale development is separated from both the antecedent ontological position of the scale developer and any inferences derived from subsequent test scores. Critically, the internal structure of the scale will be unaffected by either of these. However, without a description of that ontological position within which to consider the meanings of those test scores, these scores may be interpreted quite differently. Essentially, the input of the antecedent ontological position of the scale developer may affect the output without disturbing the internal development process associated with the scale itself. The structure is the same; the result may be different (DeVellis, 2017).

Within the context of PWDs, the scale development process would not vary significantly in terms of its internal structure regardless of which model of disability provided ontological influence. Each of these models could support the same scale categories and items. The difference would only be evident at the output level.

Four models of disability, when applied to the various categories of workplace interactions, could generate similar items within the CADE Scale. However, although the internal structure of this process is similar for each of these models, the output is dependent upon a prior ontological relationship to disability.

Without a recognition and analysis of this antecedent ontological perspective in which the scale is developed, any interpretation of the inferences generated from respondent scores becomes subject to a claim of ontological bias. This challenge is illustrated through an example item taken from the Attitudes Toward Disabled Persons (ATDP) Scale (Yuker et al., 1970), one of the most frequently applied by researchers in measures of attitudes toward PWDs (Wang et al., 2021). Item Five of the ATDP Scale states that "Disabled people are the same as anyone else" (p. 113).

Without being provided with sufficient information to determine and evaluate the ontological perspective within which this item has been drafted, two distinct interpretations, and scores, would be possible. First, this item may be understood to support the equality of PWDs. Second, it may be evaluated as supporting their inherent differences.

If the item is based upon a medical model of disability, test scores that are in support of the similarity of PWDs would be interpreted as representing a respondent's disagreement with that model's assumption that PWDs are inherently different from others. Within a medical model framework, PWDs are responsible for making best efforts to recover from what Parsons (1951) suggested was their *deviant behaviour*. These *deviants* were obliged to normalize their social relationships with the IWOD community. However, within a social model perspective, those same test scores would indicate that a respondent acknowledged that any perceived differences between PWDs and IWODs are external to the individual and socially imposed. Any required behavioural change rested with society, not the individual PWD (Oliver, 1990). Adherents to one or the other of these models of disability would form disparate inferences from the same data.

Scale developers, by omitting a clear ontological position within the overall test development process, create a second challenge. Reviewers are unable to examine and determine the intended theoretical standpoint of the scale itself. A systematic review of scales created to measure attitudes toward PWDs indicated that none of these provided information regarding the ontological orientation of the scale developer (Breen, 2018b). A further analysis of the several individual items within these scales indicated that, within each scale, different items relied on different models of disability. This imbrication of theoretical perspectives within individual scales precludes a cogent evaluation of validity evidence within the empirical and theoretical evidentiary framework necessary to generate well-supported interpretations of test data. This exclusion of theoretical validity evidence, considered to be both critical and significant (AERA, 2014), introduces an unwarranted degree of speculation into subsequent analytical efforts.

As we have outlined, it is clear that there is a broad recognition of the relationship between researchers' various worldviews and findings of validity. However, there has been little effort made to move beyond this recognition to a process that provides a framework for the evaluation of this relationship as it applies to the overall validation process. The question becomes whether there is a means to address these ontological considerations in a manner that would generate additional validity evidence within the scale development process and any subsequent inferences generated through analyses of score data. We suggest two possibilities. The first occurs at a macro level through the application of several qualitative research techniques. The second occurs at a micro level, illustrated through a description of the development processes of the CADE Scale and the PBED Scale.

The Oxford English Dictionary (1997) states that an assumption is that which is taken for granted as the basis for an argument or action. Following this definition, although quantitative processes are capable of maintaining an internal coherence, they are enclosed by a set of surrounding assumptions. Within the sphere of scale development, a researcher's antecedent ontological position assumes the role of these assumptions, creating propensities, limitations, and biases (Creswell, 2013) which, in turn, inform subsequent development and implementation processes.

Qualitative researchers provide a range of recommendations regarding how best to acknowledge and evaluate the impact of these *a priori* assumptions when quantitative analyses and test data interpretations are dependent on underlying assumptions (Schatzman, 2001). Creswell (2013) describes eight distinct methods, various combinations of which may be utilized to address researcher bias which, according to that author, may well be introduced into any study. Of particular applicability with regard to ontological bias is the requirement of "*clarifying researcher bias* from the outset of the study … so that the reader understands the researcher's position and any biases or assumptions that impact the inquiry (emphasis in original)" (p. 251). That author also identifies researcher reflexivity as a method to consider a set of possible biases, recognizing that interpretations by readers may be influenced by those biases (Creswell, 2013). Researcher reflexivity includes a critical self-evaluation of possible biases and beliefs and an explicit acknowledgement that these may affect the research process (Berger, 2015).

The value of reflexivity is also described by Maxwell (2012) who suggests the application of a framework of triangulation. Described by that author as a technique of making use of several methods and sources to gather and present information, triangulation "reduces the risk that your conclusions will reflect only the systematic biases or limitations of a specific source or method" (p. 106). This reflection, and the consequent transparency generated by this process, is intended to create a more fulsome and available validation process. A clear articulation of the "personal politics" (Brennan, 2001, p. 12), in this case the ontological framework applied to the scale development process, adds to this evidence and provides transparency (Hubley & Zumbo, 2011; Messick, 1989, 1995).

The above arguments indicate that understandings of validity are interpretive, and that there is an obligation for researchers to describe and offer for inspection the framework from within which these understandings are derived. If validity is influenced by the interplay between an internally coherent epistemology and a particular ontological framework which has the potential to influence any subsequent data-driven hypotheses, there is value to be found in making these ontological assumptions visible for external scrutiny. Presenting that framework for inspection will provide the opportunity for a more broadly based and coherent analysis and critique of validity evidence. Otherwise, statements related to validity are only partially available for critique.

Workplace Attitude Measures

Self-report scales designed to measure community attitudes toward PWDs first began to appear in the 1930s. However, these early instruments did not typically present evidence in support of either the validity or reliability of individual test items or overall test scores (Yuker, Block, & Younng, 1970). Following these earliest efforts, newer measures began to examine attitudes toward PWDs within specific contexts, including the workplace, and to provide increasingly sophisticated statistical analyses of test results. However, the limited validity evidence upon which these findings have been based, especially evidence of theoretical validity, continues to raise concerns regarding possible bias and a lack of reliability (Breen, 2018b).

The few scales available to examine the relationship between co-worker attitudes and PWDs have been most frequently conceptualized as a combination of external influences on co-workers, including environmental or organizational characteristics such as legislative frameworks, corporate policies, business or strategic goals, or personal characteristics of employees with disabilities (Stone & Colella, 1996). In other examples, psychosocial relationships between co-workers and employees with disabilities have been correlated with the size of a particular workplace, the nature of the work being conducted, or the behaviour of those employees with disabilities. Those measured behaviours ranged from the degree of exhibited friendliness to levels of demonstrated obsequiousness (Colella & Varma, 2001).

Although these scales may offer useful comparisons of disability-related co-worker attitudes within one or more of these several external parameters, they tend to demonstrate one or both of two limitations. First, they describe relatively inflexible environmental correlates with these attitudes. Second, they do not speak to the interactional, motivating factors that influence these determinations. In addition, these scales do not provide potentially transformative data to those employers or co-workers whom they measure or to employees with disabilities.

Knowing that co-workers in larger organizations frequently display more positive attitudes toward employees with disabilities than do co-workers in smaller organizations (Burke et al., 2013) is of limited value to the disabled job seeker, the policy developer, or the human resources department if there is no immediate or direct action that can be taken to build upon that information. Based on these data, PWDs may choose to seek employment opportunities in large organizations that display these more positive attitudes. However, this is merely playing the odds, not changing the playing field.

Finally, those measures available to quantify workplace attitudes toward PWDs have been described as providing little formal evaluation or detailed psychometric analyses (Antonak, 1988). This observation has been more recently supported in a systematic review of current instruments (Breen, 2018b). In that latter review, none of these instruments articulated evidence of theoretical validity or indicated reliance on a specific model of disability. As described in Table 6.1, those four measures which could be analysed on an item-by-item basis revealed varying degrees of imbrication related to each of three prominent models of disability (medical, social, and embodiment models). This reliance on several models of disability within individual measures fails to consider a requirement for theoretical coherence within any validity analysis (Messick, 1990). A separate systematic review of 31 instruments measuring more general attitudes toward disability indicated

Table 6.1 Measures of workplace attitudes toward PWDs

Scale Name	*Date*	*Author(s)*	*Total Items*	*# of Items per Category*
Attitudes toward Disabled Persons (ATDP)	1970	Yuker, Block, and Younng	20	Medical – 13 items Social – 2 items Embodiment – 4 items Indeterminate – 1 item
Scale of Attitudes toward Disabled Persons (SADP)	1982	Antonak	24	Medical – 15 items Social – 6 items Embodiment – 1 item Indeterminate – 2 items
Interaction with Disabled People Scale (IDP)	1992	Gething and Wheeler	20	Medical – 3 items Social – 3 items Embodiment – 2 items Indeterminate – 12 items
Attitudes toward Employing People with Disabilities Scale (ATEPD)	2004	Loo	13	Medical – 5 items Social – 3 items Embodiment – 4 items Indeterminate – 1 item

Source: Adapted from Breen (2018b). Individual measures of workplace attitudes toward PWDs have drawn on multiple models of disability.

that a significant number of these measures were also found to have "poor overall utility" (Palad et al., 2016, p. 370).

Transparent Scale Development

The development processes of the CADE Scale (Breen, 2019) and the PBED Scale (Breen, Havaei, & Pitassi, 2019) each include an examination of applicable theoretical and empirical validity evidence. This was undertaken to provide the structural and procedural transparency that contributes to the overall evidence of ontological validity.

The methods that have been applied in the development of the CADE Scale and the PBED Scale include efforts to articulate their theoretical frameworks and to be transparent within our considerations of overall validity. Although the two scales described below followed somewhat different development processes, each was underpinned by three common supports.

First, within the context of workplace measures of attitudes toward PWDs, ontological validity evidence was operationalized as the degree to which theoretical rationales are delineated and incorporated into the development of assessment measures.

Second, as detailed in Chapter 8, an autoethnographic account of the personal history of one of us (Breen) has been provided as a personal and political framework from within which the difference model of disability and, consequently, the CADE Scale and PBED Scale, may be observed to have been developed. The purpose of that autoethnography, as well as the several commentaries provided throughout this book, is to make explicit those value implications, personal politics, and ontological positionings – and the social and cultural environments within which they are located – that have informed the development of the difference model and the two scales described below.

Third, evidence of theoretical validity was generated from within a three-part strategy. First, each of the proposed scale items was screened against the precepts of the difference model of disability. This alignment with a specific model of disability was intended to provide theoretical coherence (Breen, 2019). Second, all items within the scales presented issues that are associated with workplace circumstances. Each of these items provided an opportunity for respondents to rate their attitude toward PWDs specifically within the employment environment. In addition, the circumstances described within the scale items were crafted to allow for responses based on a comparative analysis between PWDs and IWODs. For example, Item Eight of the 20-item CADE Scale states that "Employees with disabilities are more likely than others to miss work." Finally, initial validity tests were conducted with respondents who identified as either employees or employers (Breen, 2019).

The Co-Worker Acceptance of Disabled Employees (CADE) Scale

The CADE Scale has undergone several modifications based on ongoing evaluations and initial validity tests. However, several core determinations have remained constant since the first version was developed. One of these central tenets that was of significant influence, both within the development process of the initial CADE Scale and the subsequent iterations described below, has been an effort to move beyond a descriptive analysis of attitudes toward PWDs. The CADE Scale has been designed to generate data that can be demonstrated to effectively measure, categorize, and provide support for strategies to enhance attitudes toward PWDs within the workplace.

The CADE Scale measures the level of acceptance of disabled employees by co-workers in terms of the degree of social separation or *difference* that is perceived by those co-workers. To accomplish this, the initial CADE Scale categorized and measured three variables – awareness, skills, and resources. These variables are associated with the co-workers themselves in an effort to understand *why* a co-worker accepts an employee with a disability. This analysis distinguished the initial CADE scale from other measures that evaluate the external, derivative question of *whether* co-workers are more or less accepting of disabled employees. This concept of *difference* as an underlying construct of this psychosocial relationship is discussed in more detail below.

The CADE Scale has also addressed a second limitation found within other current scales. These scales tend to measure attitudes toward categories of

PWDs that do not accurately represent workplace demographics as these relate to specific impairments. There has been a wide, and relatively inconsistent, selection of definitions and descriptions used by scale developers for the purpose of measuring attitudes toward PWDs. These have, either singly or in various categorizations, included physical disabilities, chronic illness, disabled athletes, classroom peers with physical disabilities, cerebral palsy, arm amputations, blindness, deafness, mental illness, and others (Findler, Vilchinsky, & Werner, 2007). There have also been correlations of attitude toward disability based on technical descriptions such as the 1995 World Health Organization's International Classification of Impairment, Handicap and Disability (Krahé & Altwasser, 2006).

However, none of these categories captures a realistic representation of PWDs in the workplace. In 2006, the Canadian federal government published the national Participation and Activity Limitation Survey (Statistics Canada, 2006). That survey found that the most commonly reported impairments in the workplace are, in order of frequency – hearing loss, pain, mobility, and agility. The 2012 Inclusive Public Service Survey conducted in the Northwest Territories, Canada (NWT Bureau of Statistics, unpublished) indicated that pain and mobility were the most common impairments among respondents. A similar census conducted in the Yukon Territory, Canada in 2011 (Yukon Bureau of Statistics, unpublished) listed hearing loss and pain as the two most common impairments among employees who responded to that survey. In 2017, the Canadian Survey on Disability indicated that the most frequently reported impairments in the workforce were, in order, pain-related, flexibility, mobility, and mental health-related (Statistics Canada, 2017b). In each of these, as described below, the limitations were operationalized within very broad parameters, allowing for mild, moderate, and severe categorizations.

The CADE scale addresses this discrepancy between how PWDs are actually represented in the workplace and the categorizations that have been most commonly observed in studies of attitudinal variance. Without a consideration of this issue, potentially biased data create concerns with regard to scale reliability and criterion validity. Scales that have been intended to measure co-workers' attitudes toward PWDs in the workplace could as easily have been measuring a similar but different construct.

The CADE scale presents the construct of disability to be measured as an individually perceived *negative relationship* rather than as a named, specific impairment or category of impairment, or a particular workplace environment, as a referent. Following the difference model, disability is created within the imaginary of each individual respondent. This process allows the construct of disability to be populated by an amalgam of those individuals perceived as sufficiently negatively different to rise above the horizon of social notice.

Within this context, a difference is named as a disability only when that difference is perceived as a negative attribute (Vehmas & Watson, 2014).

This perception of disability may change over time and location and is understood as a fluid social construct (Shildrick, 2012). In essence, respondents are encouraged to apply their own personal relationship to disability as a concept, rather than to particular individuals or categories of impairment, when completing the CADE Scale. Subsequently, what is measured by the CADE Scale is the generalized relationship between respondents and those whom they perceive as sufficiently different to rise above the horizon of social notice.

Background

The original CADE Scale, referred to herein as V.1, was developed in 2011 to fill a gap within the disability awareness training environment. A wide range of disability awareness training modules had been developed and delivered in North America following the original Tilting At Windmills program first introduced in 1981 by Richard Pimentel. However, there has been little progress made to quantify the effects of these training sessions on participants or, in the longer term, within organizations (Brostrand, 2006). This early version of the CADE Scale (i.e. V.1) was developed by one of us (Breen) and two colleagues (M. Hanson and Dr S. Jull) in 2011. It was first administered within a project designed to deliver and evaluate the effects of the START Model of disability awareness training to employees of the Government of the Northwest Territories in Canada (GNWT Disability Awareness Training Report, 2014, unpublished).

This first version of the CADE Scale contained 17 items designed to measure cognitive, affective, and behavioural dimensions of attitudes toward PWDs. Over the course of three years (2011–2014), a total of 337 respondents participated in 38 training sessions. Sessions comprised a full-day of training for the general population of employees. At the behest of the employer, these sessions were redesigned to be delivered in a compressed, half-day format for managers, directors, and members of the several executive groups. The scale was administered prior to and immediately following each of these training sessions. Divided into three sections, the scale presented items that corresponded to: awareness and comfort with disability (6 items); skills in working with and supporting PWDs (6 items), and; resources available to support PWDs (5 items). Respondents scored each of these items within a five-point Likert-style response format, with lower scores indicating more negative responses and higher scores indicating more positive responses.

We acknowledge that this first iteration of the CADE Scale was developed within a somewhat informal context and, consequently, was exposed to a number of potential psychometrically related critiques. However, two extremely interesting, albeit tentative, results became apparent following an Exploratory Factor Analysis (EFA) of these response data. First, although both the pre- and post- analyses revealed a three-factor model, the first factor in each demonstrated an eigenvalue almost four times that of the following two factors; in addition, each accounted for 65% of the *variance explained* by the EFA. This difference between the first and subsequent factors typically indicates that the scale should be considered as a one-factor scale (Furr & Bacharach, 2014). We described that factor as 'Comfort with PWDs in the Workplace'.

Second, the items that comprised the first factor within the pre- and post- analyses were almost completely different. Only one item from Factor One in *pre-* remained in Factor One in *post-*. The first factor of the *pre-* analysis was comprised principally of items that were based on cognitively oriented circumstances within the workplace. Conversely, most items in Factor One of the *post-* analysis were based on affect-based circumstances and relationships with PWDs in the workplace.

We had hypothesized that those items that were more directly related to affective/emotional experiences would accrue more importance to participants over the course of the training session and that these changes would correlate with a reduction in the *difference* relationship between co-workers and employees with disabilities. These results appeared to support that hypothesis, with the caveat regarding possible critiques described above. Our second hypothesis was that an exposure of participants to the realities of disability, the availability of skills and tools to remediate possible workplace limitations, and the resources available to support these remediations, would create an effect that is analogous to the concept of cognitive dissonance (Festinger, 1963). Within that construct, two incompatible thoughts held at the same time by an individual create psychological discomfort and a concurrent desire to eliminate that discomfort through a resolution of that incongruity (Mills & Harmon-Jones, 1999).

We encouraged an iterative process wherein participants were confronted with two incompatible emotional states that were in need of resolution. These two states, essentially disparate locations along a dimension of workplace attitudes toward PWDs, were separated by the degree to which the initial states were affected by participation in the START training module. This state, which we termed *affective dissonance,* provided an opportunity for participants to re-experience their affective relationships with PWDs.

The above referenced changes recorded by our EFA appeared to indicate that those items that were more directly related to affective/emotional experiences accrued more importance to participants. In addition, our comparative analyses between pre- and post- administrations of the scale indicated a general increase of 41% in overall mean scores. This increase represented a more positive relationship with PWDs. Overall, these changes appeared to be positively correlated with a reduction in the *difference* relationship between co-workers and employees with disabilities. These initial conclusions provided the incentive to continue with a more rigorous development of a second iteration of the CADE Scale.

As a second step in the development of the CADE Scale, a literature review was conducted that encompassed a wide array of scales designed to measure attitudes toward a range of othered groups. The purpose of this review was to determine whether a scale with a purpose similar to the proposed CADE Scale (V.2) was already available within a different context. Fifty-one scales were reviewed, including a selection of eight scales designed to measure generic racial attitudes and prejudices (Davis & Engel, 2011). Representation from several categories of othered groups included 41 measures of race/ethnicity/diversity, six measures related to women/gender, two measures of general prejudice, and one each of prostitution and poverty. Each of these scales demonstrated several differences from the proposed CADE Scale (V.2). These included differences in terms of their levels of specificity, a lack of intersectionality with disability, and no references to workplace accommodations (Breen, 2018a).

CADE Scale (V.2)

The development of the CADE Scale (V.2) maintained our commitment to a project that would generate data within a framework that was capable of analysis through considerations of both theoretical and empirical validity. With regard to theoretical validity, we continued with a process framed within the difference model of disability. As described in detail in Chapter 5, the difference model postulates that others' responses to disability are first generated as affective reactions, which require only the most basic mental processes and which do not require a cognitive analysis (Gawronski & Bodenhausen, 2006). Cognition is considered to be a secondary process employed to make meaning out of these initial affective responses and to provide a coherence to the worldview of the individual (Damasio, 1999, 2000; Guidano, 1995; Zajonc, 1980, 2000).

As a non-cognitive model, the difference model of disability does not require purpose, the need to generate fault, or purposeful meaning-making (Dhamoon, 2009) as an explanation for the relationship between disability and society. Instead, this relationship only comes into existence when PWDs are perceived to be sufficiently, and negatively, different.

As described below, the CADE Scale (V.2) retained this theoretical commitment with regard to both process and end result. Our second commitment, that of generating empirical evidence, included validity and reliability evidence produced first by a content validity study and second by an initial validation (pilot) study.

Content Validity Study

Evidence based on content serves as a foundation upon which test scores, including those acquired through measures such as the CADE Scale, may be evaluated and interpreted (Messick, 1980). Content validity is a determination of the degree to which the items within a test are representative of and relevant to the construct under consideration (Haynes, Richard, & Kubany, 1995). Content validity studies are typically comprised of three sections.

First, the developer of the study generates a set of items intended to broadly represent the construct under consideration. The recommended number of initial items varies from between 50% more than expected in the final scale (DeVellis, 2012), to twice as many (Miller, McIntire, & Lovler, 2011).

One of us (Breen) began the CADE Scale study in 2016. Based on the author's review of current scales (Breen, 2018b) and his own professional experience (Beck & Gable, 2001; DeVellis, 2017), a maximum number of 20 items was determined to be appropriate for the CADE Scale. Therefore, 40 items were generated for further evaluation.

To generate this initial list of items, the author conducted a systematic review of the literature (Breen, 2018a) and reviewed data from several government commissions that accept filings of human rights grievances (referred to as *complaints* in Australia and Canada; *charges* in the USA). These bodies included the Equal Employment Opportunities Commission (USA), the British Columbia Human Rights Tribunal (Canada), and the Canadian Human Rights Commission. Overall, workplace-related filings by PWDs were most commonly associated with discharge; followed by, in order of prevalence, reasonable accommodations (referred to in the UK as *workplace adjustments*); performance and supervision; and hiring. This initial list of 40 items included four subsets of 10 items – each of which addressed one of the abovementioned categories of complaint – hiring, performance, accommodations, and supervision/termination.

Finally, these 40 items were screened by the author through the difference model of disability. The purpose was to ensure that each of the scale items would present respondents with a workplace circumstance that would suggest a possible perceived difference between PWDs and IWODs. The structural coherence provided by each item having a foundation within the difference model of disability responded to the requirement to clearly delineate the normative judgments (Hubley & Zumbo, 2011) or value implications (Messick, 1998) underlying the development of the scale, thereby providing additional evidence of theoretical validity.

The second step in this process included the submission of the 40 items to a panel of SMEs for consideration and review. Garnering input from SMEs within this form of judgmental study is a commonly recommended method to gather evidence of content validity (see, for example, Beck & Gable, 2001; Lynn, 1986). Recommended numbers of SMEs vary from a minimum of three (Lynn, 1986), to between five and ten (Beck & Gable, 2001) to a maximum of 20 (Grant & Davis, 1997). However, Lynn (1986) notes that no maximum number of SMEs has been established.

With complex constructs, such as workplace attitudes toward PWDs, it is recommended that SMEs are recruited from several disciplines with varying categories of expertise (Davis, 1992). In addition, a broad geographic representation is useful if regional differences in language are anticipated (Grant & Davis, 1997), as is the case when considering the language of disability.

SMEs were recruited for participation through personal communication by the author. Each of the SMEs was either known to the author through professional contact or was well-known within the field of disability and employment. Each of the above recommendations was addressed within this process. Three categories of expertise were selected as representative of a broad understanding of workplace attitudes toward PWDs. These included: extensive delivery of disability-related training in the workplace; an understanding of the structural and functional aspects of the workplace through either an academic or practice perspective; and/or participation as a PWD in a variety of personal and professional employment relationships.

Initially, 35 SMEs were contacted either by telephone or email. Twenty-one of those contacted agreed to participate – four identified as female and 17 as male. Of these, eight SMEs had PhDs, two had LLBs, six had Masters degrees, and three had undergraduate degrees. The remaining three SMEs did not disclose this information. The geographic distribution of SMEs was relatively broad, with individuals located in Canada (11), the United States (5), Great Britain (4), and Australia (1). Eight of the SMEs identified as PWDs.

As a third step in this study, the SMEs reviewed the 40 items that had been developed by Breen (2018a; 2019) and categorized each on a four-point scale for *relevance* and *clarity* (Lynn, 1986). Items were rated for relevance as – *not relevant, somewhat relevant, quite relevant*, or *very relevant*. Ratings of *not relevant* or *somewhat relevant* were scored as *disagree* and ratings of *quite relevant* or *very relevant* were rated as *agree*. Similar categories were used for ratings of clarity.

These ratings were summed within a Content Validity Index (CVI) for each item (I-CVI rating) and for the scale as a whole (S-CVI) (Lynn, 1986). The overall CVI includes the proportion of SMEs required to agree on individual items (I-CVI ratings), as well as the scale as a whole (S-CVI rating), in order for the test to be considered content valid (Hubley & Palepu, 2007; Polit, Beck, & Owen, 2007). As the number of participating SMEs is increased, the proportion may be less than 1.0. With a panel of 10 SMEs, this proportion is calculated at 0.78 for individual items. However, no further reductions in a proportion of agreement are recommended for larger panels (Lynn, 1986). A similar proportion of agreement of 0.80 was applied to the scale as a whole (Polit et al., 2007).

As recommended by Schilling et al. (2007), written instructions to the SMEs included a statement that confirmed that all responses to the several items were to be based upon the relevance of each item to the construct under consideration, not on whether the SMEs agreed with the specific item statement. However, the response scores provided by three of the SMEs, in conjunction with several narrative comments provided by each, indicated that these SMEs were responding to their normative political beliefs. Scores for each of these three SMEs ($M=13.67$, $SD=1.53$) were much below those provided by other SMEs (M=34.8, SD=4.2). These three sets of SME scores were treated as outliers and removed from further calculations (Waltz, Strickland, & Lenz, 2010).

One further adjustment was made as the study progressed. Originally, the response data obtained from the panel of SMEs were to be calculated as one group, combining the scores of trainers, workplace experts, and PWDs with workplace experience (Davis, 1992; Grant & Davis, 1997). However, with a total of eight SMEs identifying as PWDs, an unanticipated opportunity became available. A comparative analysis of data obtained from PWDs and IWODs was conducted to determine whether these two groups generated significantly different scores. This analysis revealed that the PWD group generated lower I-CVI scores for relevance than the IWOD group in nine items, higher in three items, and the same scores in eight items. Overall, the PWD group scored an S-CVI score of 89 as compared to a score of 95 by the IWOD group. However, all overall I-CVI scores and the S-CVI scores equalled or exceeded the minimum recommended score of 0.78 (see, for example, Hubley & Palepu, 2007; Lynn, 1986; Polit, Beck, & Owen, 2007).

Finally, the CVI analyses of the SME responses indicated that 20 items scored above the 0.78 cut-off point of agreement by the SMEs. The remaining 20 items were removed, resulting in a 20-item scale. These items were organized into a measure suitable for administration as an initial validation study.

Initial Validation Study

A minimum of 200 responses is recommended for an EFA of a 20-item scale (DeVellis, 2017). Therefore, the sample size of 288 respondents recruited for this study was considered to be adequate. This sample was generated through a combination of two separate efforts. First, a description of the CADE Scale research project was published in a newspaper article on September 29, 2017 in Whitehorse, Yukon, Canada. That article also included a summary of the purpose of the project and a request to participate in the study by completing the CADE Scale. Access to the scale, through a provided URL, was described as available through a secure website that was hosted by the University of British Columbia. The introductory section of the online survey provided additional information and indicated that participation was both anonymous and confidential.

In the second part of the effort to recruit respondents, the CADE Scale was similarly described during a keynote address by Breen to participants attending a conference focused on issues of disability and employment in Albany, New York on October 12, 2017. Conference attendees were similarly invited to access the website provided and complete the survey. Each of these groups, in Whitehorse and Albany , were also encouraged to pass on the information and website address to others. The overall data collection period ran from September 29 to October 31, 2017. Participant responses were provided within a seven-point Likert-type response format, anchored by Strongly Agree (scored as 1) and Strongly Disagree (scored as 7). All response data were analysed through SPSS (v. 24).

Of the 288 respondents, over half were female (57%) and most were between the ages of 29 and 68 years (77%). The greatest percentage indicated that they had a postsecondary degree (68%). In addition, most participants indicated that they did not have a disability (78%). Key demographic information is shown in Table 6.2.

A series of EFAs was conducted on the response data obtained within the initial validation study of the 20-item CADE Scale. This analysis eliminated six items, resulting in a 14-item scale (Breen, 2019). A further EFA was conducted on this shortened version of the CADE Scale to determine the underlying components. Initially, a four-component solution was extracted explaining 53% of the variance. However, analysis of the four-component solution revealed that the first factor, with a score of 3.90 (27.86% of the variance explained), was more than three times that of the second factor at 1.27 (9.08% of the variance explained).

Similar to our analysis of the CADE Scale (V.1), such a large difference between the relative sizes of factors, particularly when subsequent differences are relatively small, indicates that only those large factors are significant (Furr & Bacharach, 2014). The relative difference of more than three times the variance explained between the first and second factors, coupled with the relatively small differences between the following factors, indicate that the CADE Scale should be understood as a one-factor scale. Furr and Bacharach (2014) suggest that such an analysis may be confirmed by a scree plot as described by Cattell (1966). The scree plot is essentially a visual representation of those eigenvalues that are considered to be significant. In this case, the scree plot also indicated only a single significant factor, thereby supporting the one-factor solution.

Additional supporting evidence for a one-factor solution was generated by conducting a Parallel Analysis (PA) of the data. In a PA, the number of variables, in this case 14 items, and participants (n=288) were input into software (Monte Carlo PCA) that generates random numbers based on a correlation matrix. That program performs a Principal Components Analysis (PCA) and determines the eigenvalues for those specified variables (Watkins, 2000, 2006). Only those factors which had generated higher numbers in the original data set are considered to be of consequence. When the PA data were compared to the CADE Scale (V.2) data, only the first factor in the original analysis produced a higher score than those generated by the PA (3.90 to 1.39). This comparison provided additional evidence for a one-factor solution. When calculated as a one-factor PCA, each of the 14 items in the reduced CADE Scale loaded with a coefficient greater than 0.30. This loading indicates that each of the items is measuring the same construct (Furr & Bacharach, 2014). The 14 item CADE Scale (V.3) is shown as Table 6.3.

Table 6.2 Participant's demographic characteristics in validation study

Age		*Education*		*Gender*		*PWD*	
Years	*# (%)*	*Completed*	*# (%)*	*Identity*	*# (%)*	*Identity*	*# (%)*
19–28	39 (14%)	Secondary	21 (7%)	Female	163 (57%)	PWD	46 (16%)
29–38	59 (20%)	College	41 (14%)	Male	104 (36%)	IWOD	224 (78%)
39–48	46 (16%)	University	82 (28%)	Other	5 (2%)	Unsure	12 (4%)
49–58	59 (20%)	Masters/PhD	90 (31%)	Prefer not to answer	8 (3%)	Prefer not to answer	5 (2%)
59–68	61 (21%)	Professional degree	27 (9%)				
69+	18 (6%)	Other	7 (2%)				
Total*	282 (97%)	Total*	268 (91%)	Total*	280 (98%)	Total*	287 (99%)

Source: Adapted from Breen (2019). Participants in initial validation study of CADE Scale are somewhat older, typically have post-secondary educations, identify most frequently as female, and closely represent the percentage of PWDs within the community.

Note

* Not all respondents answered all questions. Therefore, totals do not equal 288.

Table 6.3 The Co-worker Acceptance of Disabled Employees (CADE) Scale (V.3)

#	*Item*	*Employment-related Category*
1.	Disabled applicants should provide job-related details of their disability during the interview process.	Hiring
2.	I would be less comfortable welcoming a new employee into my work group if they had a disability.	Hiring
3.	Job candidates with disabilities are less likely than others to have the emotional stability necessary to succeed at very stressful jobs.	Hiring
4.	I would be concerned that having a disabled person as part of my work unit could negatively affect my own performance evaluation.	Performance
5.	Employees with disabilities are more likely than others to miss work.	Performance
6.	I would be more comfortable working with others who did not have disabilities.	Performance
7.	Employees with disabilities typically expect some help in performing their day-to-day tasks.	Performance
8.	I would be unhappy about being requested by a supervisor to assist a disabled co-worker with performing a brief, daily task.	Accommodation
9.	Supervisors should not have to accept additional responsibilities to manage disabled employees.	Accommodation
10.	Costs to provide accommodations for disabled employees often divert funds from other necessary expenditures.	Accommodation
11.	As a supervisor, I would be particularly uncomfortable following up with an employee who blamed a poor performance review on their disability.	Supervision/dismissal
12.	The supervision of disabled employees can be more difficult because of possible claims of discrimination.	Supervision/dismissal
13.	It would be harder for me to dismiss a disabled employee for poor performance than it would to dismiss another employee.	Supervision/dismissal
14.	Supervisors may have to spend less time with other workers in order to meet the needs of employees with disabilities.	Supervision/dismissal

Source: Adapted from Breen (2019). The 14-item CADE Scale provides balance in a measure of the four employment-related categories.

Exploratory factor analyses of scales developed to measure attitudes toward PWDs have produced both unidimensional (see, for example, Yuker et al., 1970) and multidimensional (see, for example, Antonak, 1982) solutions. Although Yuker et al. (1970) eschewed any consideration of theoretical validity as a part of scale development, those authors considered that respondent scores "may be interpreted as reflecting either the subject's perceiving the disabled as basically the same as or different from the non-disabled" (p. 42). Later writers, such as Antonak (1982) argued that the concept of disability was too complex to be interpreted as a unidimensional construct. Factor analyses of the 31 studies reviewed by Palad et al. (2016) revealed solutions that ranged from two to seven factors.

However, it is not surprising that a one-factor solution was generated from the initial validation study of the CADE Scale. As noted above, the questionnaire design was predicated upon the difference model of disability and each item was crafted within that specific framework. With the exception of the Attitudes Toward Disabled People Scale (Yuker et al., 1970), none of the scales reviewed in the systematic reviews by Breen (2018b) or Palad et al. (2016) demonstrated evidence of either theoretical validity or a unidimensional factor structure. Although many researchers indicate that the construct of disability is too complex to allow for a unidimensional factor structure (see, for example, Antonak, 1982), a comparative analysis of the relationship between factor structure and theoretical validity appears to have been unreported within the literature.

Each of the 14 items considered within the CADE Scale EFA included a relational aspect that differentiated PWDs from others. These include examples such as *less comfortable* (Item 4), *more likely than others* (Item 8), *particularly uncomfortable* (Item 16), *harder … to dismiss* (Item 18). These findings have implications for the focus of workplace interventions and training. If workplace attitudes toward PWDs are influenced by perceptions of difference, these interventions could include materials and techniques that would be different from those employed if attitudes were considered to be based on perceptions of an inability to perform certain job functions.

Several additional psychometric analyses were conducted on the response data generated through this initial validation study. Reliability indices were examined and considered to be satisfactory. A Cronbach's alpha was determined to be 0.79, which indicated a high internal consistency within the scale (DeVellis, 2017; Furr & Bacharach, 2014). The Cronbach's alpha also decreased if an item was deleted, with the exception of Item One. When Item One was deleted, Cronbach's alpha remained at 0.79. In addition, Item One showed a relatively low correlation of 0.24. However, this score was likely somewhat lower than the others due to its being distinguished as the only item to focus on an interview scenario. This item was retained for two reasons. First, it had been retained in the one-factor simple structure. Second, because it addressed a topic that has been raised as problematic by many of the SMEs in the content validity study. With the possible exception of Item One, these decreases in the Cronbach's alpha score indicate that each of the items is measuring the same construct.

Inter-item correlations and item-total correlations were also evaluated. Corrected item-total correlations that ranged from 0.23 to 0.53 were considered to be satisfactory. Inter-item correlations were small to strong, ranging from 0.04 to 0.47. The average inter-item correlation was 0.22. The CADE Scale is designed to measure a midlevel aspect of attitudes toward PWDs. These attitudes are limited to the workplace but are directed toward individuals with a range of perceived disabilities. Item-total correlations at the mid-range are more appropriate than those that are too high (>0.8); these latter correlations, for a midlevel scale, are considered to be redundant (Penfield, 2013).

The process described above provides theoretical and empirical validity evidence in support of the CADE Scale. The process that we have described is, however, subject to a number of critiques. Although SMEs were recruited from four different countries, these were all self-selected and English-speaking. A different panel of SMEs, with different skill sets and from different geographic locations, could have delivered different results. The potential for an acquiescence bias on the part of the SMEs is also a possibility. SME responses were not anonymous to Breen, who was known to many of the individuals within the panel. In addition, the potential exists for a confirmation bias on the part of Breen as the scale developer (DeVellis, 2017; Furr & Bacharach, 2014).

The potential for bias also exists within the framework of the initial validation study which was based on a convenience sample of respondents recruited through two public requests. These requests may have encouraged participants with an interest in supporting employment opportunities for PWDs, thereby introducing a positive bias into the responses. Additional validation studies administered to more diverse groups of respondents may yield different results. As such, results of this initial validation study may not be broadly generalizable.

Finally, as indicated by Messick (1990), test validity is ultimately based on an "evaluative judgment of the degree to which empirical evidence and theoretical rationales" (p. 5) actually support interpretations of test scores. Therefore, any determinations of validity formed by a review of this development process will be strengthened through further analyses of data, including those generated through a test/retest application prior to and following various workplace interventions (AERA, 2014).

The Perceived Barriers to Employing Persons with Disabilities (PBED) Scale

Introduction

A summary of the development of the Perceived Barriers to Employing Persons with Disabilities (PBED) Scale (Breen, Havaei, & Pitassi, 2019), is provided here as additional empirical validity evidence in support of the difference model of disability. The development process, the psychometric analysis of the first administration of the scale, and the input provided by a cohort of Armenian stakeholder groups, each provide additional support for the difference model of disability. This additional empirical validity evidence in support of a model of disability is analogous to and extends Messick's admonition with regard to test validity. That author states that the generation of validity evidence is a "continuous, never ending process" (Messick, 1980, p. 1019).

In Armenia, the employment of people with disabilities is considered critical for social integration and self-reliance (Osipov, 2013). In 2010, the Government of Armenia ratified the United Nations Convention on the Rights of Persons with Disabilities (United Nations, 2006) and, since that time, has been making efforts to reconceptualise disability within the framework of the International Classification of Functioning, Disability and Health (ICF). This new conceptualization includes a recognition of the relationship between disability and environmental factors. These factors include social, structural, and attitudinal barriers (WHO, 2001).

In 2014, in recognition of the importance of employment as a means to improve the socio-economic integration of PWDs, the United Nations Partnership on the Rights of Persons with Disabilities approved a joint technical cooperation project to assist the Government of Armenia in revising its strategy for disability certification[1] and rehabilitation planning procedures for PWDs. Led by the United Nations International Children's Emergency Fund (UNICEF), this project also included funding for the initial steps in the development of a national strategy to support and enhance employment opportunities for PWDs. This latter component of the project was directed by the United Nations Industrial Development Organization (UNIDO) with a mandate that included a delineation of the perceived challenges to the employment of PWDs from the perspective of employers.

One of us (Breen) was engaged by UNIDO to lead this latter aspect of the project. Ultimately, this led to the development, initial administration, and psychometric analysis of the PBED Scale. This project proceeded through several phases, framed within a Participatory Action Research (PAR) approach (Pasmore, 2001). First developed by Kurt Lewin, *action research,* including PAR, posits that social research is enhanced by incorporating the "meanings understood by participants as they act in their world" (Wallerstein & Duran, 2008, p.27).

Within this Armenian project, the PAR process was implemented to ensure that all stakeholder groups could participate and contribute their various perspectives on the issue of employment and PWDs within that country.

Initially, Breen conducted a literature review of studies developed to measure workplace attitudes toward people with disabilities (e.g. Antonak, 1982; Findler, Vilchinsky, & Werner, 2007; Yuker, Block & Younng, 1970; also see Breen, 2018b). This research indicated that none of these studies had originated in or had been applied to PWDs within Armenia. In addition, these studies, principally American, most frequently reported that employer attitudes were found to be significantly influenced by perceptions that PWDs were relatively incapable of performing required tasks within the workplace (Domzal et al., 2008).

The results of this literature review were presented through facilitated discussions with Armenian stakeholder groups over two days in October, 2016, in Yerevan, the capital of Armenia. These stakeholder group participants included five government officials, two educators, three employers, and 31 representatives from NGOs. This latter group included officials from UNICEF, UNIDO, and several Armenian organizations that provided various services on behalf of PWDs. Of these participants, six indicated that they were members of the Armenian disability community. Throughout these discussions, communications were in Armenian and English, supported by professional simultaneous translation.

In contrast to the findings obtained through the initial literature review, several participants from the several stakeholder groups indicated that the attitudes of Armenian employers toward PWDs were significantly influenced by concerns over negative perceptions of PWDs in the workplace by co-workers, supervisors, and customers.

Additional topics within this two-day session included a review of several models of disability, including the medical model, the social model, the difference model, and the biopsychosocial model (WHO, 2001). The group also considered a number of the principal arguments that have been put forward as explanations for the high unemployment rate of PWDs. These included the three factor argument put forward by Stone and Colella (1996) which recognizes legislative supports, organizational values, as well as the characteristics and attitudes of employers and people with disabilities, as contributors to this ongoing dilemma. The group generally agreed that, of these factors, the attitudes of others within the workplace are likely to be the most significant indicators of employment success for PWDs (Antonak, 1982; Findler, Vilchinsky, & Werner, 2007).

In addition, several of the participants voiced concerns regarding two additional challenges to employment success for PWDs within Armenia. These included the physical challenges to employment facing PWDs in Armenia and to negative employer and co-worker attitudes. The group concluded that, of these two, negative attitudes directed toward PWDs within the workplace were of primary significance.

Several group members also noted that there had not yet been a comprehensive measure and analysis of the overall priority of these considerations within the Armenian employer community. Therefore, it was recommended that the development and administration of a self-report questionnaire to a representative group of employers would be an effective step toward determining the issues that most significantly effected employer decisions with regard to employing PWDs. The group agreed that the data resulting from such a survey would make a valuable contribution to the development of training programs and other interventions within the workplace and as a means to inform policy intended to encourage more positive attitudes toward PWDs in Armenia.

The PAR stakeholder group provided input into three separate aspects of the proposed survey process. These included: categories and examples of questionnaire items, content of an introductory letter/materials to be forwarded to employers, and the means and scope of distribution of the survey.

The group reviewed a selection of surveys designed to measure attitudes toward people with disabilities in different contexts (see, for example, Domzal, Houtenville, & Sharma, 2008; Yuker, Block, & Younng, 1970). It was recommended that two general areas of employer concern should be explored. These included employer attitudes held toward job seekers/ employees with disabilities as individuals, and employer perceptions regarding accessibility and accommodations.

It is also of note that this information provided by the group did not offer a definition of disability against which employers could consider their responses. This decision by the PAR group was based on a recognition that the very low reported labour force attachment of PWDs in Armenia would result in few employers having direct workplace experience with individuals who could be compared to a provided definition. In addition, the group believed that measuring employers' attitudes against their own perceptions of PWDs would be an appropriate initial approach in Armenia.

Immediately following these discussions, Breen and two officials from UNIDO met with an official from the Republican Union of Employers of Armenia and with two additional employers from within the private sector. These discussions supported at least some of the recommendations made by the PAR group. These private sector and Union representatives agreed that employer attitudes toward hiring PWDs would likely be affected by perceptions of significant costs associated with workplace accommodations and with challenges in finding skilled workers with disabilities. They also agreed with the PAR group that employer attitudes toward PWDs would be influenced by perceptions of physical inaccessibility of various workplaces. However, they did not believe that negative workplace attitudes toward PWDs by supervisors, co-workers, or customers would be of significant influence.

Based on the input from the original PAR group and these additional comments, Breen developed a first iteration of the PBED Scale. The scale contained 15 items, each intended to address workplace attitudes of employers toward PWDs as individuals and attitudes toward environmental barriers. All items were presented in a seven-point Likert-type response format, with responses ranging from Strongly Disagree (1) to Strongly Agree (7), including a neutral midpoint. Item scores would be totalled after negatively worded items were reverse scored, with higher scores indicating more negative attitudes toward PWDs.

This first version of the PBED Scale was drafted in English. The survey materials were then screened through the Flesch-Kincaid Index to ensure a suitable functional reading level (Wilson & Wauson, 2010) and through the Gunning Fog Index, which indicated a satisfactory comprehension level for business communications (Wilson & Wauson, 2010). These materials were then translated into Armenian by a professional translator and then back-translated by a second translator (Brislin, 1970). Subsequent comparisons with the original English materials indicated that the Armenian version of the scale was an accurate representation of the original English version.

Following the completion of this translation process, a list of over 800 employers was compiled through consultations with the Yerevan UNIDO office, the Republican Union of Employers of Armenia, and the Armenian State Employment Agency. Each of these employer names was entered into a printed list that was manually cut into individual pieces and mixed together. A project volunteer randomly selected 180 employer names.

Each of the 180 employers was then contacted by telephone and, based on a prepared script, invited to participate in the described survey. Of these employers, 12 declined to participate. When asked to provide an explanation, each of these employers indicated that they believed that PWDs could not be effective employees. The remaining employers were advised that the survey could be, at their discretion, sent via email or delivered as a paper copy[2]. Eighty-three requested that they receive the survey by email. Seventy-three of these emailed their responses within the required time period.

The remaining 85 employers selected the paper copy option. For this latter group, project volunteers hand-delivered the survey materials. The volunteers waited while the surveys were confidentially completed and sealed into the provided envelopes by the respondents. All 85 of these surveys were completed and the envelopes returned to the project research coordinator. In total, 158 responses were returned, resulting in a survey response rate of 88%. Response data were anonymously entered into spreadsheets by the Armenian project coordinator and subsequently forwarded to Breen and colleagues for quantitative analysis.

In the second phase of this project, quantitative data from this random sample of 158 employers were used to examine the psychometric properties of the newly developed measure and to understand attitudes toward employing PWDs in Armenia. These response data were examined through the application of a series of EFAs, item correlations, and reliability indices. The resulting data, as well as those obtained through an examination of descriptive statistics, provided a basis for subsequent recommendations for Armenian policy development regarding the employment of PWDs.

To evaluate a 15-item scale through an EFA, a minimum of 150 responses is necessary (DeVellis, 2017). Therefore, the sample size of this survey (n=158) was deemed adequate for psychometric analysis. Demographic information gathered from respondents indicated that 55% were males and 45% were females. A total of 81% of respondents were younger than 49 years of age. A total of 37% of respondents worked in a mid-sized business with between 10 and 49 employees. Of the remainder,

31% worked within small businesses with fewer than 10 employees and 29% were from large businesses, with more than 50 employees.

A total of 40% of respondents indicated that their business employed at least one PWD. A total of 51% of respondents indicated that they did not and the remaining 9% were unsure. Of these, 67% of respondents from both the service sector and from the cultural and entertainment industry reported employing a minimum of one PWD. These were followed by the health and social security sector, reporting a rate of 64% and from education reporting a rate of 52%. Each of the other industry sectors reported that fewer than 50% of their organizations employed at least one PWD.

An initial EFA was conducted on the 15-item PBED Scale, using Principal Component Analysis with Oblimin rotation. This process indicated the removal of six items. As illustrated in Table 6.4, this resulted in a nine-item version of the PBED Scale (Breen, Havaei, & Pitassi, 2019). A second EFA analysis, again using Principal Component Analysis with Oblimin rotation, was conducted on this revised version of the scale to determine the underlying components. A two-factor solution was extracted, which explained 52% of the variance. The factor loadings ranged from 0.51 - 0.86 for the first subscale and 0.59 - 0.77 for the second subscale. These were well above the cut-off scores of 0.40

For each of the subscales, inter-item correlations were small to strong and statistically significant. These ranged from 0.21 to 0.53 and from 0.19 to

Table 6.4 Perceived Barriers to Employing Persons with Disabilities (PBED) Scale

#	*Item*	*Factor*
1.	Employing people with disabilities would add additional work for me.	Structural
2.	People with disabilities are unable to perform the jobs required in my company.	Structural
3.	Managers do not know how to supervise people with disabilities.	Social
4.	My customers would be uncomfortable with disabled employees.	Social
5.	Employing people with disabilities is too costly for our business.	Structural
6.	People with disabilities with suitable skills should have the opportunity to work.*	Social
7.	Our other employees would not want to work with people with disabilities.	Social
8.	People with disabilities do not have the skills needed to do the tasks that we require.	Structural
9.	The location of our business is not accessible to people with disabilities.	Structural

Source: Adapted from Breen, Havaei, and Pitassi (2019). Analysis of responses to the administration of the PBED Scale indicated a measure of both structural and social factors.

Note

* Reverse scored.

0.63 respectively. The average inter-item correlations were 0.38 for Subscale One and 0.35 for Subscale Two. Correlation between items in the first subscale and its total subscale score were strong, ranging from 0.60 to 0.76. The correlation between items in the second subscale and its total subscale score were also strong, ranging from 0.57 to 0.83. Finally, all of the items within the two subscales had item-total correlations greater than 0.5, which indicates that each appropriately provides a large amount of information (Penfield, 2013).

Reliability indices were also examined. Cronbach's alpha for the overall scale was 0.78. For the subscales, Cronbach's alphas were, respectively, 0.75 and 0.69. Corrected item-total correlations ranged from 0.37 to 0.59 (Subscale One) and 0.33 to 0.66 (Subscale Two). With two exceptions, the Cronbach's alpha decreased if that item was deleted. However, the Cronbach's alpha increased by only 0.01 when either of these was removed.

As noted, the EFA produced a multidimensional scale with two factors (Simms, 2008). The first of these was labelled *structural issues*. It included items that addressed the skill levels of PWDs, costs associated with various accommodations, and the accessibility of workplaces. Within this context, *structural issues* were considered to extend beyond any required physical accommodations to include employers' perceptions of the effects that PWDs would have on the workplace environment. These included performance measures such as overall productivity and quality control.

The second factor was labelled *social issues* and included items which addressed employers' anticipation of co-worker, customer, and supervisor reactions to PWDs in the workplace. These responses represented employers' anticipation of others' reactions to PWDs in the workplace. These items focused on perceptions of disability as a construct rather than ability or performance. Employers also indicated a belief that PWDs with suitable skills should be entitled to work. However, this belief may well have been mediated by an overarching belief that this would not typically be the case.

The findings from this first administration of the PBED Scale were significantly different from those found within several studies conducted within the USA and elsewhere. To illustrate, a large American Department of Labor survey (n=3,797) found that employer attitudes were most influenced by concerns that PWDs would be unable to perform the work required. Least frequently mentioned as a contributor to these employer attitudes was a perception that supervisors and co-workers would hold negative attitudes toward PWDs (Domzal, Houtenville, & Sharma, 2008). Similarly, an Italian study found that these employer attitudes toward PWDs in the workplace were informed principally by an expectation of poor performance (Nota et al., 2014). A French study that compared co-worker attitudes toward job applicants found that PWDs were perceived to be less competent than IWODs (Louvet, Rohmer, & Dubois, 2009).

Other studies have also offered a variety of explanations for negative workplace attitudes toward PWDs. These have included costs of accommodation (Copeland et al., 2010), a lack of positive experiences with PWDs in the workplace (Chan et al. 2010), and unpredictability on the part of PWDs (Findler, Vilchinsky, & Werner, 2007). Although this list is not exhaustive, it is of note that none of these studies identify employer concerns regarding possible negative attitudes of customers, supervisors, or co-workers.

Researchers have also suggested that employers recognize that it is desirable and appropriate to espouse positive and welcoming attitudes toward PWDs within various social circumstances but that these attitudes do not extend to economically motivated environments such as employment (Hernandez, Keys, & Balcazar, 2000). One of us (Breen) has termed this discordant relationship of attitudes toward PWDs as a demonstration of a *socially acquiescent façade of equity* (SAFE) mode of behaviour that is dependent on weightings of political correctness against perceived negative economic consequences associated with PWDs.

As described above, employer attitude surveys most often indicate that these attitudes are principally based on perceptions that PWDs are incapable of performing needed tasks. However, the results of this first administration of the PBED Scale indicate that, in Armenia, employer attitudes are influenced by their perceptions that PWDs, as individuals, would be poorly accepted by supervisors, co-workers and customers (social issues) as well as by perceptions of poor job performance (structural issues). These findings provide additional validity evidence for the difference model of disability. The significance of the relationship between employer attitudes and the factor that we named *social issues* supports the principal underlying premise of the difference model in that the items that appeared within this factor are all associated with perceived differences between PWDs and IWODs.

We also recognize that this administration of the PBED Scale indicated that employers had concerns over a number of structural barriers associated with the employment of PWDs. However, two practical issues are of significance when interpreting these data. First, in Armenia, accessible transportation and other suitable civil infrastructure are less commonly available than in the several countries more commonly serving as platforms for various measures of employer attitudes toward PWDs (e.g. the United States, the United Kingdom, Canada, Australia; see Breen, 2019). Second, the most frequently recognized and most likely to be engaged in the workforce are those PWDs with various mobility limitations (Osipov, 2013). It is possible that these two aspects of life in Armenia combined to influence the creation of the *structural issues* factor within our data analysis.

As we have referenced elsewhere within this book, our work with regard to the difference model, the CADE Scale, and the PBED Scale is ongoing and that further efforts may generate additional supporting, or contradictory, evidence. We also recognize that the findings generated from these initial applications of these two scales could be further validated through additional administrations of the final, shortened versions.

The use of a larger and more broadly representative employer sample would allow for additional psychometric analysis. A larger sample size from various locations within Armenia would also provide more broadly based demographic information, including more detailed information related to industry sectors. It would also allow for a more detailed analysis of the relationship that exists between structural and social factors which influence employer attitudes in their consideration of hiring PWDs.

Similarly, additional administrations of the CADE Scale, within a more geographically diverse and more broadly based employment environment, would also provide additional data for psychometric analysis, particularly as these would pertain to generalizability. We anticipate that these future administrations and analyses of the PBED and CADE Scales will have significant implications for the development of vocational rehabilitation strategies and the focus of employer training and awareness interventions.

Notes

1 In 2012, individuals certified as PWDs represented 6.2% of the population of Armenia. This calculation includes only those PWDs who have been certified as having impairments that have been determined to be either *medium* or *severe*. Certification is not provided to PWDs who have been rated as having either *light* or *moderate* impairments. Only those PWDs who are certified are included in disability-related statistics and are eligible for supports (Osipov, 2013).

2 This mixed method of data collection was created to account for a recognition that many employers did not have access to email. It should also be noted that although those with email access were made aware of the potential insecurity of email transmissions, none raised a concern.

7 People With Disabilities

This chapter is an effort to provide some insight into the several perspectives that have informed our current understanding of PWDs. In one sense, as we describe next, the factors that have been of significant influence include historical interpretations of disability, more immediate interpersonal and intrapersonal relationships with disability by both IWODs and PWDs, and various considerations of the future social status of disability. These several understandings are distinguished, not only by their ontological underpinnings but, by extension, whether these differences should continue to exist.

In a more meta-analytical sense, each of these factors can be understood as contributing to several relatively parallel explanations that follow from a single set of relational discrepancies or differences. As we have described earlier, various models of disability, from the moral model to those that are supported by various interpretations of identity politics, require a continuation of difference for their existence. Others, such as variations of the social model, argue for masking these same differences. The difference model, as we have described in detail, suggests that difference can be eliminated through a subsumption of disability into a greater community norm.

Regardless of these variations in understandings, it is unlikely that many PWDs or IWODs would suggest that in our present environment, particularly as it relates to employment, PWDs enjoy opportunities that are similar to those afforded to IWODs. Every analysis that has been cited within this book, and elsewhere, clearly demonstrates this discrepant reality. Our intent throughout this chapter is to provide the reader with a broad, and somewhat unvarnished, overview of perceptions of disability in order to assist in the project of extinguishing these relational discrepancies. By delineating these varied and sometimes complex relationships, some of which have existed for millennia, we have attempted to present these historical and current relationships as building blocks for future efforts to remove PWDs from our current perceived status as the *other* (Stainton, 2004).

DOI: 10.4324/9781003220695-7

It may be useful to offer a brief consideration of the larger disability community as it is related to those of us who write and speak about PWDs. Are we playing statistical games when we acknowledge that those with disabilities make up 15% of the population and that this significant minority wants specific political concessions, various entitlements, or particular ways of living? Are we suggesting that these desires are voiced on behalf of 15% of the population? The obvious dilemma is that advocates, academics, and others who purport to speak on behalf of PWDs may be implying a much bigger support base than is actually the case. If we tease apart the population of the disability community, we see that it is anything but a homogenous group, and nowhere are there indications that anyone actually speaks for more than a small segment of PWDs. This is particularly concerning when we consider that the membership of the most significant group within the disability community – the people who have no affiliation with any organization – have never indicated that they wish anyone to speak on their behalf. Instead, they are just getting on with their lives.

A Cultural and Historical Overview

Regardless of the specific environment in which various relationships between PWDs and IWODs exist, society has typically sought a means to categorize and assign rankings to its membership. Goffman (1963) refers to this ranked separation as the *ingroup* and the *outgroup*. As Davis (2000) describes, in an analysis of this divide specific to IWODs and PWDs, "Cultures perform an act of splitting. … These violent cleavages of consciousness are as primitive as our thought processes can be" (p. 53). Fujiura and Rutkowski-Kmitta (2001) argue that "We are driven to classify and count the human condition … Such has been the case with disablement" (p. 69). Stainton and Swift (1996) suggest that this differentiation is necessary to support a determination of collective and individual identities. Shakespeare (1994) notes that "for there to be normality, it is necessary for there to be abnormality" (p. 294). The following historical review provides additional illustrations of these hegemonic understandings of disability as conceptually separated from the IWOD community.

In classical Greek times, there was no abstract word to describe the concept of physical disability as a predetermined set of limitations (Edwards, 1997). Instead, disability was based on the degree to which an individual was able to engage in appropriate participation in these communities. This *community model* of disability determined the status of individuals with physical disabilities, and community participation by those with limitations was commonplace. Military service and other efforts that contributed to social necessities were carried out by those described as " … men [*sic*] with significant physical impairments" (p. 40).

Although these individuals, typically with acquired disabilities, were frequently able to maintain a reasonable level of participation in community life, those born with disabilities were often killed at birth. Those disabilities were seen as offences to the gods and required immediate resolution (Braddock & Parish, 2001). Others, including those who were deaf or mute, were typically considered as worthless or cursed (Rose, 2006). A secondary trope that emerged within classical times, and which still continues to be maintained by at least a minority, is that from suffering comes wisdom (Gagnon, 2016). Within this context, disability continues to be understood as a test of faith (Retief & Letsosa, 2018).

Following the classical period in the Western world, according to Gregory (2007), were "centuries of indifference and hostility toward the psychiatrically and mentally impaired … . (T)hey were alternately ignored, persecuted, or tortured" (p. 53). Although some theorists have argued that the rise of capitalism and modernism have created the classification of *disability* (Oliver, 1990), others suggest that, notwithstanding a lack of generic terminology, few individuals with physical disabilities survived for very long in many of the pre-capitalist economies (Charlton, 2006). Darling (2013) describes a litany of culturally related responses to infants born with visible impairments within these apparently halcyon days. These responses are best described as both immediate and fatal.

The dichotomy between those with differences that were either unrecognized or seen as benign and those that were not accepted has existed across a broad spectrum of cultures. Similar to the ancient Greeks, many African languages have no single word for disability and only name those specific limitations that have what are construed as having a negative impact on daily life. Other categories of impairment are essentially ignored (Darling, 2013).

The Renaissance period of the late 15th and early 16th centuries saw a re-emergence of the rationalism that had been in relative abeyance since classical times. This led to a revised representation of society that was based on the burgeoning scientific revolution and empiricism, which quickly spread from the natural sciences to encompass a broad range of social affairs (Rogers, 1995).

This application of a process of quantification to human relations necessitated a means to describe and measure social boundaries. The solution was the creation of the *other*, a categorization based on unreason and depravity. This was a significant transformation of disability from what had been considered, at various times, as residing somewhere along a spectrum that had ranged from the acceptance of benign difference to the focus of the wrath of the gods. This notion of *unreason*, as described by Foucault (1988), included categories described as the insane, the deranged, and the demented. Stainton (2004) argues that the oppression of PWDs reaches beyond various socially manifested political constructs, down into "the fundamental discursive nexus of reason/unreason, which is crucial ... to the very existence of the concept itself" (p. 226).

Whether this categorical separation was one of reason and unreason, individual moral or spiritual desuetude, or divine punishment, disabilities have been treated throughout history with a mixture of fear and discomfort and, occasionally, a degree of tolerance (Braddock & Parish, 2001). However, an increasingly medicalized view of disability during the 19th and 20th centuries added a new dimension to the stigmatization of PWDs. Prior to that period, all bodily representations were seen as unavoidably flawed due to the impossibility of attaining the perfection exhibited by the gods (Davis, 2006). As theoretical analyses became more empirical and widely applied during this period, including neo-Darwinian considerations of social norms, individuals who diverged from these new social standards came under increasing censure.

This new, humanist perspective appeared to many at the time to be supported by an apparent correlation between the natural and social sciences. As Gregory (2007) points out, the normal distribution curve, now more typically referred to as the bell curve, was developed by Gauss in the 1780s as a mathematical representation of a specific statistical distribution of observations. However, it quickly became apparent that the normal distribution curve could also be applied to social and biological observations. In 1825, Adolph Quetelet, a Belgian statistician, was one of the first mathematicians to recognize that this curve appeared to be applicable to social data (Rogers, 1995). Quetelet "demonstrated that the heights of French army conscripts ... could be described using the normal curve" (Gregory, 2007, p. 114). The resulting distribution revealed that conscript heights clustered around the average, or mean, and that gradually the sample numbers were reduced as a function of their increasing distance from that mean. Quetelet interpreted these findings as indicating that "the average man is seen as nature's ideal and deviations from this are nature's mistakes" (p. 115).

Additional experiments with various biological and social measures revealed similar results. However, the next step, taken by Quetelet and others, transformed the descriptive value of the normal curve into a prescriptive social litmus test. Deviations from the mean of the normal curve were interpreted, following Quetelet, as errors. These early analyses provided quasi-scientific and philosophical frameworks that supported a reinterpretation of the typical (i.e. the mean) into normal and the atypical (i.e. distanced from the mean) into abnormal.

Responses to those who were perceived as different, created within a period which saw the early development of industrialization, market economies, and rationalism, included a determination to resolve this apparent social problem. Charlton (2006) points out that this rejection of difference, based on what that author describes as institutionalized fear and loathing, presented only three possible solutions – ignore that difference, maintain what is perceived as useful, and destroy that which is perceived as detrimental.

This latter option found support within the eugenics movement. This popular and widespread movement, first named in 1883 by Francis Galton, advocated the improvement of the human species through direct intervention. These interventions included the sterilization of those considered unfit to reproduce and the killing of various institutionalized populations (Davis, 2006). PWDs were often understood as fitting into both of these categories (Pernick, 1997).

Davis (2006) notes that, when the notion of the mean, in societal terms, replaced that of degrees of imperfection, a space was created for disability. And, as theoretical analyses became more focused on social applications of neo-Darwinian thought, disability became more closely defined with *deviance* as a social analysis and increasingly conflated with "criminal activity, mental incompetence, (and) sexual licence" (p. 9).

A common theme emerges when looking back at these several historical influences on the relationship between society and disability. That commonality is whether a particular disability was *socially noticed* as a *negative difference* within a particular environment. This difference, which has included a wide range of social and activity limitations (Nagi, 1976), continues to have a significant impact on our understanding of disability.

Thinking and Feeling

The balance of this chapter examines this understanding of PWDs as *negatively different* (Deal, 2003) from two distinct perspectives and considers how each of these applies to and affects PWDs in the workplace. The first is based on macro-level analyses of individuals who self-declare their impairment through one of several categorical matrices, such as censual surveys, or who are otherwise so categorized through a variety of cognitive frameworks, such as the biopsychosocial model of disability, as outlined in the International Classification of Functioning, Disability and Health (ICF) (WHO, 2001). These frameworks, including that put forward within the ICF, understand disability as resulting from a complex matrix of environmental, social, and personal factors. Impairments, referred to variously as health conditions, diseases, disorders, injuries, or traumas, are understood as recognizable functional limitations. These impairments are necessary components of each of these macro-level definitions of disability. Without impairment, the construct of disability cannot exist (Shakespeare, 2014).

The second of these perspectives is that created by the social perception of PWDs. Those latter perceptions determine, at a more micro level, the membership of particular individuals within a pre-existing, affect-based construct of disability. That perceived membership, or determination of disability, is generated through an acognitive scan for indications of negative difference. Those who are determined to meet this test ultimately fall within the category of PWDs and those who do not are perceived as merely different. Importantly, these characterizations can be somewhat fluid (Goffman, 1963) and susceptible to influences that include prior theoretical exposure, categorical or general experience with disability, appropriate training, and individual relationships with PWDs (Stone & Colella, 1996; Wang et al., 2021)

These two approaches to understanding disability correspond closely to what we and others recognize as a categorical distinction between impairment and disability (Osborne, 1990; Shakespeare & Watson, 2001). In very broad terms, the former is associated with individual limitations, and the latter with the perceived relationship that exists between those limitations and the external environment. We have previously described a number of variants of these environmental influences in our summaries of the several models of disability (see Chapter 4) and will not do so again in this chapter. Our purpose here is to explore and describe the relationship between a population-based quantitative analysis of disability based on functional limitations and the qualitative factors that underpin individual determinations of membership within that same group from a more immediate perspective of employment.

We suggest that, within the workplace, PWDs are much more significantly defined by subjective perceptions of a negative difference than by objective considerations of impairment. These perceptions are reminiscent of the third factor put forward by Stone and Colella (1996) in their analysis of the relationship between PWDs and the workplace. This factor refers to the personal characteristics of both PWDs and co-workers, particularly as these affect the overall employment success of PWDs. These personal characteristics include the type of impairment and the responses generated by perceptions of disability. These authors hypothesized that the generation of categorical stereotypes of disability based on initial perceptions would inform interpretations of observed traits, behaviours, and characteristics of individual PWDs. We consider these relationships later in this chapter. In addition, we have extended this argument to include a set of variables created by the relationships that exist between IWODs and PWDs as well as amongst the several different groups of PWDs. Finally, we consider the additional complexity that each of these latter relationships brings to the workplace.

Counting Impairments

At the scale necessary to generate data that are suitably consistent to allow for application within many international considerations, disability is described as a result of the relationship that exists between impairment and the lived environment and is considered to be the largest minority group in the world. At its most macro level, the World Health Organization indicates that over one billion people live with disabilities (WHO, 2001). These disabilities range from those that include relatively minor functional limitations to others that exert extremely significant impacts on individual lives (WHO, 2011). However, as the language used to describe PWDs has continued to evolve (United Nations, 2006) and take on various political connotations, it has become increasingly difficult to contextualize these definitions of disability within circumstances such as employment.

To compound the challenges associated with quantitative analyses of disability, the definitions of disability within various countries are at times more exclusionary than those provided by the WHO. In some jurisdictions, such as Armenia and Russia, individuals are not considered to be PWDs, for purposes of funding supports and other state interventions, without either an identification of a particular "approved" impairment or a demonstration of a predetermined level of impairment beyond what would be described as *light* or *moderate* impairments in other jurisdictions (Osipov, 2013). The assignment of such relatively onerous guidelines, associated with either the complexity or assumed degree of social limitations associated with particular impairments, has been found to result in significantly underestimated population figures and the concomitant availability of state supports in various countries (Breen, Havaei, & Pitassi, 2019).

Finally, individual countries often make use of a variety of definitions of disability for different purposes. In Canada, for example, the federal Employment Equity Act (1995) describes PWDs as individuals who consider themselves to be disadvantaged in employment, or perceived as such, by virtue of their impairment. However, the more recent Accessible Canada Act (2019) considers a PWD to be an individual whose impairment, as it interacts with an environmental barrier, hinders equal participation in society. Each of these was developed for a specific political purpose within a developing understanding of disability. The former, based principally on a medical model of disability, is intended to apply specifically to the relationship between impairment and employment. The latter, based on the social model, is focused on more broadly based relational issues that exist between PWDs and society. However, confusion remains within organizations with regard to the appropriate definition to put forward when gathering disability-related data from employees (Breen, 2021). This definitional challenge is further compounded by a clear separation between those individuals who fit within one or more of these objectively defined definitions and the perceptions of employers when either considering their current workforce or making hiring decisions.

Defining and counting PWDs are further complicated because different societies, at different times, treat individuals with various impairments in different ways (Shakespeare & Watson, 2001). Culturally based relationships to disability are many, varied, and not always clearly delineated. Within environments such as employment, we suggest that these broad categorizations of disability neither reflect on-the-ground realities nor do they provide data that are particularly germane to the hiring, retention, and promotion of PWDs. Instead, when faced with these unclear and contradictory messages, employers are more likely to rely on their personal experience and various media representations of disability when determining what are considered to be appropriate decision-making strategies. These several influences are described in more detail next.

Within individual workplaces, the representation rates of the several categories of disability do not typically align with those same categorizations of disability as described within international, national, or regional population-based surveys. For example, the recent Canadian Survey on Disability (Statistics Canada, 2017) indicates that, of the ten described categories of disability, those PWDs who indicated that "pain" was either their only or principal disability were overrepresented in their employment rate, while all others were underrepresented (see Table 7.1). This same survey reveals that the proportion of those categories of disability that are most frequently presented within commercial and marketing media images (i.e. those with sensory limitations and wheelchair users) is relatively low, both in absolute terms and within the workplace. In addition, much of the news-related representation of disability in the media is impairment imagery, with a focus on visible limitations (Darke, 2004).

To further compound this dilemma, these same categorizations of impairment do not necessarily align with population-based understandings. For example, "mobility limitations" are described in a recent Canadian government survey as including those individuals who have some degree of difficulty

Table 7.1 Employed PWDs (15–64 years)

Disability Type	*Percentage of Identified Disabilities*	*Percentage of All Employed PWDs*
All PWDs	100	100
Pain	65	71
Flexibility	45	44
Mobility	43	35
Mental/Psychological	33	27
Dexterity	24	16
Learning	21	12
Seeing	20	16
Hearing	18	18
Memory	17	11
Developmental	5	3
Unknown	3	3

Source: Adapted from Statistics Canada, 2017b.

Note: Responses indicated that individuals lived with between two and three impairments. Therefore, the total response rates are greater than 100%.

either walking on a flat surface for 15 minutes without resting or walking up or down a flight of 12 stairs without resting (Statistics Canada, 2017d).

The 2019 American Community Survey made use of a similar definition and indicated similar results, although it applied a slightly different classification system for categorizing disability (United States Census Bureau, 2019). This discrepancy between the numbers accrued through population-level analyses of impairment and perceived workplace representations of disability raises the question of how employers, supervisors, and co-workers come to understand the construct of disability.

As would be expected, most IWODs within the workplace do not dedicate significant amounts of time to researching and developing sophisticated understandings of disability at a global level. We suggest that disability itself is more typically characterized as an amalgam of three data streams. These include PWDs who are visible within the workplace, PWDs who may be present within the personal sphere of these IWODs, and images of those PWDs who are most frequently presented within the marketing and news media.

Within the Workplace

The most frequently self-reported impairments within the workplace are pain, flexibility, mobility, and mental health (Statistics Canada, 2017b; also see Table 7.1). Of these four most frequently reported impairments, pain, flexibility, and mental health are typically considered as falling within the "invisible" category.

What is less commonly understood is that individuals who self-disclose as living with mobility impairments are also likely to remain "invisible." According to Statistics Canada, based on data extracted from the Canadian Survey on Disability (2017), wheelchair users make up only a small percentage of those survey respondents who indicated a limitation in mobility. Of 2,676,370 respondents who indicated a mobility limitation, only 224,800 (or 8.4%) were wheelchair users. (These data were obtained by the authors from Statistics Canada on January 25, 2022, following a request for a custom data tabulation. This analysis had not been previously undertaken.) As noted above, those who were calculated as individuals with mobility limitations included individuals with a broad range of limitations, many of which may not have been visible, or recognizable, within particular workplace environments. These data were gathered through two screening questions within that national survey (see CSD, 2017 [DSQ_Q085 & DSQ_Q090]).

After factoring in the proportion of those PWDs living with relatively invisible mobility limitations, it is apparent that the most common perceptions by IWODs of disability within the workplace – those with sensory impairments or wheelchair users – represent a small minority of PWDs. Wheelchair users are described by Corin de Freitas, a researcher at the

University of British Columbia, as the "charismatic megafauna of the disability world" with an associated high level of social visibility (personal communication with Breen, December 1, 2021). This term was borrowed from the field of environmental conservation, wherein it is applied to flagship species that are visible and appealing and which serve to focus public attention and promote fundraising (Albert, Luque, & Courchamp, 2018).

This discrepancy between the actual categorical makeup of PWDs within the workplace and the general perception on the part of co-workers, supervisors, and employers is further compounded by analyses that reveal that employed PWDs who live with invisible impairments are significantly less likely to self-disclose than are those with visible impairments (Nelissen et al., 2014).

At a practical level, any hiring, retention, or promotion of PWDs within the workplace depends to a significant degree on the perception of disability as a construct that is created and applied by those in positions of power or influence. Although perceptions of individual PWDs, with any attendant visible impairments or limitations, will be included in this decision-making algorithm, these choices – to hire, retain, or promote – will be driven in large part by this overriding perception of disability itself. As noted by Shakespeare (1994), PWDs are not seen as individuals but as representations of disability.

As an additional consideration regarding wheelchair users and the relationship of this category of PWDs to employment, it is useful to note that the term is applied as a simulacrum representing a variety of impairments that may require a wheelchair as an accommodation. A partial list of these impairments, as noted by Hebl and Kleck (2000), includes "amyotrophic lateral sclerosis, amputations, Friedrich's ataxia, cerebral palsy, muscular dystrophy, myasthenia gravis, polio, rheumatoid arthritis, spina bifida, spinal cord injury, spinal muscle atrophy, a stroke, traumatic brain injury, age-related mobility impairment, and temporary impairment" (p. 420). Many of these wheelchair users, depending on individual circumstances, may require significantly different categories and degrees of accommodations and may experience significantly diverse life courses.

The term "wheelchair user" as a descriptor for an impairment appears to be the only example of a general category of impairment described by its most typical accommodation. More commonly, various perceived limitations or impairments are referenced when describing, or at least when subvocalizing, various PWDs. A person with limited hearing is unlikely to be referenced as a "hearing aid user." Nor is a blind person considered a "mobility cane user" or a "guide dog user." Whether this description of those who use wheelchairs is more typically applied as a euphemism for paralysis or substituted as a descriptor for an unknown mobility impairment has not, to our knowledge, been clearly established. As well, whether this generic image is more typical of a sports model wheelchair, as more commonly used by those who are the most mobile, or a powered wheelchair that is used by those in need of additional mobility assistance, is also an unknown at this point.

To illustrate further, one of us (Breen) is a part-time wheelchair user and, on several occasions within the workplace, has encountered IWODs who have stated that "Now that I have come to know you and seen your abilities, you do not seem disabled at all." At times, these comments have become more patronizing and have included statements such as "When you are sitting behind your desk, you look just like anyone else." Remarkably, these kinds of comments appear to be delivered in an effort to break down perceived barriers, demonstrate that the IWOD is able to see beyond any presenting impairment, and dispel what are assumed to be latent concerns over inferiority on the part of the PWD.

This change in relationship, whether expressed verbally or through behaviour, is commonly experienced in the workplace by many PWDs. What has changed is not the individual PWD, but rather the perception of that individual by the IWOD. And, if initial reactions to disability are understood as perceptions of a negative difference, any subsequent perception of an individual that is discordant with this relationship requires a re-categorization of the PWD to avoid both cognitive dissonance (Seligman, 1971) and, perhaps more significantly, what we have referred to above as affective dissonance.

Goffman (1963) states that a change to a less negatively perceived disability-related status is caused by an increasing *disattention* to a specific impairment. That author cites the use of the wheelchair user to illustrate how this significant impairment can be easily *disattended* when all parties are sitting around a conference table. Goffman extends this argument by pointing out that, in other circumstances, the opposite reaction may also occur. Where a particular impairment is more attended to than would typically be the case, the change in status of the PWD moves in the opposite direction – from being merely different to negatively different. However, whether that impairment has disappeared, become viewed as circumstantially irrelevant, or been subsumed into a new perception of the individual PWD remains unclear within this analysis.

The principal issue raised within these considerations is that employers, and co-workers, face an almost Sisyphean struggle in understanding the reality of PWDs in the workplace. These challenges include ongoing analyses and interpretations of what may appear to be constantly changing relationships between specific impairments and various workplace environments.

A second challenge to understanding is associated with a recognition of the factors that may motivate various actions and attitudes on the part of PWDs (Stone & Colella, 1996). This challenge is associated with a common discrepancy between what may be assumed by IWODs to be the motivating factors behind these various behaviours and attitudes on the part of PWDs and the reality of those factors from the perspective of individual

PWDs. These misunderstandings, whether based on inappropriate applications of general assumptions regarding PWDs or simply misinformation, significantly hinder the establishment of positive relationships between PWDs and others within the workplace.

This challenge is clearly illustrated within the academic literature that focuses on co-workers' perceptions of a lack of distributive fairness with regard to providing accommodations to PWDs. These perceptions of injustice may be based on feelings that receiving an accommodation makes another's job easier, more desirable, or imposes onerous duties on others (Kensbock, Boehm, & Bourovoi, 2017). Each of these, however, does not account for an impairment-related requirement for that accommodation. Instead, only the visible results are considered. To illustrate with a commonplace example, the random or arbitrary request for an ergonomic chair by a single employee may justifiably be perceived as unfair. However, that would not be the case if that employee was a PWD with chronic lower back pain and a medical requirement for that specific accommodation. What differentiates these two scenarios is the motivating factor for the accommodation. These perceptions and subsequent reactions will not only influence the success of various accommodations; they may also determine the initial decision of the PWD to make such a request (Colella, 2001).

One of us (Breen), when in his role as the manager of the Workplace Diversity Employment Office within the Yukon government (2004–2013), chaired an ongoing Disability Resources Group that provided a meeting opportunity for PWDs who were employed by that government. Structured as a quarterly two-hour working lunch session, these meetings were open only to those PWDs and guest speakers. Participants were provided with a variety of accommodations, including a real-time text display of the discussion, attention to various dietary restrictions, seating options, and American Sign Language (ASL) interpreters who provided services for a number of Deaf participants.

The physical layout of the meetings included several tables arranged in a large, horseshoe shape, with participants sitting around the outside of this array. The Deaf participants all sat at one end of the horseshoe with the ASL interpreter facing them from across their table. At one particular meeting, Breen and the guest speaker, who on that day was the Yukon government Public Service Commissioner, sat at a small table at the open end of the horseshoe facing the approximately 40 participants.

As the lunch dishes were being removed by several servers, one of them approached one of the Deaf participants from behind and, without attracting their attention, asked if their plate should be removed. The ASL interpreter's attention was elsewhere, communicating with another participant. The Deaf person made no response and the server asked again, this time loudly enough that Breen, the Commissioner, and several others looked over in that direction. The server asked again, this time quite loudly, again received no response, and walked away emptyhanded and clearly upset.

By this point, the ASL interpreter had recognized the difficulty and had communicated the circumstances to the Deaf participants. Several of the other participants began to acknowledge what had just occurred and commented on how frequently others make incorrect assumptions about various disability-related behaviours. The Public Service Commissioner, who had been scheduled to address the group on another topic, changed her presentation to acknowledge what had just occurred and listen to these several examples of similar misunderstandings. As a final note, following the end of the meeting, Breen was able to locate the server and explain the circumstances that had led to this misunderstanding.

Personal Experience

Prior interactions with PWDs have been linked to correspondingly more positive IWOD attitudes. Following from the original intergroup contact hypothesis (Allport, 1935), research has shown "that contact effects hold equally well for groups other than races and ethnicities" (Pettigrew & Tropp, 2008). Others have extended this argument specifically to include disability, concluding that any experience with PWDs tends to lead to more positive attitudes (see, for example, Stone & Colella, 1996; Wang et al., 2021). However, other studies have provided more nuanced findings, indicating that previous interactions that have led to more generally positive attitudes toward PWDs have been themselves relatively positive (Barr & Bracchitta, 2012; McManus, Feyes, & Saucier, 2011). Additionally, these more positive attitudes are mediated by various categories of impairment (Deal, 2003). Finally, it is of note that Pettigrew and Tropp (2006), in a meta-analysis of 515 studies, indicate that contact effects are more strongly associated with affective indices than with cognitive indices.

Women and younger people have also been found to have more positive attitudes toward PWDs (Deal, 2003; Gething & Wheeler, 1992). Various arguments have been put forward to explain these phenomena. For the former, Hyde (2006) suggests that females demonstrate higher levels of empathy and have been socialized into more nurturing roles. For the latter, increased experience with PWDs in school and other social environments has been offered as a possible explanation (Mpofu, 2003). Of concern in terms of these demographic findings, employment analyses indicate that management positions are most typically held by men (Statistics Canada, 2022) and that these positions are increasingly occupied by older workers (Statistics Canada, 2019).

Attitudes toward PWDs have also been found to vary across differing social bounds and have included instances of attitudes based on perceived future challenges. In 2007, a large-scale American survey (Domzal, Houtenville, & Sharma, 2008) indicated that employers' attitudes toward PWDs were more negative with regard to employment than within other social environments. In this sample, it appeared that these negative attitudes had been constructed to support an overall predetermination not to hire PWDs. Almost 75% of these employers indicated that PWDs would be unable to perform the tasks required within their organizations. In essence, these attitudes had been generated and applied based on anticipated negative experiences rather than on first-hand knowledge.

These fractured attitudes toward PWDs, or more appropriately toward the construct of disability itself, have also been observed within narrow subdivisions of an employment environment. As noted earlier, an American study described how customer attitudes toward PWDs as serving personnel varied depending upon the reason for attending a particular restaurant. Survey respondents, presented with a hypothetical example, less frequently selected a specific location known to employ a number of PWDs as serving staff if the occasion was intended to be a romantic setting or for business purposes than if that occasion was one involving family or friends (Kuo & Kalargyrou, 2014). Each of these employment-related examples demonstrates that these attitudes were based on a hypothesized future experience rather than on prior relations.

Media Images

Media-related images, whether verbal, textual, or visual, can be further subdivided into those that include PWDs within various consumer marketing campaigns, contained within topical news items, or featured in what are frequently termed human interest stories. In the former, particularly in visual images, disability is most typically portrayed by a person using a wheelchair, whether as a product model, an athlete, or as a member of a social group. In the latter two categories, which may be less dependent upon visual representations of specific impairments, PWDs are typically described as being in need of social intervention, who demonstrate incapacity, or who are otherwise perceived as unlikely to be employed.

The media also makes use of disability as an epithet to emphasize hardship, injustice, or tragedy. The United Nations, in a recent commentary on disability and the media, states that PWDs "are often negatively stereotyped … and treated as objects of pity, charity, or medical treatment" (United Nations, 2021). A recent Belgian review of local print media found 184 articles from within 16 local magazines that referenced disability. That study found that media images of disability were most frequently focused on the "suffering, caring, fixing, and overcoming the disability" (Goethals et al., 2022, p. 757). A news article published on January 11, 2022, by the Canadian Broadcasting Corporation (CBC), Canada's public news broadcaster, reported that a landlord recently raised the rent for an apartment by 61% in a jurisdiction with no rent controls. The tenant featured in this story was described as a person with multiple disabilities. This description was clearly intended to increase viewers' sense of injustice by implying that this could occur even to a person with diminished capabilities – *as we understand PWDs to be*. Unlike other derogated group names, it appears to be acceptable to the media to make use of *disability* as a meme for enhanced suffering and incapacity. One of us, Breen, contacted the CBC Ombudsman to voice this concern. An email response by the regional news director of the CBC indicated that this article did not "convey any broader message about people with disabilities" (Breen, personal communication, January 14, 2022).

News reports often raise topics such as "the suffering of the disabled and the elderly," "transportation or other public services unfair to the disabled," or "the disabled require increased welfare services funding to meet extra costs." PWDs, although members of a broad, heterogeneous group, are often subsumed within the impairments and accommodation requirements of a specific subgroup or even an individual. A recent online news article describing a new driverless transportation shuttle in France stated that this bus featured "an automated ramp and wheelchair anchor points for disabled passengers" (New Atlas, 2021). Although the intent of the article is clearly to illustrate the inclusive aspects of this new system, the construct of disability is narrowed through its representation by wheelchair users. Wheelchair use again becomes a simulacrum of the larger group of PWDs both at a categorical level and at that of a generic functional limitation.

Media depictions of various social groups, including PWDs, have been described as *second-hand exemplars* in which indirect experiences "are often stereotypic in nature, failing to convey the real diversity of groups" (Linville, 1998, p. 443). These experiences can lead to more extreme stereotyping by failing to portray differences and diversity within groups such as PWDs.

Beginning in San Francisco in 1867, a series of what came to be called the Ugly Laws (Burgdorf & Burgdorf, 1975) were passed as municipal ordinances by a number of American cities. These laws, at the time most commonly referred to as Unsightly Beggar Ordinances, were intended to prevent those with visible disabilities, among others who were considered to be offensive to the public order, from seeking alms from passersby. Those with disabilities were also, in some instances, prevented from appearing in public at all. Sanctions included fines and jail terms.

Many of these edicts also included options for sentencing impaired transgressors to poor farms, later to alms houses, and still later to secure medical facilities. Each of these, with a corresponding increased degree of control, was, according to the Ordnances and the sentiment of the day, intended to provide a degree of care for those "pitiful creatures" forced into a life of mendicancy (Schweik, 2009, p. 102).

These latter sentencing options can collectively be understood as the beginning of *institutionalized pity* toward PWDs. Although these PWDs were considered to be criminals for transgressing these Ordnances, the option of substituting diversionary sentences for prescribed sanctions demonstrates a clear distinction between PWDs and others caught up in these same Ordnances. The last of these Unsightly Beggar Ordnances was finally repealed in Chicago in 1973. However, this same institutionalized pity associated with PWDs has continued with events such as the annual Jerry Lewis Telethon, which ended in 2014. Media Smarts (2021), Canada's Centre for Digital and Media Literacy, notes that a recent report from the Canadian Association of Broadcasters states that PWDs continue to be viewed as objects of pity. Media Smarts also indicates that wheelchair users continue to be predominant in media representations of disability.

In a recent study of media representation of Paralympic athletes (London 2012 and Rio de Janeiro 2016), a critical analysis revealed that newspapers at the time focused "on the effort, dedication, and suffering only of athletes participating in the Paralympic Games" (Martinez-Bello et al., 2021, p. 1). These authors noted that these comments created a clear separation of these athletes from those participating in the corresponding Olympic Games. In that same review, it was noted that Paralympic athletes were not treated simply as athletes but were commonly described with reference to their non-athletic endeavours, thereby diminishing their athletic achievements to a status of part-time efforts.

As a final consideration within the topic of media-generated images of PWDs, we acknowledge the challenges associated with attempts to convey the concept of disability within a visual medium such as television. The most efficient means to portray disability, without further textual or visual explanation, is to ensure that the described PWD has the *appearance* of being a PWD. At that point, no further explanation is required. This technique provides an immediate demonstration of *personification*, one of the seven factors that influence determinations of newsworthiness (Boukes, Jones, &

Vliegenthart, 2022). However, this apparent increase in reliance on personalization and negativity (i.e. tabloidization) within the mainstream media at the expense of reportage quality has been a continuing concern among media scholars (Barnett & Seymour, 1999). The challenge associated with these trends, insofar as they apply to PWDs, is that viewers, without sufficient clarifications and background information, are more likely to generalize disability based on these examples. It is unsurprising that employers, as consumers of various public news media, may well generalize these overwhelmingly negative images of disability when considering the employment of individual PWDs.

Perceiving Disability

We recognize that we are treading on sensitive ground within the following consideration of disability, particularly as these explorations of categorical separations within the disability community may raise a variety of concerns for some PWDs and theorists. These include the potential to create wedge issues associated with variations between and within several categories of disability.

We agree with Barnes (2019), who notes that categorical labels have the potential to be socially and politically divisive. As a consequence, disability theorists appear to have been generally unwilling to articulate the implications that follow from a consideration of disability as a heterogeneous construct. Instead, disability has most frequently been presented as a single group, including when used in support of furthering demands for social equality (Swain, French, & Cameron, 2003). Finkelstein (1993) is critical of those PWDs who seek to distinguish themselves from either the group as a whole or from others with different impairments. That author states that these efforts, "it is falsely believed, free the individual, or group, to consider themselves as only a variation in the pattern of normality while the others, lower down the scale, can be regarded as really disabled" (p. 13).

Examples of categorical heterogeneity have most typically been redefined as cultural or experiential variations within the larger construct of disability. A category of *impairment effects* has been developed by Thomas (1999b) to differentiate internal influences on individual impairments from those that have been understood within the social and embodiment models as being imposed from external sources. Crow (1996) has distinguished those PWDs whose impairments exist apart from any social influence. However, other scholars have acknowledged that discussions regarding the differences associated with various impairments have been kept within the disability community so as not to risk presenting a diminished or fractured presence to society at large (Shakespeare, 2014).

If, as we have proposed, disability itself is a relational construct, determined by whether the individual PWD is perceived as negatively different (i.e. above or below the horizon of social notice), we understand that some

PWDs may well be viewed as negatively different and others as merely different. Our purpose is not to create a two-tiered construct of disability but to acknowledge that this already exists, to consider its implications within the workplace, and, consequently, to take action to eliminate this structure. Our goal is to expand the concept of what Goffman (1963) described as *normal* to include all those PWDs considered to be different, including those now perceived as negatively different. We are striving for a new social norm that anticipates a range of attributes within its population; one that accepts and values all those with differences (Crow, 1996).

We recognize that a number of practice-related challenges may flow from any efforts that are perceived to disaggregate what is considered to be the world's largest minority (WHO, 2011) into several less than homogeneous subcategories. For example, arguments may be put forward that question the legitimacy of claims based on the entitlements and authority bestowed by this rubric within demands for social equality, applications for funding, and other supports (Deal, 2003). However, we suggest that the practical implications of the generalized attitudes of others toward disability are of such critical influence within the workplace that they supersede these concerns regarding a possible fracturing of the homogeneity of disability. Crow (1996) responded to a similar concern over the possible difficulties that may appear following an acknowledgement that impairment has a legitimate place within considerations of the social challenges that face PWDs. That author indicated that a continued silence would prevent advocates from effectively managing this reality. Such is also the case with maintaining what is considered by many to be a false, albeit politically expedient, image of the collective of disability.

To provide additional detail within this imaginary of PWDs, we consider two separate perspectives. The first is that of IWODs and the second is that of PWDs. Each of these is described within a relatively broad social context, although these perceptions are clearly applicable to the environment of the workplace.

The IWOD Perspective

As we have described throughout this book, the IWOD perspective of disability is, although varied due to social circumstance, cultural location, and demographic characteristics, relatively negative when compared to IWODs in the same circumstance. These comparisons are further exaggerated when PWDs are compared to IWODs in the workplace (Domzal, Houtenville, & Sharma, 2008). We suggest that this perspective is driven by two somewhat imbricated sets of influencing factors.

The first of these influences results from a frequently misconstrued perception of life as a PWD. By this, we do not refer specifically to misunderstandings associated with a particular impairment. Instead, these first influences are the perceptions and responses to disability *writ large*. These are best understood as retroductive responses to what we have described as the negative difference that is associated with PWDs. In general terms, these responses are based on assumptions regarding what circumstances must be the case in order to explain the existence of a particular phenomenon (Bhaskar & Danermark, 2006).

These assumptions are illustrated within various lists of explanations provided by different researchers in efforts to explain why IWODs may exhibit negative responses to disability. To illustrate at least some of these latter explanations, Livneh (1982) provided a detailed analysis and summary of several factors that had, at various times, been put forward. These included sociocultural conditioning, childhood influences, psychodynamic mechanisms, disability as a punishment for sin, aesthetic aversion, and threats to body image integrity. In a later review and analysis, that same author (Livneh, 2012) added several additional possibilities. These included the following: anxiety-provoking unstructured situations, minority group comparability, disability as a reminder of death, prejudice-inviting behaviours, the influence of disability-related factors, demographic variables associated with attitudes, and personality variables associated with attitudes. Others, including Goffman (1963), have attempted to delineate a more narrow, root cause for these attitudes. That author, in his seminal work of that year, proposed that *stigma*, within a number of guises and applications, was capable of accepting that mantle.

The above analyses, and other similar efforts to hypothesize a variety of causal categories in support of the "negative or aversive reaction(s) or attitude(s)" (Livneh, 2012, p. 13) toward PWDs, are attempts to explain *why* these perceptions may exist. These considerations may well be of strategic value in providing guidance and direction for further research and planning within various social environments, including the workplace. However, for our immediate purposes, we wish to draw attention, not to theoretical explanatory analyses, but rather to the behaviours themselves that illustrate and confirm the differences *between* the perceptions of PWDs by IWODs and by PWDs themselves. We illustrate these differences with three somewhat overlapping sets of examples – catastrophized perceptions, unwanted assistance, and boundary transgressions.

Catastrophized Perceptions

One of us (Breen) is an experienced wheelchair user. He has participated in competitive wheelchair sports at a national level and has a self-image of being relatively nimble and competent in his wheelchair. The wheelchair he uses is quite clearly, for those who are knowledgeable of such equipment, a high-tech sports model designed for manoeuvrability and speed.

However, Breen's self-image is clearly at odds with the perceptions of at least some IWODs. Offers of assistance are frequently made while he has been performing various tasks with demonstrable competence. These have been accompanied by comments such as "Wouldn't it be easier if I did that for you?" or "Can I push your wheelchair for a while?." This latter query, in particular, demonstrates the differences in perception that we are herein considering. Breen's wheelchair is designed exclusively for self-ambulation and has no push handles. These offers "to push" have, at times, been accompanied by somewhat fumbling efforts to push on his shoulders. He has also, at various times, been shouted at to ensure that he has been able to hear a question, been spoken to in stilted, simplistic language to encourage comprehension, and asked by a doctor if he was capable of reading the printed instructions accompanying a medical prescription.

Similar behaviours on the part of IWODs are considered to be relatively typical by many wheelchair users. Other PWDs have noted how, when with a companion, they are often overlooked by servers in restaurants or by salespeople in other service environments, with all attention being directed to the companion. These scenarios typically involve questions from IWODs such as "What would he like to eat?," "Would she like to try that on?" or "Can he manage that on his own?."

Unwanted Assistance

For wheelchair users, and others with various visible impairments, another IWOD behaviour that is frequently encountered is what is sometimes referred to as *overhelping* (Ryan, Anas, & Gruneir, 2006). Blind people being aggressively "helped" across streets that they did not wish to cross; IWODs insisting on attempting to complete words or sentences for individuals with childhood-onset fluency disorder (previously known as stuttering or stammering); and wheelchair users finding themselves being unexpectedly pushed from behind by a stranger.

In an example of this latter type of behaviour, Breen was badly injured while disembarking from an airplane in a wheelchair borrowed from the airport authority (his own wheelchair having been inadvertently left on the tarmac by airport personnel at his city of departure). The borrowed wheelchair was of a design intended principally to be pushed by an attendant. As such, the brakes were located near the top of the wheels for easy access by whoever was providing assistance. However, in this instance, Breen was wheeling the chair along the jetway when a flight attendant approached from behind and began to push the chair without first inquiring whether this assistance was required. Breen's thumbs became trapped under the brakes, resulting in a significant amount of bloodshed and difficulty in extricating his thumbs from where they were trapped.

Boundary Transgressions

Breen has, at various times, had money placed in his lap as he has wheeled along sidewalks, been patted on the head (with accompanying comments regarding how brave he must be), and has been accosted on several occasions with requests that those so intruding be allowed to pray on his behalf for his recovery. While wheeling on a downtown walkway with his partner of the time, who was also a wheelchair user, his passage was purposefully blocked by an IWOD couple who wished to relate how "cute" they thought he and his companion appeared to be.

Other PWDs report similar circumstances in which personal boundaries and social norms are ignored by others. These include intrusions that may be physical and include unwanted touching of the individual or the mobility aid. These latter intrusions have included picking up a pair of crutches that were leaning nearby a seated PWD to "try them out." Breen reports having had individuals, at various times, put a foot on either his wheelchair footrest or on top of a wheel, in apparent demonstrations of camaraderie.

These intrusions may also be verbal and include strangers inquiring about the cause of an apparent impairment or other personal medical information. Breen, early in 2022, was using his forearm crutches while walking through a supermarket in a large Canadian city. He was approached by a woman who said, "I'd hate to see the other guy!" Some PWDs have commented that these transgressions appear to be informed by perspectives that understand PWDs as children, with the associated overly familiar blurring of boundaries exhibited by some adults.

Discrepant Perceptions

We have brought attention to these differences in the perception of PWDs by IWODs for two reasons. First, we suggest that the association of *normalcy* within the self-images of IWODs and PWDs typically falls within relatively dissimilar bounds. For purposes of clarity, we distinguish normalcy from typicality as each of these concepts would be understood by these two groups. For IWODs, PWDs often fall neither within the bounds of what would be perceived as normal nor typical. However, the self-images of PWDs, although they may be perceived as atypical, most frequently exist within the bounds of normalcy (Morris, 1993). As we and others have considered, it is the rejection of PWDs by IWODs from within this bound of normalcy that has been the basis for a host of social inequities (Breen & Forwell, 2021; Oliver, 1990). In summary, normalcy is not conceptually equivalent between these two groups (Breen, 2018a; Deal, 2003).

Second, this separation between understandings of normalcy by IWODs and PWDs is further subcategorized according to specific impairments. According to Harpur, Connelly, and Blank (2017), these disadvantages related to PWDs include not only having "their rights to work discounted by laws and institutions" (p. 507), but also having these rights further compromised within a hierarchy of impairment that becomes increasingly onerous for those with mental disabilities as compared to those with physical or sensory impairments. Wickenden (2013), drawing upon the World Report on Disability (WHO & World Bank, 2011), indicates that "those with physical or visual impairments tend to be less excluded from society than those with cognitive, communication, or behavioural difficulties" (p. 16).

Mastro et al. (1996), in a review of studies that ranked various impairments, found a similar consistency in preferences on the part of respondents for sensory and mobility limitations as compared to intellectual and developmental delay, as well as to cerebral palsy and epilepsy. Additionally, these authors reported a pattern of hierarchical preference related to the severity of impairments, with more positive responses directed toward those with apparently more mild impairments. Others have indicated that these preference hierarchies are, to some extent, context related; however, certain impairments such as amputations typically remain near the top, while others remain near the bottom (Yuker, 1988).

For purposes of employment, this hierarchy of impairments, as described by Deal (2003), could as easily be considered as a hierarchy of exclusion from the workforce. Based on data provided within the Canadian Survey on Disability (2017), of the ten described categories of impairment included in that survey (see Table 7.1), the three categories of learning, memory, and developmental impairments have the lowest rates of employment. These are also the categories that are, as noted above, most commonly ranked near the bottom of various perceived hierarchies of impairment.

These ranked exclusions, based on a rating by others of the degree to which various categories and degrees of impairments are considered to be more or less appealing, have been found within measures that have analysed social distancing, attitudes toward athletes with impairments, and general preferences toward particular categories of impairment (Mastro et al., 1996). We use the term *appealing* here to represent a broad array of terms that have been applied to denote a gradation of attitudes toward PWDs, along a dimension variously described as discomfort in social settings (Gething & Wheeler, 1992), viewed as lesser persons (Loo, 2004), capable of limited activity (Ozawa & Yaeda, 2007), and perceived difference (Yuker, Block, & Younng, 1970). Hughes (2019) encapsulates these "pre-reflective" negative attitudes within the IWOD community as derivatives of "fear, hatred, and disgust" (p. 89).

Each of these terms can be interpreted as attempting to capture and describe the relative distance from a central norm that is occupied by various categories of impairment. This common effort to distinguish PWDs from IWODs is clear, whether framed within downward comparison theory (Wills, 1981), as a response to existential anxiety, terror management, or another of the several theoretical structures that have been hypothesized as supports for these relationships (Dovidio, Major, & Crocker, 2000).

The PWD Perspective

A similar relationship between PWDs, as represented within and between various categories of impairment, has been less fully explored than that which exists between IWODs and PWDs. There are, to our knowledge, few broadly based analyses that focus on the relationships that exist between various groups within the overarching construct of disability. However, it is well established that these hierarchical categorizations of various impairments exist within the PWD community (Harpur, 2019; Shakespeare, Gillespie-Sells, & Davies, 1996). As noted by Wills (1981), "persons experiencing negative affect can enhance their subjective well-being through comparison with a less fortunate other" (p. 245). As we describe, this hierarchical separation appears to be increasingly active within what has been historically presented as a relatively homogenous PWD community.

Oliver (1996) states that the key elements necessary to identify PWDs are as follows: "the presence of an impairment; the experience of externally imposed restrictions; self-identification as a disabled person" (p. 5). However, the necessity of each of these elements has more recently come under scrutiny. And, as a result, the definition of disability as a shared identity among these groups has begun to fracture.

Several groups who are viewed by many IWODs and some PWDs as falling within this category do not necessarily consider themselves to be PWDs (Watson, 2002). *(We would like to state that we are attempting to portray the several descriptions that follow from a position of ontological neutrality. However, we acknowledge possible critiques associated with unintentional bias – Breen & Forwell.)* Perhaps most clearly representing this position is the Deaf community, whose members distinguish their self-identity from that of PWDs and suggest that, principally by virtue of their distinct non-verbal language(s), they are a separate and identifiable cultural minority (Shakespeare, 2014).

Other, similarly persuasive distinguishing characteristics have been put forward by some members of other groups who have, until relatively recently, been considered by others and by themselves to be members of the disability community. These include Blind individuals, those with learning disabilities (referred to as "learning difficulties" in the UK), and many individuals who maintain a clear separation between neurodiversity, including autism, and disability (Jaarsma & Welin, 2012). In addition, many seniors and youth living with various impairments and chronic illnesses do not identify as PWDs (Priestley, 1999; Shakespeare, 2014).

These several rejections of a disability identity, including those who refute the classification of various personal characteristics as impairments, express a common theme (Watson, 2002). They each perceive that the identity of disability is inapplicable to their personal or group circumstance. Some, such as the Deaf community, suggest that membership in the disability community is tacitly imposed by others, including both the IWOD community and some PWDs, due to a lack of recognition of a cultural separation driven by communication differences. Many within the learning disabilities community reject the label of disability, suggesting that learning disabilities themselves are most typically found within individuals who have typical or superior levels of intelligence (Gates & Mafuba, 2016).

Although each group puts forward different explanations for this rejection of membership within the PWD community, two common sentiments are recognizable. First, the construct of disability is understood by many as implying negative associations with skills and abilities. Rather than deny these specific implications, these groups have removed themselves from the field. Although these disavowals are understood by some researchers as failures to accept individual limitations (Livneh & Antonak, 1997; Olney & Kim, 2001), each of these groups offers a cogent explanation for their rejection of this rubric.

The second, and more complex, of these explanations can be illustrated by the statement with which many of us are familiar – "I may have challenges, but I am not disabled!" This determination raises the question of what it means to be a PWD and, by extension, what is the meaning of disability. We suggest that disability is understood by many as a definitional *remainder*. The question of "Who are people with disabilities?" is often answered through a valenced and affective response to difference from the perceived norm. Whenever such a perception cannot place the observed individual within that pre-existing norm, the individual becomes a member of the group that does not fit within this construct.

As described in Chapter 5, this affective response precedes a cognitively driven effort to create synchrony with a pre-existing worldview. However, the perceived difference that generates this response is only that – difference from a previously accepted norm. PWDs are, collectively, what is external to what is considered by the perceiver to be safe, normal, and without concern. We are what is left over – the remainder. It is only when the cognitive self takes over, in an effort to categorize and cohere these perceptions, that specific differences are seized upon and inserted as explanatory placeholders. We can imagine a filtering or sorting process occurring within the observer that screens for and flags any characteristics that could have raised these initial affect-based responses to negative difference. What we are now experiencing with the growing number of rejections of this imaginary is a determination to reject that rejection. Essentially, these individuals and groups who may be considered as PWDs by others are clearly stating that they are not to be included in this list of placeholders.

This rejection extends what Watson (2002) has described as an alternate model within Disability Studies in which that author has rejected the existence of a disability identity based on shared experiences. Instead, Watson suggests that identities of disability exist "only as opposites, they are multiple and temporal" (p. 509). We argue that, although these identities may well be multiple and temporal, they are no longer envisioned as opposites. What is left over is not necessarily the opposite of anything except in the most trite definition of not being a member of the category within which it is not included. To illustrate with a somewhat homely example, animals that are not dogs would not be considered to be the opposite of dogs. They are what *remains* when all of the dogs are accounted for. This growing rejection of the disability epithet by these several groups may well be described by the summary statement "We are not your remainder!"

Apart from those individuals described above who perceive themselves as residing outside of the construct of disability, there is another group whose concerns focus on the categorization of impairments within a definition of disability that is typically framed as a homogeneous, albeit somewhat amorphous, construct. These concerns focus on what are perceived to be characterizations associated with particular individuals or with particular groups of PWDs that are stereotypically generalized to an overly wide and often inappropriate swath of PWDs. This stereotyping, whether of the abilities, skills, attitudes, or performance of a relatively narrow example to the group as a whole, is understood as capable of negatively impacting the larger cohort. This is of particular concern, for example, when media stories regarding PWDs most frequently focus on a particular challenge for an individual or group but which refer to the specific individuals generically as PWDs.

At the time of this writing, Canada is beginning to loosen a number of COVID-related restrictions. A headline from February 2022 on the Canadian public radio broadcaster states that "As restrictions loosen up, advocates for people with disabilities say their needs haven't been considered" (CBC, 2022). That radio article interviews two people who are wheelchair users, one of whom had also identified as immunocompromised. Each describes a number of challenges that they have faced as they continue to manage through this pandemic. A final interviewee, a university professor engaged in a related study, indicated there existed a lack of community support for PWDs.

Each of the concerns and comments put forward within these interviews is completely creditable and deserving of immediate attention. However, the absence of any qualification of the characteristics of those PWDs who are in need of that "community support" leaves the listener with a generalized, and unwarranted, image of all PWDs as requiring the described assistance.

A final and potentially sensitive topic within any consideration of the heterogeneity of those individuals who comprise the broad category of PWDs is particularly applicable to employment. An internet search of keyword combinations that include *disability/ability/perception* reveals millions of results that reference famous people with disabilities, advice on how PWDs should "play to their strengths," and various disability-related resources. There are also significant amounts of data, released through various government and non-government organizations, that describe rates of employment by category of disability, including corresponding subcategories based on the severity of particular impairments (see, for example, CSD, 2017). A second internet search reveals thousands of journal articles that explore the self-perception of PWDs as these perceptions are influenced by the majority IWOD community. However, there is very little published academic material that considers the inter-categorical relationships that exist between PWDs who identify as living with different impairments (Deal, 2006; Mastro et al., 1996).

This topic may be best framed as those relationships between PWDs who do not wish to distinguish themselves entirely from membership within the disability community but who, at the same time, wish to separate themselves from others within this group. For purposes of this comparison, we have separated this group from those who have entirely disassociated themselves from the disability community. We will refer to that first group as *rejecters* and this second group as *distinguishers*.

This latter group, the distinguishers, is differentiated from the IWODs and the rejecters. Neither of these other two groups see themselves as PWDs. The IWODs because they do not perceive any personal similarity to the characteristics and limitations that are typically assigned to PWDs by the IWOD community. The rejecters because they perceive those personal characteristics that others may describe as limitations or impairments as mere differences that do not warrant those descriptions. Both of these groups understand themselves to be outside of any definition of disability.

The distinguishers maintain self-images that include impairment. On their own, these categorical separations may be considered to generate little tension. Instead, as described by Davis (2002), these separations may only illustrate a developing confidence within the larger group that allows for an acknowledgement that many impairment groups have little in common with each other. It would be unsurprising that, for example, wheelchair users may choose to distinguish themselves from individuals living with sensory impairments and vice versa. Associated life courses, possible habilitation and rehabilitation regimes, and various accommodations required with regard to employment, transportation, and other social interactions would be quite different for each of these groups. These significant differences do, however, support the notion that PWDs do not share an overarching and common identity group (Watson, 2002).

But there is another caveat attached to these discrepant self-images. Not all impairments are perceived by the distinguishers to be of equal value (Watson, 2002). These categories of impairment are, at times, further subcategorized hierarchically based on complexity, duration, and degrees of independence. The perceived value, or legitimacy, of these several demarcations has been variously interpreted and ranked. Some PWDs with more complex circumstances associated with their impairments view others who are more mobile, independent, or who otherwise face fewer daily challenges as "elitist" and not "genuine" PWDs (Deal, 2003, p. 898).

In other circumstances, those who face fewer challenges, and who may be more mobile and independent, see those at the opposite end of this dimension of complexity as negatively influencing the perception of others with regard to the likely or typical limitations associated with a particular category of limitation (Mastro et al., 1996). These same authors also reported on interviews with elite athletes who had participated in the

Paralympic Games. These revealed a "hierarchy of stigmatised disabilities" (p. 199) within several categories of impairment. Most pronounced within this particular hierarchy were feelings of prejudice and discrimination experienced by athletes living with cerebral palsy. This group indicated that they were "not accepted by athletes with spinal cord injuries and amputations" (p. 200).

Similarly, Deal (2003) provides a review of the attitudes that PWDs may exhibit toward others with various impairments. That author suggests that these hierarchical perspectives may be influenced by considerations of one or more of several dimensions of impairment. These include the complexity and appearance of a particular impairment, as well as whether there may be competition between various impairments for resources, services, or other supports.

The various efforts that have been implemented by several groups to separate from or distinguish themselves within the construct of disability indicate a growing determination not to be identified as a part of a homogenous whole. Writers within the field have addressed this issue from different perspectives. Dovidio, Major, and Crocker (2000) indicate that by stigmatizing others, the stigmatizing individual may enhance their own status. Finkelstein (1993) argues that some PWDs may choose to differentiate themselves from others, whom they view as residing on a lower level within a disability hierarchy, in order to present themselves as less impaired or relatively *normal* (italics added). Separate identities clearly exist within individual impairment groups. Deal (2003) points out that a review of the research indicates that the ranking and assigning of degrees of stigma associated with this hierarchy has been variably associated with a range of impairments.

These efforts at distinguishment, particularly as they apply to employment environments, are analogous to other self-promoting efforts made by job applicants and by those seeking advancement or other benefits within a competitive workplace environment. We suggest that many PWDs are likely to believe that employers, although they may initially react to a perception of generic difference, do not necessarily categorize an individual solely as a member of the relatively difficult to define construct of disability but also as a person using a wheelchair, a person with limited vision, or a member of some other impairment-related group. Similar to others within a competitive work environment, it is unsurprising that PWDs would make efforts to portray themselves in what could be perceived as a positive light. With little evidence available to indicate a common bond with all other PWDs, coupled with a lack of shared experience beyond a commonality of discrimination in the workplace, the increased efforts on the part of some PWDs to either separate from, or at least distinguish themselves from, the generic community of impairment is to be expected.

We do not suggest that these categorizations necessarily apply to all PWDs who identify as PWDs. However, research suggests that individuals often perceive a greater number of subcategories within their own in-group than within various out-groups (Linville, 1998).

The Horns of a Dilemma

There are two distinct challenges that present themselves within this homogeneity versus heterogeneity analysis. First, if the current trend toward heterogeneity continues, disability as a *remainder* will be occupied increasingly by several distinct subgroups. This will include those with limited political resources, those whose impairment characteristics are less frequently associated with typicality, and those whose impairments are extremely complex. Although this separation is most immediately noticeable when considering the rejecters, the distinguishers will be contributing to a striation of the construct of disability into degrees of quasi-typicality.

This separation of characteristics into mere differences, and into impairments that are considered to be more or less challenging, may well be of some social benefit to the rejecters and to the distinguishers who distance themselves from those PWDs who are perceived as living with more limiting impairments. Within the framework of employment, we have described several examples of impairments *disappearing* following demonstrations of skills and abilities. In addition, those with particular impairments, limitations, or differences that are generally perceived by IWODs as relatively minimal barriers may understand those who are in the *remainder* category of disability as competing with them for employment opportunities, service delivery, and social policy development (Deal, 2003). These potentially internecine relationships between various categories of those who may or may not choose to identify as PWDs extend the Stone and Colella (1996) hypothesis that the various behavioural characteristics of PWDs could contribute to the workplace relationships between PWDs and IWODs. Not only could these relationships be informed by the responses of PWDs to the attitudes of IWODs, but they could also be influenced by the relationships between these several newly separated groups.

Finally, this growing rejection of the label of disability has also created an unanticipated challenge associated with gathering demographic data. For example, the 2017 Canadian Survey on Disability is a national data-gathering tool designed to provide guiding analytics on topics that include national and regional disability-related demographics, employment rates, as well as rates and categories of accommodation requirements and solutions. That survey does not ask respondents to indicate whether they believe they are a PWD. Instead, this definition is inferred from a formula that cross-references responses to queries related to a range of daily living activities and whether these activities are problematic and/or the degree of difficulty that is associated with these activities (Statistics Canada, 2017c, 2017d). Demographic information, which depends upon the responses to these queries, may now be increasingly under-reporting the number of individuals who would otherwise be considered as PWDs.

The consideration here is not that these responses should be considered incorrect or inappropriate. However, this possibility of under-reporting may negatively affect a variety of positive programme initiatives intended to be of benefit for PWDs. For example, various government or industry-sponsored Employment Equity initiatives (referred to in some jurisdictions as Affirmative Action initiatives) are intended to increase employment representation of PWDs to levels that are at parity with population numbers. If these numbers are under-reported as they align with the screening definitions of disability within data-gathering surveys, employers will be seeking parity for PWDs at a lower rate of representation than would otherwise be the case. At a minimum, this challenge may require a reconsideration of the data-gathering strategies employed by the various agencies responsible for generating this information.

Skills, Abilities, and PWDs

One additional barrier may further obscure a more fulsome consideration of the construct of disability as either a collection of parts or as a unified whole. That is the political difficulty that arises when distinguishing the relationships between PWDs and the larger community as they exist today from what many of those within this latter community believe that these relationships should be now and in the future.

This challenge is particularly evident within considerations of employment. It does not refer to arguments that describe or decry the current state of employment or those that advocate for more equitable opportunities for PWDs. Instead, it refers to what may be considered by many to be the politically incorrect analysis of the disability community as being comprised of individuals with varying degrees of ability, skill, and employment potential. In much the same way that the disability community has gone to some lengths to minimize or eliminate its relationship with impairment when communicating with the IWOD community (Shakespeare, 2006), we suggest that a similar embargo has been placed on the topic of the differentiation of abilities, both between and within various categories of impairment. This embargo against public discussions associated with employability appears to have been widely adopted by both PWDs and IWODs, although for different reasons. On the part of PWDs, any public musings regarding the rankings of abilities could easily be misconstrued as creating an arbitrary boundary around employability. This determination could be understood as providing evidence for a reduction in the overall ratio of "employable" PWDs to the employer community. It could also provide support for limiting the availability of workplace accommodations only to those PWDs deemed to qualify under this arbitrary rubric.

On the part of IWODs, entering into such a discussion, whether on an individual or categorical basis, would be fraught with the possibility of human rights complaints and, in some cases, with a public repudiation of previously entrenched, or at least stated, corporate values. However, a lack of public discussion does not imply that this topic is not well recognized in practice. Harpur (2019), in an analysis of the Concluding Observations issued by the United Nations CRPD Committee (United Nations General Assembly, 2006), indicates that remedial legislation within various countries has frequently treated psychosocial impairments, including intellectual and other medical conditions associated with brain operation, less favourably than physical and sensory impairments within a context of employment. Harpur also states that there is "deeply embedded prejudice against people with mental disabilities, particularly as compared to other disability categories" (p. 14).

Other Social Influences

The preponderance of media imagery of disability is negative. These negative representations contribute significantly to workplace hesitation in the hiring of PWDs. However, it is also clear there are many positive media references to individuals and groups of PWDs. These include coverage of the Paralympics and other sporting events, to extraordinary personal accomplishments, and to evocative images of disability within the sports, fashion, and entertainment industries (see, for example, Rick Hansen, Viktoria Modesta, Aimee Mullins). However, we suggest that individuals such as these are removed from the category of PWDs by virtue of their accomplishments.

Rather than being incorporated into the larger collective of PWDs, these *high achievers* are perceived as residing outside of that group. They are, as denoted in media coverage during the 2012 Paralympics, *the superhumans* (Crow, 2014). And this phenomenon is not limited to current times. Mordecai (Three-Finger) Brown [*sic*], a baseball pitcher for the Chicago Cubs in the first decade of the 20th century, was made a media star for his ability to throw a "famously tricky curveball" (Schweik, 2009, p. 92). American baseball has also been the home of a number of other famous PWDs. Jim Abbott, born without a right hand, pitched for several Major League teams over the course of ten years. Elsworth Hoy, who was deaf, played for the Chicago White Sox in the last decade of the 19th century. When Hoy made an exceptional play, fans would stand and wave their hats to show their appreciation.

In the face of these accomplishments, the negative difference required to signal the category of disability is transformed into mere difference. As with the high achievers noted above, and in similar circumstances with other derogated groups, changing the membership status of an individual often appears to be a much more commonplace resolution to this dissonance than is a re-analysis of an entire group (Crow, 2014).

In spite of international legislative and educational efforts that have been implemented since the 1980s, studies continue to indicate that employers do not hire PWDs in numbers that are proportionate to their labour market representation. As we have previously described, these decisions have been most frequently explained as a function of misinformation. Perceived lack of skills and abilities, perceptions of increased costs, presumed management difficulties, and anticipated negative responses from co-workers and customers have all been found in various degrees to influence the hiring algorithm.

However, it is difficult not to reflect on whether the issue is based on these particular inputs that are understood as influencing this hiring algorithm or whether the problem is with the algorithm itself. We suggest that these concerns are not principally defined in terms of categories of disability such as sensory, mobility, intellectual, or psychological, nor are they considered in terms of degree, duration, complexity, or cost. Instead, they are determined, in large part, as a result of a cognitive analysis of an affective response to negative difference. As described above, this cognitive analysis may include mediating factors from prior workplace or personal experience, personal characteristics of the observer or of the PWD, and exposure to various media images of disability. However, its principal influence remains its preceding affective response to a perception of negative difference.

Evolving Challenges

Rapidly advancing legal and ethical considerations of disability have recently taken place at the same time as unprecedented scientific developments. This conjunctive process has begun to present major tensions in how we understand disability (Breen, 2015). From both ethical and scientific standpoints, disability is increasingly seen by many, IWODs and PWDs alike, as a state within which a person is both entitled to be and capable of being *cured*. It should be noted that, within this context, *cure* represents the elimination or reduction of impairment, without regard to the means or ethical implications associated with such an intervention.

A deepening understanding of human rights has combined with previously unparalleled scientific developments to create an environment that will have a significant impact on the collective consciousness associated with disability. One of the most challenging questions that arises from this convergence of ethics and science is the relationship between disability and individual choice. This is illustrated by the ongoing complexity developing within the relationship between disability and *cure*.

To illustrate, we consider the implications of a hypothetical ability to repair all spinal cord lesions within a reasonably short period of time. An individual's social location would immediately move from one that includes limitations imposed by personal impairment, as well as political and social barriers, to one of an able-bodied individual with a temporary illness or injury. The social model of disability, which posits disability as being created through environmental restrictions (Oliver, 1990; Oliver & Barnes, 2012), may well be superseded by a return to a neo-medical model, complete with interventions leading to repair and rehabilitation.

Even without an easily available *cure* option as described above, there is another aspect to this concept that requires consideration. Consider the advent of personal use exoskeletons that may soon offer many of those with spinal cord injuries an opportunity to walk, albeit without being *cured* in the traditional sense.

Although currently available devices have substantial limitations and are extremely costly, ongoing research will undoubtedly result in functional improvements and cost reductions over the next several years. Those PWDs who are able to much more readily access the next generation of exoskeletons may be faced with an extremely difficult choice. To stand or not to stand. To walk or not to walk. Each of these responses is fraught with challenges. At stake would be a reconsideration of one's personal identity as well as a variety of external social implications. These latter would include the perceptions of others and the continued entitlement to what are today considered to be necessary accommodations. Whether related to age, duration of impairment, or cultural identity, it is likely that some wheelchair users would prefer to remain seated.

And exoskeletons are merely the tip of that technological iceberg. Continuously enhanced function and affordability permeate the world of high-tech electronics. From home computers to electric vehicles, the speed of development of these consumer goods has been without precedent within the world of manufacturing. Audial descriptions of the surrounding environment are now communicated in real time to those who are blind (see, for example, Aira Tech). Thought-controlled artificial limbs and retinal prostheses, both described within the concept of *cyborg culture* (Barfield & Williams, 2017), have begun to appear within the sphere of medical technology. These, and many other electronic and bio-chemical advancements, will soon provide opportunities to significantly change the face of disability.

If the social model and the neo-medical model are posited at opposite ends of the continuum of the disability metaphor, the question arises as to the degree to which individuals will be perceived as retaining a right to determine their own location in the wake of these ongoing medical advances. If so, one could anticipate a significant backlash toward those who decide to stay sitting in place. We would need to look no further than the current COVID-19 pandemic and the socially divisive hostilities that have arisen over vaccination to foreground this concern.

The ability, whether merely perceived or not, to abandon one's impairment, coupled with the apparent choice not to do so, has the potential to create a significantly increased resistance to the overall acceptance of PWDs within the workplace. Any refusal to accept whatever *cure* is offered may provide additional support for those who argue that PWDs are using their impairments to gain some advantage.

The rationale behind what is referred to in Canada as Employment Equity may suffer the same fate as other forms of accommodation. The current level of incredulity found within segments of the population that oppose active measures to enhance employment opportunities for PWDs may well grow if those latter individuals are increasingly seen as malingerers. And, perhaps surprisingly to some, this image of disability remains current in many environments. Crow (2014), in an analysis of images associated with welfare services reform that appeared in the British press in 2012, found that PWDs are often portrayed as "fraudster(s) and scrounger (s)" (p. 169). Any apparently unfounded rejection of a *cure* by PWDs may be interpreted by some as further evidence to support the elimination of procedural, physical, or other accommodations.

In addition, there is a singular issue associated with accommodations related to employment that distinguishes this from other daily living categories. Employment is competitive. Building a ramp does not particularly inconvenience those who prefer stairs. The replacement of door knobs with levers works well for everyone. But securing a job necessarily implies that someone else did not get that job. The individual who retains his or her disability and continues to rely on positive employment programmes or various accommodations associated with what may be viewed as *unnecessary* disabilities may well face reduced acceptance in a competitive work environment.

If *choice* becomes the defining image of disability, a revisiting of the notion of disability as *deviant behaviour* as articulated by Parsons (1951) may well re-surface. This position maintains that individuals with impairments are not at fault for their limitations but that they have a moral responsibility and social duty to make efforts to regain what that author describes as proper functioning. This responsibility includes seeking and accepting appropriate medical advice.

For those who choose to remain *uncured,* what Siminski (2003) describes as the blame and responsibility and what Goffman (1963) refers to as the stigma of disability may well be perceived by some others to land squarely in the lap of those who so choose. The attributes of impairment and disability, which have been separated by social model adherents (Oliver, 1990), will now appear to some to be reconnected through the mechanism of personal choice. The additional premise of *oppression,* as required by the UK social model of disability (Shakespeare & Watson, 2001), creates a further complication. Specifically, choosing to retain an impairment weakens this premise to such a degree that it virtually disappears.

Although the North American social model has rejected the premise of *oppression* in favour of a minority-rights paradigm (Barnes, Mercer, & Shakespeare, 1999; Davis, 2013), this model also maintains a perspective that seeks to explain disability by assigning responsibility to the IWOD majority. Shakespeare (2004) argues that "rather than a social theory of disability, we need a social theory of embodiment" (p. 20). However, the embodiment model brings us back again to explaining disability as a difference from the norm (Darling, 2013), without a consideration of whether this state of difference is optional. If optional, any biological basis for disability appears to vanish (Hacking, 1999). This will leave those who wish to *stay seated* or are required to do so in a very tenuous position.

Who Do We Think We Are?

A topic that has received little consideration within the ongoing politics associated with PWDs and the larger IWOD community encompasses the iterative effects of the intra-psychical changes within PWDs brought about through the application of the newest models of disability. We acknowledge that the social model, in particular, has served as a rallying point from which many PWDs have been able to transform their own self-perceptions from those characterized by tragedy and personal responsibility to one in which society itself is held responsible for maintaining many of these inequities (Oliver, 1990).

And, at least in one sense, these new models are of uncontested value. They have laid bare society's overwhelming efforts to keep those of us who have been perceived as negatively different out of sight, out of mind, and certainly out of any meaningful social relationships. Eugenics, sterilizations, institutions, special schools, and special employment are topics familiar to many of us (Swain, French, & Cameron, 2003). What has not been adequately considered within these models are the unintended consequences of such relatively new social positionings. Although the embodiment models have, to an extent, softened the cudgel blow of responsibility wielded by the most ardent of the social modelists toward the IWOD community, each of these models maintains, and requires, a separation of identity between PWDs and IWODs. This separation serves as a receptacle for the burdens of responsibility, guilt, and blame.

As we have described in detail throughout this book, this separation is only possible within a cognitively framed analysis. To illustrate the effects that this pendulum swing of responsibility has generated, Crow (1996), arguing in support of a social model of disability, and in opposition to a medical model approach, stated that "(medical model) research will strive to 'cure' an individual of their walking difficulty, whilst ignoring the social factors which make not walking into a problem" (p. 215). Although we agree with Crow's statement that social factors can exacerbate this problem, it is virtually inconceivable to imagine that *not being able to walk* would not always be a problem.

Other social modelists have also suggested that suitable social environments would make significant impairments inconsequential. Oliver (2009), citing himself (Oliver, 1978), states that "the aim of research should not be to make the legless normal … but to create a social environment where to be legless is irrelevant" (p. 19).

At a more community scale, Finkelstein (1988) describes an imagined village in which all inhabitants are wheelchair users. Although this allegory is intended to illustrate how newly arrived IWOD inhabitants become the *able-bodied disabled* due, in part, to an inappropriate built environment and the development of ill-conceived remediative efforts, the underlying premise is that wheelchair use *qua* wheelchair use is only, at best, tangentially related to paralysis.

Although claims that people are disabled by society are effective in highlighting the obstacles created by the larger community, these are a subset of the overall list of environmental barriers which can only, at best, be partially remediated. As Shakespeare (2014) notes, "people with impairments will always be disadvantaged by their bodies" (p. 36). These limitations are real and cannot be wished away by rejecting a personal relationship to impairment. More pointedly, Shakespeare and Watson (2001) had earlier stated that "most (social model) activists concede behind closed doors that they talk about aches and pains and urinary tract infections" (p. 6) while, at the same time, those same activists deny that these are relevant.

It has been argued that progressive disability politics must engage with impairment, including the acknowledgement of limitations that may be associated with impairments (Crow, 1996; Thomas, 1999b). However, we suggest that this does not go far enough. A truly progressive disability politics requires that we engage with our relationships with ourselves. We suggest that real disability pride is exhibited when we freely acknowledge our impairments and still demand respect from society.

At risk of being politically incorrect, it is at times cringeworthy to observe some disability theorists' attempts to eliminate the functional relationship between individual limitations and specific impairments through sophistry and logical legerdemain. Neither those of us who live with disabilities nor IWODs of any stripe are likely to accept these statements at face value. At best, they may be understood as metaphors. However, as is much more likely, they create an image of PWDs as being out of touch with reality and determined to have no relationship with their own impairments beyond serving as locations for oppression. Although these arguments, and associated self-images, have been instrumental in initiating a well-documented shift in society's understanding regarding a range of entitlements associated with PWDs, they have also created a theoretical barrier.

These intrapersonal relationships are as much at issue as our relationships with the larger community. With the latter, we will resolve accommodation needs through attitude change, technological advances, adjustments to the built environment, medical support, and our own determination. However, with the former, we must approach other aspects of our reality from a perspective of *difference*. Otherwise, we will continue to maintain an adversarial relationship with the IWOD community and remain trapped in an endless circle of blame.

This raises the seemingly paradoxical question of how we can be both *different* and, to use Goffman's (1963) quotidian language, a part of the *ingroup* at the same time. As we have considered throughout this book, the solution is one of expanding the construct of *normal* to include a much more broadly based membership. The core premise is that the equality of rights and privileges that we as disability advocates support, and to which all PWDs are entitled, does not necessarily imply an equality of performance, capacity, or ability (Harpur, 2019).

When one cannot perambulate up a mountain, one cannot perambulate up a mountain. A wheelchair user who may be unable to scale a mountain through their own physical effort may discover alternate ways of reaching that peak. These could include a video of an expedition carried out by others, a helicopter ride to the summit, or more currently, a real-time view through a live-streamed camera drone. What is never discussed in these efforts to eliminate perceptions of limitations are the day-to-day realities that do not disappear through the installation of ramps, the development of modern wheelchairs, or even exoskeletons. Whether these limitations are related to the many functions performed by personal assistants, various hygiene requirements, or other daily living supports, it is disingenuous to ignore these realities. By presenting wheelchair users as though these PWDs do not have a personal existence separate from that appliance, and that any individual impairments are somehow extinguished through appropriate accessibility options, is both trite and deceptive.

8 An Autoethnographic Journey

Autoethnographic approaches range from the evocative to more traditional analytical ethnographic forms (Anderson, 2006). This axis supports individual and co-constructed narratives, interviews, reflexive analyses, and performance-based constructions; each with various degrees of connection to traditional analysis and/or scholarly literature.

Since the mid-1980s, various forms of autoethnography have emerged as a means to foreground the relationship between the researcher and a particular social or cultural experience (Méndez, 2013). On the one hand, autoethnography is considered to be an approach to research that provides for a systematic analysis of personal experience as a means to understand these social or cultural phenomena (Ellis, Adams & Bochner, 2011). On the other hand, autoethnography is understood as a means to produce research that, while grounded in personal experience, enhances our capacity to empathize with people who are different from us (Ellis & Bochner, 2000). That common appeal to personal experience, regardless of its presentation format, has two possible goals. The first of these is to expose underlying meaning (Reisman, 2008). The second, as with other forms of narrative inquiry, is to create a conductory process that links the particular to the more theoretical (Breen, 2017). Each of these goals is addressed within our autoethnographical project. We attempt to expose the underlying meanings associated with a lived experience and to extrapolate these meanings for application to the larger reality facing PWDs within the context of employment.

Our purpose is to provide the reader with a nomological framework, essentially a universe of qualitative evidentiary support, within which the difference model may be evaluated. That process, of describing and considering the effects of a qualitatively derived framework, contributes to the ontological validity of the construct under analysis.

Ontological validity can be described as both the process through which qualitative evidence is gathered and applied and the bridge itself that links the qualitative and the quantitative. Created through an analysis of the relationship and effect of the former on the latter, ontological validity brings descriptive clarity to the worldview of the researcher. Although the effect

DOI: 10.4324/9781003220695-8

of personal history on philosophical positions associated with disability studies, including support for particular models of disability, is noted by several writers within the field (Oliver, 2009; Thomas, 1999a), none have, prior to this work, provided detailed descriptions of that history as evidence of validity.

Ontological validity is a relatively new addition (Breen, 2018) to the five sources of validity evidence, as described by AERA (2014), that have been considered as the principal components within current unitary validity theory. This addition of ontological validity fits within a recommended process of ongoing revision, reconceptualization, and evolution within the validity complex (Messick, 1980).

As described by Anderson (2006), an analytic autoethnographical account includes several informing attributes. First, the author(s) must be publicly visible as member(s) of the research group. This status may be through *opportunity* or *conversion* (Adler & Adler, 1987; as cited in Anderson, 2006). The former of these may occur through being born into the group, acquired through illness, or other chance circumstance. The latter status may be a result of an acquired intimacy with the topic through professional or other social participation. In either case, the researcher must also be committed to making use of this autoethnographic form to support or inform an analytically based enhancement of an understanding of a larger social phenomenon.

Our decision to frame the following narrative within the analytical autoethnographical form is both strategic and clearly applicable to our personal circumstances. First, it is a means to add evidentiary support to the ontological validity associated with the difference model of disability. Second, our selection of the analytic autoethnographic framework is informed by our prior work and personal circumstances. Breen, as an individual with a virtually lifelong mobility limitation, an advocate for disability rights, and a practitioner and researcher in the field of employment and disability; Forwell as a long-time scholar, educator, and researcher whose academic efforts include the impact of a range of neurological conditions on employment, significant life transitions, and successful living with disabilities.

We present an autoethnographic account of the timeline, influences, and milestone events that led to the development of the difference model of disability and, consequently, to the development of two scales of attitude measurement in the workplace. The format has been developed around a series of motivating questions posed by Forwell to Breen. Breen's responses, presented within this framework of analytic autoethnography, will describe and consider the impact of the many professional and lived experiences that have generated this project. This journey, which serves as an extended example of ontological validity, will provide the reader with what Geertz (1971) describes as a "thick" description of the world of disability and employment, as seen through Breen's eyes. According to this prescription, the goal is to offer a description that allows readers to more clearly perceive the complex cultural and social environment that both informs and provides meaning to the life of an individual PWD.

Childhood and Youth

Forwell: What comes to mind when you recall your childhood and youth? In retrospect, can you provide any examples of what may have distinguished this period of your life due to your mobility limitations?

Breen: I started public school in 1959. In a middle-class neighbourhood in Winnipeg, Manitoba, Canada. Winnipeg is located in the centre of the Canadian prairie, and, at the time, had a population of approximately half a million. The climate went from +30 C. in the summer to −30° C. in the winter. Lots of sun; lots of snow. I was the only kid with a visible disability in my school district. I now suspect that this extended to any disability at all.

In many ways, I grew up as a minority of one. Born in 1953, I was one of the last wave of children to contract polio later that year. This was all shortly before the introduction of the Salk vaccine in 1955. In those days, disability was an unspoken term. Similar to the then-normative prohibitions against acknowledgements and considerations of cancer, sexual orientation, or various forms of discrimination, disability as a social construct was not for discussion. Neither the language nor the emotional structure was yet in place for these acknowledgements. I clearly recall that there were very few discussions within my family regarding what we would now refer to as impairment. Instead, the focus was much more directed toward mobility improvements.

As a child, I wore leg braces, used crutches, and was somewhat overweight. The latter is due both to genetics and to my mother's post-war, Jewish, middle-class notion of food as representative of everything from hospitality to a demonstration of financial security to emotional support.

During my early childhood, I was relatively oblivious to much of the "edge of the bell curve" social reality that was playing out around me. In my pre- and early-school years, I underwent a variety of surgeries, all intended to enhance my mobility and reduce my reliance on various orthopaedic appliances. In the short term, these resulted in several stays in various hospitals, extended periods away from school, and interruptions in friendships. In many ways, my family treated these singular events as just a different "normal." This was my personal reality that blended relatively seamlessly with that of the rest of my immediate family. However, this was not always the case within a larger social context.

That I was in regular school at all was a significant anomaly for this period. The school system put pressure on my parents to have me enrolled in what was described at the time as a special school for *crippled children*. The term *crippled children* encompassed everyone from kids with sensory limitations, cognitive and developmental delay, seizure activity, and those of us with mobility impairments. In short, any visible or invisible limitation that implied a difference from a mid-20th century, middle-class norm. At that time, these differences were simply not acceptable within the regular school system.

That is, until that system met my mother. As described many years later by my father, who often entertained himself with a degree of political incorrectness, there was only one difference between my mother and a pit bull during that battle – that difference was lipstick. Needless to say, I enrolled in first grade at our local elementary school. Fortunately, the suburb of Winnipeg in which we lived was quite flat and expansive. The local schools, built in the early 1950s, were all single-storey structures and relatively accessible for a child walking with leg braces and crutches. Although my mother's ferocity tended to spill over into more than a small degree of overprotectiveness, within a couple of years, I was allowed to walk the two blocks to school with a friend who was willing to accommodate my slow pace.

Although I was reasonably mobile during this period, my stamina was not particularly good. I clearly remember the first Hallowe'en night that my older brother and I were allowed to go out "trick or treating" on our own without parental accompaniment. Although it was quite a cold and snowy evening, this was relatively typical for the weather in Winnipeg at the end of October. I cannot recall our Hallowe'en costumes; I do, however, remember wearing a parka, winter boots, and mitts over top of whatever I was dressed up to be.

Needless to say, although carefully restricted to an area close to our house, my brother and I managed to extend our tour somewhat in order to fill our "loot bags" with a sizeable number of candies and chocolates. However, by the time we were part way home, I was exhausted. Luckily, I had recently learned about an ingenious method for transporting goods that had been developed by various Indigenous cultures while living traditional lives on the Great Plains of North America. This device, called a travois (pronounced trăv′-wa), consisted of a pair of wooden poles that were typically attached to a horse and dragged along the ground, with various goods tied between the poles. My brother and I improvised, with me lying on the snowy ground holding my crutches over my head so that he could drag me home. I managed to balance the loot bags on top of my parka, with the hood pulled up to keep snow from going down my neck.

Another significant memory from this period followed a transfer to a new school for Grades Four to Six. That followed a series of tests that determined that a select few of us had been deemed suitable for an enriched educational experience in a different kind of special program. That program included enriched training in mathematics, language, and basic sciences. I mention this change in venue because of a unique experience that has stayed with me quite clearly for the past 60 years. This new school was a dozen blocks away from our house. My mother drove me to school and picked me up at the end of the school day. She would stop briefly in a "no parking" zone in front of the school waiting for me and then we would head back home. One day, a police car followed us from the school into the back lane behind our house and pulled up behind us when my mother parked the car in the carport. The officer walked up to the car and peered at me inside. He advised my mother that he was following up on a complaint about my mother continuously stopping in the "no parking" zone in front of the school; he advised that he was making sure that I really was a "crippled kid." He then turned around and left without further comment.

Jumping ahead by several years in my recollections, I find myself as a 17-year-old, in my final year of high school. The year was 1970. As with many of that generation, my mind was turned much more frequently to *sex, drugs, and rock 'n' roll* (albeit with varying degrees of success) than to mathematics, physics, or chemistry. Fortunately, I had already been able to shed Latin and a few other particularly onerous subjects along the way. This was also a time when I had been forced to transition from wearing a single leg brace and using a cane, as I had been able to do for several years, to forearm crutches. Pressure sores from the brace had made its continued use impossible for a period.

This combination of attitude and physical demand led me to a significant, if rather teenaged, revelation. I would quit attending school, arguing that my new physical circumstance was too upsetting to allow me to continue in that public environment. Surprisingly, this argument was accepted. Of course, looking back on this episode, it is quite likely that my teenaged bravado was a response to a real discomfort with a significantly changed physical appearance. The school provided me with an indefinite leave and my parents begrudgingly acquiesced. This was in October, shortly after our first of a series of monthly subject tests that were administered over the course of the year, and which accounted for half of our final grade standings. The other half of our grades would be determined by final exam scores. The only exception to writing the exams was based on cumulative test scores that averaged over 80%, in which case, exemptions to the exams would be granted. Average test scores would simply be doubled to calculate final grades.

I stayed at home during the day, ostensibly by myself, while my parents worked. In reality, friends would drop by, providing various forms of entertainment. Once, during a particularly foolish episode, a friend and I went horseback riding, whereupon, due to an improperly cinched saddle, I fell off the horse and cracked two ribs. This remained a somewhat painful secret for the next few weeks. However, that was not the principal lesson learned during this prolonged period of truancy.

As final exams approached, the school indicated to my parents that I would be held back from graduating and that I would have to repeat the year. I arranged to meet with the principal and argued that I was still a student in good standing at the school, as evidenced by various communications over the year. Since, for medical reasons, I had been only able to write one set of tests, in which I had an average score exceeding the required 80%, I was entitled to the same opportunity for exemptions from writing exams as were other students. Furthermore, my final marks should be those scored on my initial set of tests. Anything else, I argued, would be discriminatory and unfair.

Although not articulated in so many words at the time, the lesson for me was undeniable. It was clear that the argument that I had put forward had no real merit. And yet, with virtually no apparent concern regarding my not having learned the curriculum that year, the school agreed to my demands. Looking back on this experience, it is apparent that my disability had been the motivating factor in this decision on the part of the school. The principal was not willing to cause another problem for what he perceived as this already heavily burdened student.

Adult Experiences

Forwell: Can you recall any highlights from your working life that you think helped to shape your commitment to the difference model of disability?

Breen: Following my negotiated graduation from high school, I began what felt like a predetermined program at university. First, an undergraduate degree in general arts. And then, on to law school. Upon reflection, it is clear that this path had been normalized, through ongoing family discussions, and not inconsiderable pressure, until I had assumed it as the necessary road for me to take in order to eventually find gainful employment. However, the times, my own youthful lack of concern over my future economic security, and a sense of not belonging to my middle-class suburban upbringing, left me quite disinterested in pursuing further education at that time.

Although I was unaware of it at the time, I now understand this sense of unbelonging as being substantially influenced by my own perceived disconnection between my own physical reality and what was generally considered as *normal* within a suburban environment in the 1960s.

Although I faced relatively few examples of direct discrimination, albeit with a number of notable exceptions, my social relations were almost exclusively contained within a mantle of difference. In a very important sense, being perceived through this lens at this time was virtually unavoidable. I was, at the time, a relative anomaly.

This sense of perceived difference was framed across a broad range of mediators. These included – intimidating, friendly, unfortunate, brave, and motivated. However, each of these shared a common sentiment in that they existed at all. Having a descriptive adjective attached to my identity permeated that identity and created a degree of perceived difference that was relatively independent of a particular valence.

With the exception of the very elderly, there were virtually no PWDs who were visible within my local environment. During this period, those individuals living with what would now be considered to be commonplace impairments were typically shunted off to special schools or other cloistered institutions, or were kept closeted by families. Disability, like a host of other topics including sexual orientation, suicide, addictions, or specific diseases such as cancer, fell outside of acceptable social discourse.

I began to find an increasing camaraderie within the hippie community in our city. Almost by definition, members of this community were both alienated from the social norms of the period and accepting of others who held similar sentiments. Having moved away from my parents' home, I shared a small apartment with a friend in an old house that accommodated an eclectic assortment of young, disenchanted, and disenfranchised counterculturalists.

I later realized that, during this period, none of my friends and acquaintances ever posed the intrusive disability-related questions that I had until that point accepted as normal. As I have since discovered, those of us with visible disabilities are routinely subjected to intrusions into what would otherwise be clearly demarcated physical and psychological boundaries. As a young adult with virtually no contact with other PWDs, or with the bourgeoning academic and topical literature that had begun to appear on the topic of disability, I had no experience or training in how best to fend off unwanted and untoward questions and comments. My early responses during this period were based principally on how my brother and I had been raised to be polite and not offend others. However, it quickly became apparent that this was not the only available option.

Discussions within my group often turned to how best to respond to others who poked fun at our adopted lifestyle, appearance, and manner of dress. Several described themselves as "counterpunchers." If so accosted, it was fair to be as outlandish in response as one could imagine. In addition, on more than one occasion, while in the company of one or another of my colleagues, I had faced a variety of intrusions associated with my mobility impairment. These ranged from blatant questions, such as "What happened to you?" to general comments of sympathy for my circumstance, to suggestions from strangers that they would pray for me. My friends, several of whom were a few years older than me, had pointed out that if I found these comments to be offensive, as they recognized that I clearly did, I was free to respond as I felt appropriate. I took this lesson to heart and, although I may be slightly embarrassed in looking back at some of the more outlandish responses, at the time, I enjoyed being quite rude.

During this period when I had temporarily abandoned my academic efforts, I began to work with a group of leather workers in a small retail store, producing many of the *de rigueur* products of the day – belts, sandals, and leather clothing. Having spent considerable time tinkering at various projects with my father, who had an eclectic range of craft skills, I was quite comfortable with a variety of tools and enjoyed the problem-solving involved in designing and making various items. It was also, during this period, that I began to recognize that there could be significant situational variations in how others perceived me with regard to my mobility impairment. I was a young, long-haired "hippie" craftsperson, who, at the time, made use of a stylish walking cane and a relatively invisible leg brace which I had affixed to a hand-made sandal. Depending on the specific situation, I was either vilified or praised for my counterculture existence, appreciated as a craftsperson, or seen principally as a PWD. My recognition of the situational variation in the degree to which my impairment either came to the foreground or was effectively relegated to a position of relative disattention eventually led me to conclude that disability itself was a purely relational construct.

My father was an independent businessperson, having worked in the cattle industry since the age of 14. He had grown up in a tiny community in rural Manitoba where his parents owned the general store. Unlike our family's middle-class, suburban friends and acquaintances, my father could ride a horse, was a crack shot, and I once watched him rope a steer. From him, I learned problem-solving and a comfort level with the precariousness of small enterprise. Although he, and the rest of my family, had continued to encourage me to continue my education with an eye to law school, I was attracted, instead, to self-employment. My first business venture was, along with a partner, the opening of a small leather goods shop in downtown Winnipeg. I had negotiated with a large retail clothing store to rent space in order to open our newly formed Mr Gumby's Leather Shoppe. (*Those of you of a certain vintage will notice the reference to Monty Python's Flying Circus.*)

The next few years included relocating to a small farmhouse purchased with friends in rural Manitoba. After a year of no running water, an outhouse, and splitting firewood, I finally decided to return to university, where I completed a Bachelor's degree in philosophy and classical studies. At this point, much against my better judgement, I succumbed to renewed family pressure and entered law school. Stability, financial security, and a certain prestige were, of course, the arguments put forward; these were coupled with not-so-subtle hints of my needing a career that would accommodate my physical limitations.

However, I knew almost immediately this was not going to be an option for me. Leaving law school after a year, and a brief stint working for a local sports fishing store, I started a home healthcare manufacturing company. I designed and produced a variety of products, including orientation and mobility canes for individuals who were blind, support canes for others, and a variety of other products and accessories. We exported our products to several countries and became a principal supplier of canes to the Canadian National Institute for the Blind.

> For several years, my healthcare business was located within what was referred to as the "old garment district" in Winnipeg. Many of these buildings had been built in the 1920s and were showing significant signs of their age. I rented the top floor of a building that was serviced by an antiquated passenger elevator that the building owner, who owned and managed a clothing store on the main floor, insisted on operating. A larger, freight elevator was located elsewhere in the building but was not available to the public. When a passenger arrived and pushed a service button, the owner would come out of his store and operate the manual controls of the elevator. We had become acquaintances over time and often chatted about business or politics. One day, as I stood behind him in the elevator, the building owner began to complain about how the government was wasting so much money on social programs, particularly a new venture to encourage employers to "hire the handicapped." As these words came out of his mouth, I could see the back of his neck become bright red. He, of course, could not make eye contact as we reached my floor and I left the elevator. Although I approached him the next day, it became clear that his solution to this embarrassing situation was to pretend this conversation had never happened.

I owned and managed this company through most of the 1980s. During this same period, I also became involved in competitive wheelchair sports. On a whim, I had responded to a radio news item describing a range of available wheelchair sports opportunities for PWDs. I mention this because, for many years, I had paid virtually no conscious attention to disability, either in terms of my own identity or that of the larger disability community. Sports was my first exposure to a large group of people who lived with various disabilities.

This connection to other PWDs affected me profoundly. As the novice member of both a wheelchair basketball and wheelchair racquetball team,

I was certainly unskilled, both in the games and with my new sports wheelchair. I recall tipping out of my wheelchair as I tried to enter a racquetball court for the first time. Red-faced, and to a chorus of laughter, I managed to persevere and eventually acquired enough skill to be selected to the Canadian National Wheelchair Racquetball Team. My perseverance had resulted in considerable improvement to my sports and wheelchair skills, including learning to ride escalators and wheel down staircases. It also exposed me to what, at the time, I considered to be the most outrageously risqué locker room humour. This was principally directed toward PWDs, or *crips*, as most of us referred to ourselves only when in the company of others with impairments. Of course, disability-related language has changed significantly since that time. Crip has come to be included in a much more mainstream set of minority descriptors, taking its personal-as-political place alongside *queer* and others.

This exposure to disability led me to a re-evaluation of my relationship to disability itself. Based on the range of individuals whom I had encountered within the sports community, each with their own skills, education, and training, I decided that I would only hire new employees who lived with disabilities. This was considered ill-advised by the small coterie of advisors whom I relied upon for business advice of various kinds. However, by the time that I sold that business in 1990, I had hired, among others, a lathe operator who was blind, a hard-of-hearing salesperson, a production worker with uncontrollable seizure activity, and another with virtually no short-term memory who was supported by my production manager in a rather unique manner. Every time, this individual returned to his workstation, either after a break or at the beginning of a shift, the manager would demonstrate the particular function that he, the production worker, had been performing so that he could return to his task. When looking back on this situation, and recalling that this occurred in the mid-1980s, the lesson learned was not that this technique was an effective solution to this particular challenge, but that it was completely accepted as a norm within that micro-environment. At the time, I did not have the knowledge of many of the larger social changes, and associated language, that were becoming prevalent within the academy and elsewhere. However, it was becoming increasingly clear to me that the attitudes of others toward disability were of critical importance in developing a new and expanded sense of *normal*.

Many years after first learning to negotiate an escalator in my wheelchair, my wife and I were in the UK while I attended the University of Leeds for a semester as a visiting scholar. One day, while sightseeing in London, we exited a subway at a station that had no elevator. Instead, it had what I thought at the time was perhaps the longest escalator ever created. It appeared to be traversing three storeys within the station. Without giving the issue much thought, I wheeled on and started to go up. After moving along for several meters, my wife commented that no one was getting on the escalator behind us, even though there was quite a large crowd milling around at the bottom of the escalator. This episode reinforced for me how disability, as perceived by others, is not necessarily particularly similar to the self-perceptions of PWDs.

In 1986, Canada instituted its first Employment Equity legislation. Consequently, governments and corporations were anxious to provide disability-related training to management. At the time, a friend of mine managed a national organization dedicated to improving employment opportunities for people with disabilities. He approached me to provide training sessions on the topic. He felt that my experience, both as a person living with a disability and as a small business owner, could be valuable in helping to convince generally sceptical managers within public and private organizations of the benefits associated with hiring PWDs.

As I became more involved in this work, I was fortunate to be able to travel across Canada delivering various training and workshops to governments and large corporations. I believe that these various sessions were valuable to at least some of these participants who came to see PWDs in a positive and capable light. In retrospect, I realize that the value for me was my exposure to hundreds of people who had the ability to influence the lives of PWDs, to hear of their concerns, and to begin to understand the systemic workplace bias that existed toward PWDs. I also realized that the benefit for some of the participants was simply having an opportunity to see a PWD in a role that was unexpected.

At the time, I used a bright red sports wheelchair, wore flamboyant neckties, and sported long, curly hair. At the end of various sessions, when asked for comments, participants would frequently indicate how my hair and tie were still quite noticeable, but that my wheelchair had disappeared. Although, as referenced elsewhere, this "disappearing wheelchair" scenario is not always a sought-after or positive result of familiarity with a PWD, at the time these comments appeared to be indicative of an enhanced sense of comfort on the part of a relatively inexperienced audience.

Unfortunately, not all of these training interactions were successful. During an obligatory disability awareness training session that I was delivering to members of management of a Canadian public utility company, it became apparent that the consensus in the room was that this training was considered to be offensive and a waste of time. As one participant opined, their organization already treated everyone the same. He explained that everyone who worked as a manager for the company had worked his [*sic*] way up after having been required to start in the field as a *pole climber*. In response, and in keeping with the new Employment Equity language, I pointed out that fairness did not imply treating everyone the same but rather treating everyone according to their needs. This was absolutely unacceptable to this group. What became apparent, as my presentation continued, was that the participants' real concern was that allowing a wider group of people into the roles now occupied by a relatively homogenous collection of middle-aged, white men could jeopardize opportunities for additional promotions before retirement. These comments reinforced my perception that members of the larger community saw disability through a situational lens. That lens was focused on the immediate relationship that existed between IWODs and PWDs rather than on PWDs themselves.

As my consultancy began to take more of my time and offer opportunities for travel, I sold my manufacturing business and relocated to the Yukon Territory in Canada's north. I had been hired to conduct an organizational review of a local NGO and subsequently accepted a management contract that had been offered to me by its board of directors. That organization provided supported employment services for adults with a wide range of disabilities and also owned a manufacturing company that produced a variety of wooden products for the mining industry. That latter company was a social enterprise with a dual mandate. It needed to make a profit and it was created to provide employment for PWDs. My responsibility was to find employment opportunities for PWDs within the community and to grow the manufacturing company to increase available internal positions.

I found that there were two advantages to working within a small city in northern Canada. First, I was able to make personal contact with a significant percentage of the business community and to engage owners and managers in frank discussions regarding disability and employment. Second, the local governments, both federal and territorial, were willing to fund a variety of practice-based research projects. As a consequence, I was able to establish partnerships with several business sectors to develop employment training programs for our clients and other members of the disability community.[1] These endeavours provided me with significant insight into how PWDs were viewed, and categorized, by employers. Most noticeable to me was that many employers separated PWDs into two groups, which could be generally categorized as what Goffman (1963) had categorized as the *ingroup* and the *outgroup*. However, what was most intriguing were the determinants of the membership of each of these groups. Those individuals with disabilities who were perceived as being able to *perform* within the specific context under consideration, in this case within a specific employment environment, were considered to be within the *ingroup*. Those who could not were in the *outgroup*.

The lesson for me was that membership in either the *ingroup* or the *outgroup* by individual PWDs was not tied specifically to a particular disability, to its complexity, or to what may appear to be overall life challenges. Rather, that membership was categorized relative to a particular employment context. These were not examples of the "disappearing disability" such as described above in my training sessions. Instead, these situations reflected the point at which these differences were perceived as sufficiently negative to rise above what I later termed *the horizon of social notice*.

A second example of my own workplace experience, which ultimately contributed to the development of the difference model, occurred when I was employed by the Yukon government in northern Canada between 2004 and 2013. I had been hired to create and manage a new Workplace Diversity Employment Office. That government had been concerned over a discrepancy between the territorial population-based representation of disability, which was approximately 12.5%, and the much lower self-reported representation rate of PWDs within the government workforce. That workforce numbered approximately 4,000 people with only 4.4% self-reporting as PWDs. During the period, we introduced several initiatives to recruit new employees with disabilities and to encourage self-disclosure amongst current employees.

At that time, I was also providing disability awareness training sessions with a co-facilitator who was hard of hearing. Although my training partner had acquired very advanced hearing aids, he pointed out a significant problem associated with using the multi-line telephones that were common within our organization. In essence, increasing the volume of the telephone resulted in a concurrent increase in distortion, making telephone communication particularly challenging for individuals who wore hearing aids. To resolve this challenge, we sourced a small device that attached directly to the telephone receiver cord and which provided controls for both volume and tone adjustment. This allowed for managing any distortion as the volume was increased and it solved the problem – for $30.00.

In addition, based on a then-recent internal equity census within the Yukon government, I knew that there were a significant number of government employees who had indicated that they were also hard of hearing. To address this challenge of telephone communication, I purchased 100 of these devices through my discretionary accommodations fund, sent an email to all government employees advising that we were aware of this problem, and invited everyone who could benefit to obtain a unit, at no charge, through our office. Two things happened almost immediately. First, all of these devices were distributed within two weeks. Second, I began to receive telephone calls and emails asking about the availability of other accommodation options from managers and supervisors who had previously failed to recognize the availability of such solutions.

My lesson learned was that this project had changed perceptions regarding PWDs; specifically, that various limitations associated with impairments were no longer perceived as unmanageable, core characteristics of PWDs. Instead, they had begun to be perceived as peripheral challenges to be overcome. These responses clearly supported my developing belief that without these changes in attitude, the various requested accommodations would not have been sought out.

Forwell: Could you reflect on any moments when you recognized that your life, as a PWD, would be challenging for others without disabilities to understand?

Breen: I think that it would be useful to frame my response by first comparing my own self-image with how I am seen by many people. What is most interesting to me is that these can, at times, be almost mirror images. I see myself as part of that *normal* that we have discussed. Not only do I lead a social and economic life that is relatively common in early 21st-century Canada, I perceive myself, including my methods of mobility, as normal. Of course, these may not be normal for others but, for me, getting up in the morning and going to the kitchen to make coffee is a normal event. I do not think about the technique or skill required to move from our bedroom to the kitchen any more than another would if ambulating without the aid of crutches. I perceive my physical activities as normal, regardless of whether they may appear challenging, awkward, or hesitant to another. And regardless of whether they are, in fact, more complicated or time-consuming. I think that, in many ways, this issue of appearance is key to understanding these challenges of understanding.

Although these reflections are associated with physical appearance, including what I will call *appearance in motion*, it is easy to extrapolate these same considerations as applying to other PWDs with other impairments. Essentially, if others, those we have named as IWODs, are unable to understand me from a performatively normal perspective, the only option remaining is to assign some degree of abnormality. In one sense, I face the same dilemma when I consider how the typical IWOD ambulates. I have no understanding of the mechanics or balance requirements involved in keeping someone bipedally upright while ambulating. The difference is that I am surrounded by bipedally upright IWODs. It is difficult not to assign a degree of normalcy to this group, even though I may not understand either the process or the skill set required to carry off this unimaginable task.

This impetus to assign normalcy to our own behaviours was illustrated to me quite vividly one day in 1988 when I was the keynote speaker at a gathering in celebration of a federally funded Canadian project called National Access Awareness Week. I had been requested to speak to a group of business and government employees who had been invited to listen to my presentation on the topic of employment and disability. This was at a time shortly after the Canadian government had passed its first Employment Equity Act. Employers were anxious to learn of its implications and to consider strategies to hire PWDs. I had been delivering disability awareness training sessions across the country and, consequently, been invited to speak at this gathering. My work, at the time, had been focused on presenting what is still known as the business case argument for employing PWDs. That included describing a litany of benefits and reminding employers of various financial and behavioural myths associated with PWDs in the workplace. Although I had begun to consider the primacy of attitudes toward PWDs, which later was to become a cornerstone of the difference model, I had not developed this line of reasoning to a point of public consideration.

I had arrived at the venue just shortly before I was scheduled to speak. As I approached the stage in my wheelchair, I realized that there was no ramp and that it was going to be impossible to reach the podium and microphone. As can be imagined, a certain degree of chaos ensued. We found a solution by my transferring from my wheelchair onto the front of the stage where I sat cross-legged, holding a portable microphone. Unable to pass up this teaching moment, I put aside my prepared notes and related an image that had crossed my mind as we had attempted to find a way to save this presentation. Here is what I said:

> As I was sitting here in my wheelchair waiting for the microphone to be disengaged from the podium, I had a fleeting image of myself that I would like to relate to you. In that image I was walking along a country road but I could only see myself above the waist. My lower body was hidden by a hedge. I realized in that moment that I had never dreamed or had a waking image of myself walking unless I was similarly obscured. Until that moment, this had never occurred to me. I would like to suggest to all of you in the audience that none of you have ever been able to experience life using a wheelchair without a similar degree of obscurancy. I suggest that you would be unable to visualize the mechanics required to hop up a curb, or, more dramatically, go down a flight of stairs. These difficulties in understanding the reality of others are what feed myths, create anxiety, and foster avoidance when opportunities arise to hire people with disabilities.

I am also aware of being viewed, in some circumstances, as anything but a member of that group of normals. These discrepancies show themselves in a number of ways, although I think that the common link is that others who hold these perspectives are not able to see through the "disability" images that they have formed to recognize who I am as a person. When my skills, my abilities, my capacities, my character, are unable to percolate through this screen, it becomes impossible for another to know me. Although each of us is aware that we have various limitations, whether in physical appearance or stature, agility, intellectual ability, or other human traits, PWDs and other derogated groups have limitations assigned by virtue of their membership in that group.

I can recall a number of examples of being personally invisible to others, appearing only as a token of whatever image of disability was in the mind of an observer. One such example is from my youth, I think I was 18 years old, and I was trying to find a summer job before I started my first year of university. At the time, I walked with a leg brace and a cane and was quite mobile. I approached a local outlet of a national chain of hardware and automobile parts that had advertised for a part-time employee within the service centre. The job involved working behind a service counter and retrieving various products in the warehouse as requested by customers. I was told by the department manager that it was foolish of me to apply for a job like this. He had no interest in hearing about my skills. That was the extent of my job interview.

Another time, it was 1986, I applied to the Canadian Astronaut Program (CAP). I had developed, in partnership with a friend who was a medical doctor with an interest in neural stimulation, two experiments to be conducted in an environment of micro-gravity. One was a measure of muscle response to electrical stimulation and the other was a comparison of the psychological effects of prolonged weightlessness between an astronaut with a mobility impairment and an IWOD. Although that organization indicated an early interest in our experiment designs, I was contacted by a member of the CAP and confidentially advised that I was wasting my time. Regardless of the impairment, the CAP would never entertain an application from a PWD.

Forwell: Do you have any final thoughts that may help readers to understand what it means to be a PWD?

Breen: I do. And I would like to preface these remarks by acknowledging that they are commonly voiced by many other PWDs, some of whom are friends and colleagues and others who have written on the topic within various academic, fictional, and artistic formats. What I would ask readers to consider is the effect that living within an environment that continuously reinforces the difference, and particularly the negative difference, that is perceived to exist between IWODs and PWDs. These perceptions are manifested in many ways, including the neotenous nature that is often assigned to PWDs, assumptions of general incapability, inappropriately intrusive actions, or other behaviours that demonstrate perceived power imbalances or assumptions of diminished humanity on the part of PWDs. To illustrate within a personal context, I have been patted on the head by strangers when passing in my wheelchair. I have had money placed in my lap as I wheeled along various sidewalks. I have been cursed at for refusing offered assistance. And I have been asked by a stranger (my taxi driver) if I can have sex. (I responded "Not right now. I am quite tired.")

Throughout my youth and adult life, I have learned that it is not always necessary to offer acquiescent responses to intrusions such as I have described. However, the caveat is that responses that are unexpected, even if not particularly impolite, are frequently considered to be uncivil and, as I have been advised more than once, "I was just curious. There is no need to be rude!"

I would also like to say that the examples that I have given here are not necessarily typical of my various social relationships. Most people, including friends, acquaintances, colleagues, and strangers, are thoughtful and considerate and, most commonly, pay little attention to any differences that may be apparent. However, it is the minority that is of most influence. I know many PWDs, and I include myself in this number, who have spent time practising responses to unwanted intrusions, essentially preparing for the next situation by pre-empting a next example of "what I should have said."

Note

1 These several training programs, and the underlying MAST (Motivation, Assistance, Skills Training) framework, have been described in detail elsewhere. See – Breen, J. (2000). *Creating vocational success for adults with FAS*. Edmonton, AB: Muttart Foundation.

9 Final Thoughts

The purpose of this book has been to offer an alternative to the current cognitively based models of disability. We have provided a new framework that will assist in the achievement of fair and equitable employment opportunities for PWDs. We believe that the difference model, presented as an affect-based construct, provides a pragmatic basis for understanding workplace relationships between PWDs and IWODs. Furthermore, we believe that this perspective can and will lead to an improvement in these relationships and, consequently, to enhanced employment opportunities for PWDs. As we have described throughout this book, this belief is supported by quantitative and qualitative evidence.

We have demonstrated how we have applied this model to the development of tools that address and measure workplace attitudes. These have included training programs and tests designed to monitor attitudes toward PWDs. We have also considered how the data generated from these measures can inform novel workplace interventions and vocational planning.

It is our hope that this paradigm shift from current models of disability will provide students and teachers of disability studies, corporate champions, and vocational rehabilitation practitioners, with new insights in support of the many strategic efforts required for PWDs to reach a position of equity within the broad scheme of employment. We also hope that this same paradigm shift will provide PWDs with a sense of normativity that supersedes a divisive identity politics and which, instead, advocates for our entitled seat at a larger community table. However, although our hopes and aspirations are clear, we recognize that this work has only begun.

Becoming *Different*

It is time to strip away all of the arbitrary examples used to externalize responsibility for our various limitations. We all know that history has generally not been kind to disability. However, it is time to stop trumpeting

DOI: 10.4324/9781003220695-9

the hackneyed refrain of blame and start living with *difference*. Pointing out the responsibility of others, whether based on specific disabilities, severity, or environmental reality, each framed within shameful examples from past periods when generally horrible treatment of everyone who was not within the majority was the norm, is neither helpful nor productive.

Those of us who came of age during "the '60s" recall the intransigent nature of social norms that had become entrenched in a system, particularly when that system had not yet had sufficient reason to reflect on its values. We changed that. We gave society a reason to reflect, and ultimately to begin to change its values. We have done it again as it pertains to disability. But it is time to move on.

This is no longer a period of glory for disability activists; it is a period of bureaucracy. We no longer need to ask if this issue is on the table. It is. To transport Dr King's words, we need no longer continue to accept *the tranquillizing drug of gradualism*. Our time is now. As Dr King said 52 years ago, it is time for us to cash our cheque. And, at least in part, the impetus for this timing is somewhat disconcerting to some of us who have been at this for a considerable period. Our shiny new weapon, our legitimacy, our ace-in-the-hole, is simply ageing. The baby boom generation is quickly becoming the greatest ally that the disability movement has ever had. That quiet, internal discussion within "the movement" over the legitimacy of age-related disability is now out in the open and beyond debate.

What is left but the meaning assigned to ways of living? This meaning cannot be seen as only flowing from IWODs to PWDs. We, as people who live with impairments, are the subject, not the object, of that equation. However, we need to ask what meanings we assign to ourselves. Of course, the environment affects us, whether it is the built environment, the work environment, or the environment of relationships. Our own impairments create limitations that may be moderated to various degrees by a growing range of accommodations. To postulate otherwise makes us appear to others as annoyingly naïve, arrogant, or self-absorbed. These are the same others with whom we are negotiating for our entitlements – and employment.

Perhaps it all comes down to "What do you want?" Is it more important to be seen to be extracting your accommodations from a resentful society than to merely negotiate for what you need? If a comprehensive and coherent delivery of Universal Design (now often referred to as Inclusive Design) were to be implemented, in both the metaphorical and substantive senses, would not *oppression* disappear? This, we believe, would more than outweigh any cost to those whose identity is extracted from the struggle. Of course, there would still be opportunities to continue drumming the oppressions of historical examples of discrimination, but for what purpose?

We have presented the difference model as one which is disassociated from blame. As we described, we have used this term in a very specific sense that is derived from the affective nature of the difference model itself. There is no blame attached to perception. We believe that applications of the difference model within the employment environment will foster the construction of relationships between IWODs and PWDs that build upon this basic notion, resulting in a more equitable and successful workplace for all.

References

Abberley, P. (1987). The concept of oppression and the development of a social theory of disability. *Disability, Handicap and Society*, *2*(1), 5–19.

Accessible Canada Act, SC 2019, c 10. Retrieved on February 3, 2022 from: https://canlii.ca/t/53rfw

Albert, C., Luque, G., & Courchamp, F. (2018) The twenty most charismatic species. *PLoS ONE, 13*(7), e0199149. Retrieved on March 12, 2022 from 10.1371/journal.pone.0199149

American Educational Research Association, American Psychological Association, National Council on Measurement in Education, & Joint Committee on Standards for Educational and Psychological Testing. (U.S.). [AERA]. (2014). *Standards for educational and psychological testing*. Washington, DC: American Educational Research Association.

Albrecht, G. (1992). *The disability business: Rehabilitation in America*. Newbury Park, CA: Sage.

Albrecht, G. (2002). American pragmatism, sociology and the development of disability studies. In C. Barnes, M. Oliver, & L. Barton (Eds.), *Disability studies today* (pp. 18–37). Cambridge, UK: Polity Press.

Allport, G. (1935). Attitudes. In C. Murchison (Ed.), *Handbook of social psychology* (pp. 798–844). Worcester, MA: Clark University Press.

Altman, B. (2001). Disability definitions, models, classification schemes, and applications. In G. Albrecht, K. Seelman, & M. Bury (Eds.), *Handbook of disability studies* (pp. 97–122). Thousand Oaks, CA: Sage.

Americans with Disabilities Act of 1990, Pub. L. No. 101-336, 104 Stat. 328 (1990).

Anastasiou, D., & Kauffman, J. (2013). The social model of disability: Dichotomy between impairment and disability. *Journal of Medicine and Philosophy*, *38*(4), 441–459.

Andrews, E. (2017). Disability models. In M. Budd, S. Gough, S. Wegener, & W. Stiers (Eds.), *Practical psychology in medical rehabilitation* (pp. 77–83). Switzerland: Springer.

Anderson, L. (2006). Analytic autoethnography. *Journal of Contemporary Ethnography*, *35*(4), 373–395.

Antonak, R. (1982). Development and psychometric analysis of the Scale of Attitudes Toward Disabled Persons. *Journal of Applied Rehabilitation Counseling*, *13*(2), 22–29.

Antonak, R. (1988). Methods to measure attitudes toward people who are disabled. In H. Yuker (Ed.), *Attitudes toward persons with disabilities* (pp. 109–126). New York, NY: Springer.

Antonak, R., & Livneh, H. (2000). Measurement of attitudes towards persons with disabilities. *Disability and Rehabilitation, 22*(5), 211–224.

Aptowicz, C. (2014). *Dr. Mutter's marvels.* New York, NY: Penguin Random House.

Araten-Bergman, T. (2016). Managers' hiring intentions and the actual hiring of qualified workers with disabilities. *International Journal of Human Resource Management, 27*(14), 1510–1530.

Azjen, I. (1991). The theory of planned behavior. *Organizational Behavior and Human Decision Processes, 50*(2), 179–211.

Barfield, W., & Williams, A. (2017). Cyborgs and enhancement technology. *Philosophies, 2*(4). 10.3390/philosophies2010004

Barnes, C. (1999). Disability studies: New or not so new directions? *Disability and Society, 14*(4), 577–580.

Barnes, C. (2003). What a difference a decade makes: Reflections on doing 'emancipatory' disability research. *Disability and Society, 18*(1), 3–17.

Barnes. C. (2012). Understanding the social model of disability. In N. Watson, A. Roulstone, & C. Thomas (Eds.), *Routledge handbook of disability studies* (pp. 12–28). Abingdon, UK: Routledge.

Barnes, C. (2014). Reflections on doing emancipatory disability research. In J. Swain, S. French, C. Barnes, & C. Thomas (Eds.), *Disabling barriers, enabling environments (3rd ed.)* (pp. 37–44). London, UK: Sage.

Barnes, C. (2019). Understanding the social model of disability: Past, present and future. In N. Watson & S. Vehmas (Eds.), *Routledge handbook of disability studies (2nd ed.)* (pp. 14–31). London, UK: Taylor & Francis.

Barnes, C., & Mercer, G. (2001). Disability culture – Assimilation or inclusion. In G. Albrecht, K. Seelman, & M. Bury (Eds.), *The handbook of disability studies* (pp. 515–534). Thousand Oaks, CA: Sage.

Barnes, C., & Mercer, G. (2003). *Disability.* Cambridge, UK: Polity Press.

Barnes, C., & Mercer, G. (2010). *Exploring disability: A sociological introduction.* Cambridge, UK: Polity Press.

Barnes, C., Mercer, G., & Shakespeare, T. (1999). *Exploring disability: A sociological introduction.* Cambridge, UK: Polity Press.

Barnett, S., & Seymour, E. (1999). *A shrinking iceberg travelling south: Changing trends in British television.* London, UK: Campaign for Quality Television.

Barr, J., & Bracchitta, K. (2012). Attitudes toward individuals with disabilities: The effects of age, gender, and relationship. *Journal of Relationships Research, 3*, 10–17.

Beattie, J., Anderson, R., & Antonak, R. (1997). Modifying attitudes of prospective educators toward students with disabilities and their integration into regular classrooms. *Journal of Psychology, 131*(3), 245–259.

Beaudry, J-B. (2016). Beyond (models of) disability? *Journal of Medicine and Philosophy, 41*, 210–228.

Beck, C., & Gable, R. (2001). Ensuring content validity: An illustration of the process. *Journal of Nursing Measurement, 9*(2), 201–215.

Becker, G. (1957). *The economics of discrimination.* Chicago, IL: University of Chicago Press.

Beckett, A., & Campbell, T. (2014). The social model of disability as an oppositional device. *Disability and Society, 30*(2), 270–283.

Berger, R. (2015). Now I see it, now I don't: Researcher's position and reflexivity in qualitative research. *Qualitative Research, 15*(2), 219–234.

Bhaskar, R. (1989). *Reclaiming reality*. London, UK: Verso.

Bhaskar, R., & Danermark, B. (2006). Metatheory, interdisciplinarity and disability research: A critical realist perspective. *Scandinavian Journal of Disability Research*, *8*(4), 278–297.

Bickenbach, J., Jerome, E., Chatterji, S., Badley, E., & Ustun, T. (1999). Models of disablement, universalism and the international classification of impairments, disabilities and handicaps. *Social Science and Medicine*, *48*(9), 1173–1187.

Birch, S., & Longmore, P. (Eds.). (2009). *Encyclopedia of American disability history*. (Volumes 1-3). New York, NY: Facts on File.

Blascovich, J., Mendes, W., Hunter, S., Lickel, B., & Kowai-Bell, N. (2001). Perceiver threat in social interactions with stigmatized others. *Journal of Personality and Social Psychology*, *80*, 253–267.

Blumer, H. (1969). *Symbolic interactionism: Perspective and method*. Englewood Cliffs, NJ: Prentice-Hall.

Bogdan, R., & Taylor, S. (1989). Relationships with severely disabled people: The social construction of humanness. *Social Problems*, *36*(2), 135–148.

Bonaccio, S., Connelly, C., Gellatly, I., Jetha, A., & Martin Ginis, K. (2019). The participation of people with disabilities in the workplace across the employment cycle: Employer concerns and research evidence. *Journal of Business and Psychology*. 10.1007/s10869-018-9602-5

Boorse, C. (1977). Health as a theoretical concept. *Philosophy of Science*, *44*(4), 542–573.

Boukes, M., Jones, N., & Vliegenthart, R. (2022). Newsworthiness and story prominence: How the presence of news factors relates to upfront position and length of news stories. *Journalism*, *23*(1), 98–116.

Braddock, D., & Bachelder, L. (1994). The glass ceiling and persons with disabilities. *Federal Publications (Institute on Disability and Human Development. Public Policy Monograph Series #56)*. Chicago, IL: University of Illinois at Chicago. https://hdl.handle.net/1813/77511

Braddock, D., & Parish, S. (2001). An institutional history of disability. In G. Albrecht., K. Seelman, & M. Bury (Eds.), *The handbook of disability studies* (pp. 11–68). Thousand Oaks, CA: Sage.

Breen, J. (2015). The exoskeleton generation – Disability redux. *Disability and Society*, *30*(10), 1568–1572.

Breen, J. (2017). Disability as difference – A fictional representation. *The Qualitative Report*, *22*(10), 2722–2741.

Breen, J. (2018a). The co-worker acceptance of disabled employees (CADE) scale: A study to gather evidence of content validity. (PhD dissertation) http://hdl.handle.net/2429/67749

Breen, J. (2018b). Attitudes toward employees with disabilities: A systematic review of self-report measures. *Australian Journal of Rehabilitation Counselling*, *24*(2), 67–87.

Breen, J. (2019). Developing the Co-Worker Acceptance of Disabled Employees (CADE) Scale. *Australian Journal of Rehabilitation Counselling*, *25*(1), 1–14.

Breen, J., & Forwell, S. (2020). The Difference Model of disability: A change in direction for vocational rehabilitation practice. *Australian Journal of Rehabilitation Counselling*. 10.1017/jrc.2020.2

Breen, J. & Forwell, S. (2021). The difference model of disability: A focus on employment. In N. Ferreira, I. Potgieter, & M. Coetzee (Eds.), *Agile coping in the digital era: Emerging issues for research and practice* (pp. 275–298). Cham, Switzerland: Springer Nature.

Breen, J., Havaei, F., & Pitassi, C. (2019). Employer attitudes toward hiring persons with disabilities in Armenia. *Disability and Rehabilitation, 41*(18), 2135–2142.

Brennan, R. (2001). Some problems, pitfalls, and paradoxes in educational measurement. *Educational Measurement: Issues and Practice, 20*(4), 6–18.

Brislin, R. (1970). Back-translation for cross-cultural research. *Journal of Cross-Cultural Psychology, 1*(3), 185–216.

Brostrand, H. (2006). Tilting at windmills: Changing attitudes toward people with disabilities. *Journal of Rehabilitation, 72*(1), 4–9.

Bruyère, S., VanLooy, S., von Schrader, S., & Barrington, L. (2016). Disability and employment: Framing the problem, and our transdisciplinary approach. In S. Bruyère (Ed.), *Disability and employer practices: Research across the disciplines* (pp. 1–26). Ithaca, NY: Cornell University Press.

Buller, D. (2005). *Adapting minds*. Cambridge, MA: MIT Press.

Burgdorf, M., & Burgdorf, R., Jr. (1975). A history of unequal treatment: The qualifications of handicapped persons as a 'suspect class' under the equal protection clause. *Santa Clara Law Review, 15*(4), 855–888.

Burke, J., Bezyak, J., Fraser, R., Pete, J., Ditchman, N., & Chan, F. (2013). Employers' attitudes towards hiring and retaining people with disabilities: A review of the literature. *Australian Journal of Rehabilitative Counselling, 19*(1), 21–38.

Burkhauser, R., Houtenville, A., & Rovba, L. (2005). *Rising poverty in the midst of plenty: The case of working-age people with disabilities over the business cycles of the 1980s and 1990s*. Ithaca, NY: Rehabilitation Research and Training Center for Economic Research on Employment Policy for People with Disabilities, Cornell University.

Burkhauser, R., & Stapleton, D. (2004). The decline in the employment rate for people with disabilities: Bad data, bad health, or bad policy? *Journal of Vocational Rehabilitation, 20*(3), 185–201.

Campbell, F. (2005). Legislating disability. In S. Tremain (Ed.), *Foucault and the government of disability* (pp. 108–130). Ann Arbor, MI: The University of Michigan Press.

Canadian Broadcasting Corporation. (2022). As restrictions loosen up, advocates for people with disabilities say their needs haven't been considered. *The Current*. Retrieved on February 10, 2022 from: https://www.cbc.ca/radio/thecurrent/the-current-for-feb-7-2022-1.6342202/as-restrictions-loosen-up-advocates-for-people-with-disabilities-say-their-needs-haven-t-been-considered-1.6344715

Cattell, R. (1966). The scree test for the number of factors. *Multivariate Behavioral Research, 1*(2), 245–276.

Chan, F., Gelman, J., Ditchman, N., Kim, J., & Chiu, C. (2009). The world health organization ICF model as a conceptual framework of disability. In F. Chan, E. da Silva Cardoso, & J. Chronister (Eds.), *A handbook for evidence-based practitioners in rehabilitation* (pp. 23–50). New York, NY: Springer.

Chan, F., Strausser, D., Maher, D., Lee, E-J., Jones, R., & Johnson, E. (2010). Demand-side factors related to employment of people with disabilities: A survey of employers in the Midwest region of the United States. *Journal of Occupational Rehabilitation, 20*, 412–419.

Chan, F., Tansey, T., Iwanaga, K., Bezyak, J., Wehman, P., Phillips, B., Strauser, D., & Anderson, C. (2021). Company characteristics, disability inclusion practices, and employment of people with disabilities in the post COVID-19 job economy: A cross sectional survey study. *Journal of Occupational Rehabilitation, 31*(3), 463–473.

Charlton, J. (2006). The dimensions of disability oppression: An overview. In L. Davis (Ed.), *The Disability Studies Reader (2nd ed.)* (pp. 217–227). New York, NY: Routledge.

Charmaz, K. (1991). Turning points and fictional identities. In D. Maines (Ed.), *Social organization and social process* (pp. 71–86). New York, NY: Aldine de Gruyter.

Charmaz, K. (2000). Grounded theory: Objectivist and constructivist methods. In N. Denzin, & Y. Lincoln (Eds.), *Handbook of qualitative research* (pp. 509–535). Thousand Oaks, CA: Sage.

Chordiya, R. (2022). Organizational inclusion and turnover intentions of federal employees with disabilities. *Review of Public Personnel Administration, 42*(1), 60–87.

Clayton, S., Barr, B., Nylen, L., Burström, B., Thielen, K., Diderichson, F., Dahl, E., & Whitehead, M. (2011). Effectiveness of return-to-work interventions for disabled people: A systematic review of government initiatives focused on changing the behaviour of employers. *European Journal of Public Health, 22*(3), 434–439.

Cluley, V., Fyson, R., & Pilnick, A. (2020). Theorizing disability: A practical and representative ontology of learning disability. *Disability and Society, 35*(2), 235–257.

Colella, A. (2001). Coworker distributive fairness judgments of the workplace accommodation of employees with disabilities. *The Academy of Management Review, 26*(1), 100–116.

Colella, A., & Varma, A. (2001). The impact of subordinate disability on leader-member exchange relationships. *Academy of Management Journal, 44*(2), 304–315.

Collier, A. (1994). *Critical realism*. London, UK: Verso.

Connolly, W. (2002). *Identity/difference: Democratic negotiations of political paradox*. Minneapolis, MN: University of Minnesota Press.

Copeland, J., Chan, F., Bezyak, J., & Fraser, R. (2010). Assessing cognitive and affective reactions of employers toward people with disabilities in the workplace. *Journal of Occupational Rehabilitation, 20*(4), 427–434.

Corker, M. (1999a). Differences, conflations and foundations: The limits to 'accurate' theoretical representation of disabled people's experience? *Disability and Society, 14*(5), 627–642.

Corker, M. (1999b). New disability discourse, the principle of optimization and social change. In M. Corker, & S. French (Eds.), *Disability discourse* (pp. 192–209). Buckingham, UK: Open University Press.

Craig, D., & Bigby, C. (2015). Critical realism in social work research: Examining participation of people with intellectual disability. *Australian Social Work, 68*(3), 309–323.

Creamer, D. (2012). Disability theology. *Religion Compass, 6*(7), 339–346.

Creswell, J. (2013). *Qualitative inquiry and research design*. Los Angeles: Sage.

Crow, L. (1996). Including all of our lives: Renewing the social model of disability. In J. Morris (Ed.), *Encounters with strangers: Feminism and disability* (pp. 206–226). London, UK: The Women's Press.

Crow, L. (2014). Scroungers and superhumans: Images of disability from the summer of 2012: A visual inquiry. *Journal of Visual Culture, 13*(2), 168–181.

Damasio, A. (1999). *The feeling of what happens: Body and emotion in the making of consciousness*. New York: Harcourt Brace.

Damasio, A. (2010). *Self comes to mind*. New York: Pantheon Books.

Danermark, B., Ekstrom, M., Jakobsen, L., & Karlsson, J. (2002). *Explaining society: Critical realism in the social sciences*. London, UK: Routledge.

Danermark, B., & Gellerstedt, L. (2004). Social justice: Redistribution and recognition – A non-reductionist perspective on disability. *Disability and Society, 19*(4), 340–352.

Danforth, S. (2001). A pragmatic evaluation of three models of disability in special education. *Journal of Developmental and Physical Disabilities, 13*(4), 343–359.

Darcy, S., Taylor, T., & Green, J. (2016). 'But I can do the job': Examining disability employment practice through human rights complaint cases. *Disability and Society, 31*(9), 1242–1274.

Darke, P. (2004). The changing face of representations of disability in the media. In J. Swain, S. French, C. Barnes, & C. Thomas (Eds.), *Disabling barriers – Enabling environments (2nd ed.)* (pp. 101–105). London, UK: Sage.

Darling, R. (2013). *Disability and identity*. Boulder, CO: Lynne Rienner Publishers.

Davis, L. (1992). Instrument review: Getting the most from your panel of experts. *Applied Nursing Research, 5*(4), 194–197.

Davis, L. (2000). Nude Venuses, Medusa's body, and phantom limbs: Disability and visuality. In D. Mitchell, & S. Snyder (Eds.), *The body and physical difference* (pp. 51–70). Ann Arbor, MI: The University of Michigan Press.

Davis, L. (2001). Identity politics, disability, and culture. In G. Albrecht, K. Seelman, & M. Bury (Eds.), *The handbook of disability studies* (pp. 535–545). Thousand Oaks, CA: Sage.

Davis. L. (2002). *Bending over backwards: Disability, dismodernism and other difficult positions*. London, UK: New York University Press.

Davis, L. (2006). The end of identity politics and the beginning of dismodernism: On disability as an unstable category. In L., Davis (Ed.), *The disability studies reader (2nd ed.)* (pp. 231–242). New York, NY: Routledge.

Davis, L. (2013). The end of identity politics: On disability as an unstable category. In L., Davis (Ed.), *The disability studies reader* (*4th ed.*) (pp. 263–277), Oxford, UK: Routledge.

Davis, L., & Engel, R. (Eds.). (2011). *Measuring race and ethnicity*. New York: Springer.

de Jonge, J. (2012). *Rethinking rational choice theory: A companion on rational and moral action*. London, UK: Palgrave MacMillan.

Deal, M. (2003). Disabled people's attitudes toward other impairment groups: A hierarchy of impairments. *Disability and Society, 18*(7), 897–910.

DeVellis, R. (2012). *Scale development: Theory and applications (3rd ed.)*. Thousand Oaks, CA: Sage.

DeVellis, R. (2017). *Scale development: Theory and applications (4th ed.)*. Los Angeles, CA: Sage.

DeWall, C., & Bushman, B. (2011). Social acceptance and rejection: The sweet and the bitter. *Current Directions in Psychological Science, 20*(4), 256–260.

Dhamoon, R. (2009). *Identity/difference politics: How difference is produced and why it matters*. Vancouver, BC: UBC Press.

Disabled World. (2021, August 8). Disabilities: Definition, types and models of disability. *Disabled World*. Retrieved November 11, 2021 from: www.disabled-world.com/definitions/disability-models.php

Domzal, C., Houtenville, A., & Sharma, R. (2008). *Survey of employer perspectives on the employment of people with disabilities: Technical report*. (Prepared under contract to the Office of Disability and Employment Policy, U.S. Department of Labor.) McLean, VA: CESSI.

Donoghue, C. (2003). Challenging the authority of the medical definition of disability: An analysis of the resistance to the social constructionist paradigm. *Disability and Society*, *18*(2), 199–208.

Dovidio, J., & Hebl, M. (2013). Discrimination at the level of the individual: Cognitive and affective factors. In R. Dipboye, & A. Colella (Eds.), *Discrimination at work: The psychological and organizational bases* (pp. 11–36). Mahwah, NJ: Erlbaum Associates.

Dovidio, J., Major, B., & Crocker, J. (2000). Stigma: Introduction and overview. In T. Heatherton, R. Kleck, M. Hebl, & J. Hull (Eds.), *The social psychology of stigma* (pp. 1–28). London, UK: Guilford Press.

Dovidio, J., Pagotto, L., & Hebl, M. (2011). Implicit attitudes and discrimination against people with physical disabilities. In R. Weiner, & S. Willborn (Eds.), *Disability and aging discrimination* (pp. 157–183). New York, NY: Springer.

Downing, S. (2003). Validity: On the meaningful interpretation of assessment data. *Medical Education*, *37*(9), 830–837.

Eagly, A., & Chaiken, S. (1993). *The psychology of attitudes*. Fort Worth, TX: Harcourt, Brace and Jovanovich.

Eagly, A., & Telaak, K. (1972). Width of the latitude of acceptance as a determinant of attitude change. *Journal of Personality and Social Psychology*, *23*(3), 388–397.

Edwards, M. (1997). Construction of physical disability in the ancient Greek world: The community concept. In D. Mitchell, & S. Snyder (Eds.), *The body and physical difference: Discourses of disability* (pp. 35–50). Ann Arbor, MI: University of Michigan Press.

Eiesland, N. (2005). Encountering the disabled god. *Publications of the Modern Language Association of America*, *120*(2), 584–586.

Ellis, C., Adams, T., & Bochner, A. (2011). Autoethnography: An overview. *Historical Social Research*, *36*(4), 273–290.

Ellis, C., & Bochner, A. (2000). Autoethnography, personal narrative, reflexivity. In N. Denzin, & Y. Lincoln (Eds.), *Handbook of qualitative research (2nd ed.)* (pp. 733–768). Thousand Oaks, CA: Sage.

Employment Equity Act (S.C. 1995, c. 44). Retrieved on February 3, 2022 from: https://laws-lois.justice.gc.ca/eng/acts/E-5.401/page-1.html

Esler, M., Hastings, J., Lambert, G., Kaye, D., Jennings, G., & Seals, D. (2002). The influence on aging on the human sympathetic nervous system and brain norepinephrine turnover. *American Journal of Physiology: Regulatory Integrative and Comparative Physiology*, *282*(3), R909–R916.

Fay, B. (1996). *Contemporary philosophy of social science*. Oxford, UK: Blackwell Publishers.

Festinger, L. (1963). *Theory of cognitive dissonance*. Stanford, CA: Stanford University Press.

Findler, L., Vilchinsky, N., & Werner, S. (2007). The multidimensional attitudes scale toward persons with disabilities (MAS): Construction and validation. *Rehabilitation Counseling Bulletin*, *50*(3), 166–176.

Fink, J. (2008). Unintended consequences: How antidiscrimination litigation increases group bias in employer-defendants. *New Mexico Law Review*, *38*, 333–372.

Finkelstein, V. (1988). To deny or not to deny disability. *Physiotherapy*, *74*(12), 650–652.

Finkelstein, V. (1991). Disability: An administrative challenge? In M. Oliver (Ed.), *Social work – Disabling people and disabling environments* (pp. 1–15). London, UK: Jessica Kingsley Publishers.

Finkelstein, V. (1993). The commonality of disability. In J. Swain, V. Finkelstein, S. French, & M. Oliver (Eds.), *Disabling barriers – Enabling environments*. London, UK: Sage.

Fishbein, M., & Ajzen, I. (1975). *Belief, attitude, intention and behavior: An introduction to theory and research*. Reading, MA: Addison-Wesley.

Fiske, S. (2004). Seek out the magician: Contrarian tricks of mere simplicity make affect appear and disappear from social psychology. In R. Zajonc (Ed.), *The selected works of R.B. Zajonc* (pp. 1–10). Hoboken, NJ: Wiley.

Fiske, S., Cuddy, A., Glick, P., & Xu, J. (2002). A model of (often mixed) stereotype content: Competence and warmth respectively follow from perceived status and competition. *Journal of Personality and Social Psychology*, *82*, 878–902.

Ferreira, N., Potgieter, I., & Coetzee, M. (2021). *Agile coping in the digital workplace: Emerging issues for research and practice*. Cham, Switzerland: Springer Nature.

French, S., & Swain, J. (2001). The relationship between disabled people and health and welfare professionals. In G. Albrecht, K. Seelman, & M. Bury (Eds.), *The handbook of disability studies* (pp. 734–753). Thousand Oaks, CA: Sage.

Friedman, C. (2020). The relationship between disability prejudice and disability employment rates. *Work*, *65*(3), 591–598.

Foucault, M. (1988). *Madness and civilization: A history of insanity in the age of reason*. New York, NY: Vintage-Random House.

Fougeyrollas, P., & Beauregard, L. (2001). Disability: An interactive person-environment social creation. In Albrecht, G., Seelman, K., & Bury, M. (Eds.), *Handbook of disability studies* (pp.171–194). Thousand Oaks, CA: Sage.

Fujiura, G., & Rutkowski-Kmitta, V. (2001). Counting disability. In G. Albrecht, K. Seelman, & M. Bury (Eds.), *The handbook of disability studies* (pp. 69–95). Thousand Oaks, CA: Sage.

Furr, R., & Bacharach, V. (2014). *Psychometrics: An introduction (2nd ed.)*. Thousand Oaks, CA: Sage.

Gates, B., & Mafuba, K. (2016). Use of the term "learning disabilities" in the United Kingdom: Issues for international researchers and practitioners. *Learning Disabilities: A Contemporary Journal*, *14*(1), 9–23.

Gagnon, J. (2016). Lessons in suffering: Greek tragedy's teachings on disability through Sophocles' *Philoctetes*. *New Political Science*, *38*(3), 335–353.

Galvin, R. (2003). The paradox of disability culture: The need to combine versus the imperative to let go. *Disability and Society*, *18*(5), 675–690.

Garland-Thomson, R. (2006). Integrating disability, transforming feminist theory. In L. Davis, (Ed.), *The disability studies reader (2nd ed.)* (pp. 257–272). New York, NY: Routledge.

Gawronski, B., & Bodenhausen, G. (2006). Associative and propositional processes in evaluation: An integrative review of implicit and explicit attitude change. *Psychological Bulletin*, *132*(5), 692–731.

Geertz, C. (1973). *The interpretation of cultures*. New York, NY: Basic Books.

Gething, L., & Wheeler, B. (1992). The interaction with disabled persons scale: A new Australian instrument to measure attitudes towards people with disabilities. *Australian Journal of Psychology*, *44*(2), 75–82.

Gheidar, Y., & ShamiZanjani, M. (2020). *Conceptualizing the digital employee experience*, *19*(3), 131–135.

Gillies, J. (2012). University graduates with disabilities: The transition to the workforce. *Disability Studies Quarterly*, *32*(3), 21. 10.18061/dsq.v32i3.3281.

Ginsberg, F., & Rapp, R. (2013). Disability worlds. *Annual Review of Anthropology*, *42*, 53–68.

Glaser, B. (1992). *Basics of grounded theory analysis: Emergence vs. forcing*. Mill Valley, CA: Sociology Press.

Goethals, T., Mortelmans, D., Van den Bulck, H., Van den Heurck, W., & Van Hove, G. (2022). I am not your metaphor: Frames and counter-frames in the representation of disability. *Disability and Society*, *37*(5), 746–764.

Goffman, E. (1963). *Stigma: Notes on the management of spoiled identity*. Englewood Cliffs, NJ: Prentice Hall.

Goodley, D. (2013). Dis/entangling critical disability studies. *Disability and Society*, *28*(5), 631–644.

Goodley, D., Hughes, B., & Davis, L. (2012). *Disability and social theory*. Houndmills, UK: Palgrave Macmillan.

Grant, J., & Davis, L. (1997). Selection and use of content experts for instrument development. *Research in Nursing & Health*, *20*(3), 269–274.

Gregory, R. (2007). *Psychological testing: History, principles, and applications*. Boston, MA: Allyn & Bacon.

Guglielmi, R. (1999). Psychophysiological assessment and prejudice: Past research, current status, and future directions. *Personality and Social Psychology Review*, *3*, 123–157.

Guidano, V. (1987). *Complexity of the self: A developmental approach to psychopathology and therapy*. New York, NY: The Guilford Press.

Guidano, V. (1995). Constructivist psychotherapy: A theoretical framework. In *Constructivism in psychotherapy* (no author) (pp. 93–108). Washington, DC: American Psychological Association.

Gustavsson, A. (2004). The role of theory in disability research – Springboard or straight-jacket? *Scandinavian Journal of Disability Research*, *6*(1), 55–70.

Hacking, I. (1999). *The social construction of what?* Cambridge, MA: Harvard University Press.

Haegele, J., & Hodge, S. (2016). Disability discourse: Overview and critiques of the medical and social models. *Quest*, *68*(2), 193–206.

Harpur, P. (2012). From disability to ability: Changing the phrasing of the debate. *Disability and Society*, *27*(3), 325–337.

Harpur, P. (2019). *Ableism at work: Disablement and hierarchies of impairment*. Cambridge, UK: Cambridge University Press.

Harpur, P., Connolly, U., & Blanck, P. (2017). Socially constructed hierarchies of impairments: The case of Australian and Irish workers' access to compensation for injuries. *Journal of Occupational Rehabilitation*, *27*(4), 507–519.

Haynes, S., Richard, D., & Kubany, E. (1995). Content validity in psychological assessment: A functional approach to concepts and methods. *Psychological Assessment*, *7*(3), 238–247.

Hebl, M., & Kleck, R. (2000). The social consequences of physical disability. In T. Heatherton, R. Kleck, M. Hebl, & J. Hull (Eds.), *The social psychology of stigma* (pp. 419–439). New York, NY: Guilford Press.

Hernandez, B., Keys, C., & Balcazar, F. (2000). Employer attitudes toward workers with disabilities and their ADA employment rights: A literature review. *Journal of Psychology, 66*(4), 4–16.

Hinojosa-Laborde, C., Chapa, I., Lange, D., & Haywood, J. (1999). Gender differences in sympathetic nervous system regulation. *Clinical and Experimental Pharmacology and Physiology, 26*(2), 122–126.

Hoehl, S., Hellmer, K., Johansson, M., & Gredeback, G. (2017). Itsy bitsy spider … : Infants react with increased arousal to spiders and snakes. *Frontiers in Psychology, 8*, 1710. 10.3389/fpsyg.2017.01710

Hubley, A., & Palepu, A. (2007). Injection drug user quality of life scale (IDUQOL): Findings from a content validation survey. *Health and Quality of Life Outcomes*, 5, Article 47, 1–13.

Hubley, A., & Zumbo, B. (1996). A dialectic on validity: Where we have been and where we are going. *The Journal of General Psychology, 123*(3), 207–215. 10.1080/00221309.1996.9921273.

Hubley, A., & Zumbo, B. (2011). Validity and the consequences of test interpretation and use. *Social Indicators Research, 103*(2), 219–230. 10.1007/s11205-011-9843-4

Hubley, A., & Zumbo, B. (2013). Psychometric characteristics of assessment procedures: An overview. In K. Geisinger (Ed.), *APA handbook of testing and assessment in psychology: Vol. 1. Test theory and testing and assessment in industrial and organizational psychology* (pp. 3–19). Washington, DC: American Psychological Association.

Hughes, B. (2005). What can a Foucauldian analysis contribute? In S. Tremain (Ed.), *Foucault and the government of disability* (pp. 77–92). Ann Arbor, MI: University of Michigan Press.

Hughes, B. (2009). Wounded/monstrous/abject: A critique of the disabled body in the sociological imaginary. *Disability and Society, 24*(4), 399–410.

Hughes, B. (2019). Invalidating emotions in the non-disabled imaginary. In N. Watson, & S. Vehmas (Eds.), *Routledge handbook of disability studies (2nd ed.)* (pp. 89–101). London, UK: Taylor & Francis.

Hughes, B., & Paterson, K. (1997). The social model of disability and the disappearing body: Towards a sociology of impairment. *Disability and Society, 12*(3), 325–340.

Hunt, C., & Hunt, B. (2004). Changing attitudes toward people with disabilities: Experimenting with an educational intervention. *Journal of Managerial Issues, 16*(2), 266–280.

Hyde, J. (2006). *Half the human experience: The psychology of women*. Boston, MA: Houghton Mifflin.

Imrie, R. (2004). Demystifying disability: A review of the international classification of functioning, disability and health. *Sociology of Health and Illness, 26*(3), 287–305.

Jaarsma, P., & Welin, S. (2012). Autism as a natural human variation: Reflections on the claims of the neurodiversity movement. *Health Care Analysis, 20*(1), 20–30.

Job Accommodation Network [JAN] (2015). *Workplace accommodations: Low cost, high impact*. Retrieved on March 31, 2020 from: http://AskJAN.org/media/lowcosthighimpact.html

Judge, T., & Cable, D. (2004). The effect of physical height on workplace success and income: Preliminary test of a theoretical model. *Journal of Applied Psychology, 89*(3), 428–441.

Kane, M. (2001). Current concerns in validity theory. *Journal of Educational Measurement, 38*(4), 319–342.

Kane M. (2016). Explicating validity. *Assessments in Education: Principles, Policies and Practice*, *23*(2), 198–211.

Kaye, H., Jans, L., & Jones, E. (2011). Why don't employers hire and retain workers with disabilities? *Journal of Occupational Rehabilitation*, *21*(4), 526–536.

Kennedy, J., & Olney, M. (2001). Job discrimination in the post-ADA era: Estimates from the 1994 and 1995 National Health Interview Surveys. *Rehabilitation Counseling Bulletin*, *45*(1), 24–30.

Kensbock, J., Boehm, S., & Bourovoi, K. (2017). Is there a downside of job accommodations? An employee perspective on individual change processes. *Frontiers in Psychology*, *8*, 1536. 10.3389/fpsyg.2017.01536

Kidd, M., Sloane, P., & Ferko, I. (2000). Disability and the labour market: An analysis of British males. *Journal of Health Economics*, *19*(6), 961–981.

Kleck, R., Ono, H., & Hastorf, A. (1966). The effects of physical deviance upon face-to-face interaction. *Human Relations*, 19(4), 425, 436.

Kools, S., McCarthy, M., Durham, R., & Robrecht, L. (1996). Dimensional analysis: Broadening the conception of grounded theory. *Qualitative Health Research*, *6*(3), 312–330.

Krahé, B. & Altwasser, C. (2006). Changing negative attitudes towards persons with physical disabilities: An experimental intervention. *Journal of Community and Applied Psychology*, *16*, 59–69.

Kuo, P-J., & Kalargyrou, V. (2014). Consumer perspectives on service staff with disabilities in the hospitality industry. *International Journal of Contemporary Hospitality Management*, *26*(2), 164–182.

Lave, C., & March, J. (1975). *An introduction to models in the social sciences*. New York, NY: Harper & Row.

Lid, I. (2016). Implementing universal design in a Norwegian context: Balancing core values and practical priorities. *Disability Studies Quarterly*, *36*(2), (n.p.) 10.18061/dsq.v36i2.3234

Link, B., & Phelan, J. (2001). Conceptualizing stigma. *Annual Review of Sociology*, *27*, 363–385.

Linton, S. (1998). *Claiming disability: Knowledge and identity*. New York, NY: New York University Press.

Linville, P. (1998). The heterogeneity of homogeneity. In J. Darley & J. Cooper (Eds.), *Attribution and social interaction: The legacy of Edward E. Jones* (pp. 423–462). Washington, DC: American Psychological Association.

Livneh, H. (1982). On the origins of negative attitudes toward people with disabilities. *Rehabilitation Literature*, *43*(11–12), 338–347.

Livneh, H. (2012). On the origins of negative attitudes toward people with disabilities. In I. Marini, & M. Stebnicki (Eds.), *The psychological and social impact of illness and disability (6th ed.)* (pp. 13–25). New York, NY: Springer.

Livneh, H., & Antonak, R. (1997). *Psychosocial adaptation to chronic illness and disability*. Gaithersburg, MD: Aspen.

Loevinger, J. (1957). Objective tests as instruments of psychological theory. *Psychological Reports*, *3*(3), 635–694.

Loo, R. (2004). Attitudes toward employing persons with disabilities: A test of the sympathy-discomfort categories. *Journal of Applied Social Psychology*, *34*(10), 2200–2214.

Louvet, E. (2007). Social judgment toward job applicants with disabilities: Perception of personal qualities and competence. *Rehabilitation Psychology, 52*(3), 297–303.

Louvet, E., Rohmer, O., & Dubois, N. (2009). Social judgment of people with a disability in the workplace: How to make a good impression on employers. *Swiss Journal of Psychology, 68*(3), 153–159.

Loukács, G. (1923, 1971). *History and class consciousness* (trans. R. Livingstone). Cambridge, MA: MIT Press.

Lynn, M. (1986). Determination and quantification of content validity. *Nursing Research, 35*(6), 382–386.

Mackelprang, R. (2010). Disability controversies: Past, present, and future. *Journal of Social Work in Disability and Rehabilitation, 9*(2), 87–98.

Martinez-Bello, V., del Mar Bernabé-Villodre, M., Garcia-Ochoa, Y., Torrent-Trilles, L., & Vega-Perona, H. (2021). The representation of athletes during Paralympic and Olympic Games: A Foucauldian analysis of the construction of difference in newspapers. *Disability and Society*, ahead-of-print, pp. 1–23. 10.1080/09687599.2021.1983413

Marx, K. (1867, 1996). *Das Kapital.* Washington, DC: Regnery Publishing.

Mastro, J., Burton, A., Rosendahl, M., & Sherrill, C. (1996). Attitudes of elite athletes with impairments toward one another: A hierarchy of preference. *Adapted Physical Activity Quarterly, 13*(2), 197–210.

Maxwell, J. (2012). *A realist approach for qualitative research.* Thousand Oaks, CA: Sage.

McKee, D., & Chappel, J. (1992). Spirituality and medical practice. *The Journal of Family Practice, 35*(2), 205–208.

McManus, J., Feyes, K., & Saucier, D. (2011). Contact and knowledge as predictors of attitudes toward individuals with intellectual disabilities. *Journal of Social and Personal Relationships, 28*(5), 579–590.

Mead, G. H. (1934). *Mind, self, and society.* Chicago, IL: University of Chicago Press.

Media Smarts. (2021, November 29). Common portrayals of persons with disabilities. https://mediasmarts.ca/diversity-media/persons-disabilities/common-portrayals-persons-disabilities

Méndez, M. (2013). Autoethnography as a research method: Advantages, limitations and criticisms. *Columbian Applied Linguistics Journal, 15*(2), 279–287.

Messick, S. (1980). Test validity and the ethics of assessment. *American Psychologist, 35*(11), 1012–1027.

Messick, S. (1989). Validity. In R. Linn (Ed.), *Educational measurement (3rd ed.)* (pp. 13–103). New York, NY: American Council on Education & Macmillan Publishing.

Messick, S. (1990). *Validity of test interpretation and use.* Research Rep. No. 90-11. Princeton, NJ: Educational Testing Service.

Messick, S. (1994). The interplay of evidence and consequences in the validation of performance assessments. *Educational Researcher, 23*(2), 13–23.

Messick, S. (1995). Validity of psychological assessment: Validation of inferences from persons' responses and performances as scientific inquiry into score meaning. *American Psychologist, 50*(9), 741–749. 10.1037/0003-066X.50.9.741

Messick, S. (1998). Test validity: A matter of consequence. *Social Indicators Research, 45*, 35–44.

Miller, L., McIntire, S., & Lovler, R. (2011). *Foundations of psychological testing: A practical approach (3rd ed.).* Los Angeles, CA: Sage.

Mills, J., & Harmon-Jones, E. (Eds.) (1999). *Cognitive dissonance: Progress on a pivotal theory in social psychology*. Washington, DC: American Psychological Association.

Mitchell, D., & Snyder, S. (2012). Minority model: From liberal to neoliberal futures of disability. In N. Watson (Ed.), *Routledge handbook of disability studies* (pp. 41–50). London, UK: Taylor and Francis.

Mitra, S. (2006). The capability approach and disability. *Journal of Disability Policy Studies, 16*(4), 236–247.

Morris, J. (1993). Prejudice. In J. Swain, V. Finkelstein, S. French, & M. Oliver (Eds.), *Disabling barriers – Enabling environments* (pp. 101–106). London, UK: Sage.

Morris, R. (2019). Disabled people and employment – A UK perspective. In N. Watson, & S. Vehmas (Eds.), *Routledge handbook of disability studies (2nd ed.)* (pp. 250–264). London, UK: Taylor & Francis.

Mpofu, E. (2003). Enhancing social acceptance of early adolescents with physical disabilities: Effects of role salience, peer interaction, and academic support interventions. *International Journal of Disability, Development, and Education, 50*, 435–454.

Nagi, S. (1976). An epidemiology of disability among adults in the United States. *Milbank Memorial Fund Quarterly, 54*(4), 439–467.

Ndzwayiba, N., & Ned, L. (2017). The complexity of disability inclusion in the workplace: A South African study. In B. Altman (Ed.), *Factors in studying employment for persons with disability (Vol. 10)* (pp. 127–154). Somerville, MA: Emerald Publishing.

Nelissen, P., Vornholt, K., van Ruitenbeek, G., Hülsheger, U., & Uitdewilligen, S. (2014). Disclosure or non-disclosure – Is this the question? *Industrial and Organizational Psychology – Perspectives on Science and Practice*, 7(2), 231–235.

New Atlas. (2021, November 29). First driverless vehicle approved to operate on public roads in Europe. https://newatlas.com/automotive/easymile-shuttle-first-europe-public-roads-level-4autonomy/?utm_source=New+Atlas+Subscribers&utm_campaign=bc5d2af360-EMAIL_CAMPAIGN_2021_11_29_09_08&utm_medium=email&utm_term=0_65b67362bd-bc5d2af360-91110585

Nota, L., Santilli, S., Ginevra, M. et al. (2014). Employer attitudes towards the work inclusion of people with disability. *JARID, 27*(6), 511–520.

Oliver, M. (1990). *The politics of disablement*. London, UK: MacMillan Press.

Oliver, M. (1992b). Intellectual masturbation: A rejoinder to Söder and Booth. *European Journal of Special Needs Education*, 7(1), 20–28.

Oliver, M. (1996). *Understanding disability: From theory to practice*. Basingstoke, UK: Macmillan.

Oliver, M. (2004). If I had a hammer: The social model in action. In J. Swain, S. French, C. Barnes, & C. Thomas (Eds.), *Disabling barriers - Enabling environments (2nd ed.)* (pp. 7–12). London: Sage.

Oliver, M. (2009). *Understanding disability (2nd ed.)*. Houndmills, UK: Palgrave MacMillan.

Oliver, M. (2013). The social model of disability: Thirty years on. *Disability and Society, 28*(7), 1024–1026.

Oliver, M. & Barnes, C. (2012). *The new politics of disablement*. New York, NY: Palgrave Macmillan.

Olney, F., & Kim, A. (2001). Beyond adjustment: Integration of cognitive disability into identity. *Disability and Society, 16*(4), 563–583.

Osipov, V. (2013). *Employment of people with disabilities in Armenia: Needs and barriers*. International Organization for Migration (IOM) 27.

Owens, J. (2015). Exploring the critiques of the social model of disability: The transformative possibility of Arendt's notion of power. *Sociology of Health and Illness, 37*(3), 385–403.

Ozawa, A., & Yaeda, J. (2007). Employer attitudes toward employing persons with psychiatric disability in Japan. *Journal of Vocational Rehabilitation, 26*(2), 105–113.

Palad, Y., Barquia, R., Domingo, H., Flores, C., Padilla, L., & Ramel, J. (2016). Scoping review of instruments measuring attitudes toward disability. *Disability and Health Journal, 9*(3), 354–374.

Parsons, T. (1951). *The social system (2nd ed.).* London, UK: Routledge. https://doi-org.ezproxy.library.ubc.ca/10.4324/9780203992951

Pasmore, W. (2001). Action research in the workplace: The socio-technical perspective. In P. Reason, & P. Bradbury (Eds.), *Handbook of action research: Participative inquiry and practice (3rd ed.)* (pp. 38–47). London, UK: Sage.

Peirce, C. (1923). *Chance, love, and logic: Philosophical essays.* New York, NY: Barnes and Noble.

Penfield, R. (2013). Item analysis. In K. Geisinger (Ed.), *APA handbook of testing and assessment in psychology: Vol. 1. Test theory and assessment in industrial and organizational psychology* (pp. 121–138). Washington, DC: APA.

Pernick, M. (1997). Eugenics and public health in American history. *American Journal of Public Health, 87*(11), 1767–1772.

Pettigrew, T., & Tropp, L. (2006). A meta-analytic test of intergroup contact theory. *Journal of Personality and Social Psychology, 90*(5), 751–783.

Pettigrew, T., & Tropp, L. (2008). How does intergroup contact reduce prejudice? Meta-analytic tests of three mediators. *European Journal of Social Psychology, 38*(6), 922–934.

Plaskoff, J. (2017). Employee experience: The new human resource management approach, *Strategic HR Review, 16*(3), 136–141.

Polit, D., Beck, C., & Owen, S. (2007). Is the CVI an acceptable indicator of content validity? Appraisal and recommendations. *Research in Nursing and Health, 30*(6), 459–467.

Popovich, P., Scherbaum, C., Scherbaum, K., & Polinko, N. (2003). The assessment of attitudes toward individuals with disabilities in the workplace. *The Journal of Psychology, 137*(2), 163–177.

Poulton, R., & Menzies, R. (2002). Non-associative fear acquisition: A review of the evidence from retrospective and longitudinal research. *Behaviour Research and Therapy, 40*(2), 127–149.

Priestley, M. (1998). Constructions and creations: Idealism, materialism and disability theory. *Disability and Society, 13*(1), 75–95.

Priestley, M. (1999). Discourse and identity: Disabled children in mainstream high schools. In M. Corker, & S. French (Eds.), *Disability discourse* (pp. 92–102). Buckingham, UK: Open University Press.

Pruett, S., & Chan, F. (2006). The development and psychometric validation of the Disability Attitude Implicit Association Test. *Rehabilitation Psychology, 51*(3), 202–213.

Quadflieg, S., Mason, M., & Macrae, C. (2010). Social cognitive neural processes. In J. Dovidio, M. Hewstone, P. Glick, & V. Esses (Eds.), *Handbook of prejudice, stereotyping, and discrimination* (pp. 65–80). Los Angeles, CA: Sage.

Reindal, S. (2008). A social relational model of disability: A theoretical framework for special needs education. *European Journal of Special Needs Education, 23*(2), 135–146.

Reisman, C. (2008). *Narrative methods for the human sciences.* Los Angeles, CA: Sage.

Retief, M., & Letsosa, R. (2018). Models of disability: A brief overview. *HTS Teologiese Studies/ Theological Studies, 74*(1), a4738. 10.4102/hts.v74i1.4738

Rioux, M. (1997). Disability: The place of judgment in a world of fact. *Journal of Intellectual Disability Research, 41*(2), 102–111.

Rioux, M., & Patton, L. (2014). Employment equity and disability: Moving forward to achieve employment integration and fulfil promises of inclusion and participation. In C. Agócs (Ed.), *Employment equity in Canada: The legacy of the Abella report* (pp. 133–155). Toronto, ON: University of Toronto Press.

Rogers, T. (1995). *The psychological testing enterprise: An introduction.* Pacific Grove, CA: Brooks/Cole.

Rorty, A. (Ed.). (1966). *Pragmatic philosophy.* Garden City, NY: Doubleday.

Rose, M. (2006). Deaf and dumb in ancient Greece. In L. Davis, (Ed.), *The disability studies reader (2nd ed.)* (pp. 17–32). New York, NY: Routledge.

Ross, K. (2001). All ears: Radio, reception and discourses of disability. *Media, Culture and Society, 23*(4), 19–437.

Russell, M. (2002). What disability civil rights cannot do: Employment and political economy. *Disability & Society, 17*(2), 117–135.

Ryan, E., Anas, A., & Gruneir, A. (2006). Evaluations of overhelping and underhelping communication. *Journal of Language and Social Psychology, 25*(1), 97–107.

Saleh, M., & Bruyère, S. (2018). Leveraging employer practices in global regulatory frameworks to improve employment outcomes for people with disabilities. *Social Inclusion, 6*(1), 18–28.

Schatzman, L. (1991). Dimensional analysis: Notes on an alternative approach to the grounding of theory in qualitative research. In D. Maines (Ed.), *Social organization* and *social process* (pp. 303–314). New York, NY: Aldine de Gruyter.

Schilling, L., Dixon, J., Knafl, K., Grey, M., Ives, B., & Lynn, M. (2007). Determining content validity of a self-report instrument for adolescents using a heterogeneous expert panel. *Nursing Research,* 56(5), 361–366.

Schur, L., Kruse, D., & Blanck, P. (2005). Corporate culture and the employment of persons with disabilities. *Behavioral Sciences and the Law, 23*(1), 3–20.

Schur, L., Kruse, D., Blasi, J., & Blanck, P. (2008). Is disability disabling in all workplaces? Workplace disparities and corporate culture. *Industrial Relations: A Journal of Economy and Society, 48*(3), 381–410.

Schweik, S. (2009). *The ugly laws: Disability in public.* New York, NY: New York University Press.

Seligman, M. (1971). Phobias and preparedness. *Behavior Therapy, 2*(3), 307–320.

Shah, P., & Mountain, D. (2007). The medical model is dead – Long live the medical model. *British Journal of Psychiatry, 191,* 375–377.

Shah, S. & Priestley, M. (2011). *Disability and social change.* Bristol, UK: Polity Press.

Shakespeare, T. (1994). Cultural representation of disabled people: Dustbins for disavowal? *Disability and Society, 9*(3), 283–299.

Shakespeare, T. (1996). Disability, identity and difference. In C. Barnes, & G. Mercer, (Eds.), *Exploring the divide* (pp. 94–113). Leeds, UK: The Disability Press.

Shakespeare, T. (2004). Social models and other life strategies. *Scandinavian Journal of Disability Research, 6*(1), 8–21.

Shakespeare, T. (2006). The social model of disability. In L. Davis, (Ed.), *The disability studies reader (2nd ed.)* (pp. 197–204). New York, NY: Routledge.

Shakespeare, T. (2014). *Disability rights and wrongs revisited (2nd ed.).* London, UK: Routledge.

Shakespeare, T., Gillespie-Sells, K., & Davies, D. (1996). *The sexual politics of disability: Untold desires.* London, UK: Cassell.

Shakespeare, T., & Watson, N. (2001). The social model of disability: An outdated ideology? In S. Barnartt & B. Altman (Eds.), *Exploring theories and expanding methodologies: Where are we and where do we need to go? Research in social sciences and disability (Vol. 2)* (pp. 9–28). Amsterdam, NL: Emerald.

Shakespeare, T., & Watson, N. (2010). Beyond models: Understanding the complexity of disabled people's lives. In G. Scambler & S. Scambler (Eds.), *New directions in the sociology of chronic and disabling conditions.* (pp. 57–76). Hampshire, UK: Palgrave MacMillan.

Sherry, M. (2004). Overlaps and contradictions between queer theory and disability studies. *Disability and Society, 19*(7), 769–783.

Shildrick, M. (2009). *Dangerous discourses of disability, subjectivity and sexuality.* Hampshire, UK: Palgrave MacMillan.

Shilling, C. (2002). Culture, the 'sick role' and the consumption of health. *British Journal of Sociology, 53*(4), 621–638.

Siebers, T. (2008). *Disability theory.* Ann Arbor, MI: University of Michigan Press.

Silvers, A. (2003). On the possibility and desirability of constructing a neutral conception of disability. *Theoretical Medicine, 24*(6), 471–487.

Siminski, P. (2003). Patterns of disability and norms of participation through the life course: Empirical support for a social model of disability. *Disability and Society, 18*(6), 707–718.

Simms, L. (2008). Classical and modern methods of psychological scale construction. *Social and Personality Psychology Compass, 2*(1), 414–433.

Sireci, S. (1998). The construct of content validity. *Social Indicators Research, 45*(1–3), 83–117.

Stainton, T. (2004). Reason's other: The emergence of the disabled subject in the northern renaissance. *Disability and Society, 19*(3), 225–243.

Stainton, T., & Swift, K. (1996). "Difference" and social work curriculum. *Canadian Social Work Review, 13*(1), 75–87.

Stark, S. (2001). Creating disability in the home: The role of environmental barriers in the United States. *Disability and Society, 16*(10), 37–49.

Statistics Canada. (2006). PALS Survey. Retrieved on January 7, 2015 from: http://www.statcan.gc.ca/daily-quotidien/080724/dq080724a-eng.htm

Statistics Canada. (2013). Canadian Survey on Disability Data Tables. Retrieved on May 18, 2018 from: http://www.statcan.gc.ca/pub/89-654-x/89-654-x2013001-eng.pdf

Statistics Canada (2017a). Workplace accommodations of employees with disabilities in Canada, 2017. Retrieved on March 31, 2020 from: https://www150.statcan.gc.ca/n1/en/pub/89-654-x/89-654-x2019001-eng.pdf?st=Cf4zHE5L

Statistics Canada (2017b). Canadian Survey on Disability, 2017: Type of disability for persons with disabilities aged 15 years and over (Table 13-10-0376-01). Retrieved on June 4, 2022 from: https://www150.statcan.gc.ca/t1/tbl1/en/tv.action?pid=1310037601

Statistics Canada (2017c). Canadian Survey on Disability, 2017: Concepts and methods guide. Retrieved on February 9, 2022 from: https://www150.statcan.gc.ca/n1/pub/89-654-x/2018001/sc-ce-eng.htm

Statistics Canada (2017d). Canadian Survey on Disability, 2017: Disability Screening Questions. Retrieved on June 6, 2022 from: https://www23.statcan.gc.ca/imdb/p3Instr.pl?Function=assembleInstr&lang=en&Item_Id=348023#qb353069

Statistics Canada [Ouellet-Léveillé, B., & Milan, A.]. (2019). Results from the 2016 census: Occupations with older workers. Retrieved on June 22, 2022 from: https://www150.statcan.gc.ca/n1/pub/75-006-x/2019001/article/00011-eng.htm

Statistics Canada (2022). Proportion of women and men employed in management positions, annual. Table: 14-10-0335-03. Retrieved on June 22, 2022 from: https://www150.statcan.gc.ca/t1/tbl1/en/tv.action?pid=1410033503

Stone, D., & Colella, A. (1996). A model of factors affecting the treatment of disabled individuals in organizations. *Academy of Management Review*, *21*(2), 352–401.

Strauss, A., & Corbin, J. (1990). *Basics of qualitative research: Grounded theory procedures and techniques*. Newbury Park, CA: Sage.

Sundar, V., O'Neill, J., Houtenville, A., Phillips, K., Keirns, T., Smith, A., & Katz, E. (2018). Striving to work and overcoming barriers: Employment strategies and successes of people with disabilities. *Journal of Vocational Rehabilitation*, *48*(1), 93–109.

Swain, J., & French, S. (2000). Towards an affirmation model of disability. *Disability and Society*, *15*(4), 569–582.

Swain, J., French, S., & Cameron, C. (2003). *Controversial issues in a disabling society*. Buckingham, UK: Open University Press.

Taura, M. (2011). Evaluation of anthropomorphic status of Hausas of northern Nigeria. *Bajopas*, *4*(2), 80–82.

Taylor, S., & Bogdan, R. (1989). On accepting relationships between people with mental retardation and non-disabled people: Towards an understanding of acceptance. *Disability, Handicap and Society*, *4*(1), 21–36.

Thomas, C. (1999a). Narrative identity and the disabled self. In M. Corker, & S. French (Eds.), *Disability discourse* (pp. 47–55). Buckingham, UK: Open University Press.

Thomas, C. (1999b). *Female forms: Experiencing and understanding disability*. Buckingham, UK: Open University Press.

Thomas, C. (2004). How is disability understood? An examination of sociological approaches. *Disability and Society*, *19*(6), 569–583.

Thomas, C. (2007). *Sociologies of disability and illness*. Hampshire, UK: Palgrave MacMillan.

Thomas, C. (2012). Theorizing disability and chronic illness: Where next for perspectives in medical sociology? *Social Theory and Health; London*, *10*(3), 209–228.

Thurstone, L. (1928). Attitudes can be measured. *Journal of American Sociology*, *33*(4), 529–554.

Titchkosky, T. (2001). Disability: A rose by any other name? "People-first" language in Canadian society. *Canadian Review of Sociology*, *38*(2), 125–140.

Treasury Board of Canada Secretariat. (2018). *Employment equity in the public service of Canada (2017-2018)*. Cat. No. BT1-28E-PDF. Retrieved on February 7, 2022 from: https://www.canada.ca/content/dam/tbs-sct/documents/employment-equity-report/20190315-eng.pdf

Trieschmann, R. (1988). *Spinal cord injuries – Psychological, social and vocational rehabilitation (2nd ed.)*. New York: Demos.

Turcotte, M. (2014). *Persons with disabilities and employment.* (Catalogue No. 75-006-X). Statistics Canada. Retrieved on September 4, 2020 from: http://www.statcan.gc.ca/pub/75-006-x/2014001/article/14115-eng.pdf

Turner, B. (2001). Disability and the sociology of the body. In G. Albrecht, K. Seelman, & M. Bury (Eds.), *The handbook of disability studies* (pp. 252–264). Thousand Oaks, CA: Sage.

United Nations. (2021). (no author). Promoting an accurate image and enhancing the voice of persons with disabilities in the media. *Department of Economic and Social Affairs (Disability)* (n.p.). Retrieved on November 4, 2021 from: https://www.un.org/development/desa/disabilities/resources/disability-and-the-media.html#menu-header-menu

United Nations General Assembly. (2006). Convention on the rights of persons with disabilities. *Treaty Series, 2515,* 3. Retrieved on February 23, 2022 from: https://www.refworld.org/docid/45f973632.html

United States Census Bureau (2019). American Community Survey. Retrieved on January 26, 2022 from: https://data.census.gov/cedsci/table?q =disability%20employment&tid=ACSDT1Y2019.B18120

United States Equal Employment Opportunity Commission. (2022). The EEO status of workers with disabilities in the federal sector. Retrieved on October 2, 2022 from: https://www.eeoc.gov/sites/default/files/202204/EEO%20Status%20of%20Workers%20with%20Disabilities%20in%20the%20Federal%20Sector.pdf

UPIAS (1976). *Fundamental principles of disability.* London: Union of the Physically Impaired Against Segregation. Retrieved on June 5, 2017 from: http://disability-studies.leeds.ac.uk/files/library/UPIAS-fundamental-principles.pdf

Vehmas, S., & Watson, N. (2014). Moral wrongs, disadvantages, and disability: A critique of critical disability studies. *Disability and Society, 29*(4), 638–650.

Vernon, A., & Swain, J. (2002). Theorizing divisions and hierarchies: Towards a commonality or diversity? In C. Barnes, M. Oliver, & L. Barton (Eds.), *Disability studies today* (pp. 77–97). Cambridge, UK: Polity Press.

Vilchinsky, N., & Findler, L. (2010). Attitudes toward people with disabilities: The perspective of attachment theory. *Rehabilitation Psychology, 55*(3), 298–306.

Vivanti, G. (2020). Ask the editor: What is the most appropriate way to talk about individuals with a diagnosis of autism? *Journal of Autism and Developmental Disorders, 50*(2), 691–693.

Vornholt, K., Uitdewilligen, S., & Nijhuis, J. (2013). Factors affecting the acceptance of people with disabilities at work: A literature review. *Journal of Occupational Rehabilitation, 23,* 463–475.

Wallerstein, N., & Duran, B. (2008). The theoretical, historical, and practice roots of CBPR. In M. Minkler, & N. Wallerstein (Eds.), *Community-based participatory action research for health: From process to outcomes (2nd ed.)* (pp. 25–39). San Francisco, CA: Jossey-Bass.

Waltz, C., Strickland, O., & Lenz, E. (2005). *Measurement in nursing and health research (3rd ed.).* New York: Springer.

Waltz, C., Strickland, O., & Lenz, E. (2010). *Measurement in nursing and health research (4th ed.).* New York: Springer.

Wang, Z., Xu, X., Han, Q., Chen, Y., Jiang, J., & Ni, G-Z. (2021). Factors associated with public attitudes towards persons with disabilities: A systematic review. *BMC Public Health, 21,* 1058. 10.1186/s12889-021-11139-3

Watkins, M. (2000). *Monte Carlo PCA for parallel analysis* [computer software] (pp. 432–442). State College, PA: Ed & Psych Associates.

Watkins, M. (2006). Determining parallel analysis criteria. *Journal of Modern Applied Statistical Methods, 5*(2), 344–346.

Watson, N. (2002). Well, I know this is going to sound strange to you, but I don't see myself as a disabled person: Identity and disability. *Disability and Society, 17*(5), 509–527.

Watson, N. (2012). Researching disablement. In N. Watson, A. Roulstone, & C. Thomas (Eds.), *Routledge handbook of disability studies* (pp. 93–105). London, UK: Taylor & Francis.

Wendell, S. (1997). *The rejected body*. New York, NY: Routledge.

White, K. (2002). *An introduction to the sociology of health and illness*. London, UK: Sage.

Wickenden, M. (2013). Widening the SLP lens: How can we improve the wellbeing of people with communication disabilities globally. *International Journal of Speech-Language Pathology, 15*(1), 14–20.

Williams, S. (1999). Is anybody there? Critical realism, chronic illness and the disability debate. *Sociology of Health and Illness, 21*(6), 797–819.

Williams, G. (2001). Theorizing disability. In G. Albrecht, K. Seelman, & M. Bury (Eds.), *The handbook of disability studies* (pp. 123–145). Thousand Oaks, CA: Sage.

Wills, T. (1981). Downward comparison principles in social psychology. *Psychological Bulletin, 90*(2), 245–271.

Wilson, K., & Wauson, J. (2010). *The AMA handbook of business writing*. New York, NY: American Management Association.

Winance, M. (2007). Being normally different? Changes to normalization processes: From alignment to work on the norm. *Disability and Society, 22*(6), 625–638.

Wolbring, G. (2008). The politics of ableism. *Development, 51*(2), 252–258.

World Health Organization (2001). *International classification of functioning, disability and health – ICF short version*. Geneva, CH: WHO.

World Health Organization (2011). *World report on disability*. Malta: WHO. Retrieved on September 14, 2021 from: https://documents1.worldbank.org/curated/en/665131468331271288/pdf/627830WP0World00PUBLIC00BOX361491B0.pdf

Young, M. (1990). *Justice and the politics of difference*. Princeton, NJ: Princeton University Press.

Yuker, H. (1988). *Attitudes toward persons with disabilities*. New York, NY: Springer.

Yuker, H., Block, J., & Younng, J. (1970). *The measurement of attitudes toward disabled persons*. Albertson, NY: Insurance Company of North America.

Zajonc, R. (1980). Feeling and thinking: Preferences need no inferences. *American Psychologist, 35*(2), 151–175.

Zajonc, R. (2000). Closing the debate over the independence of affect. In J. Forgas (Ed.), *Feeling and thinking: The role of affect in social cognition* (pp. 31–58). Cambridge, UK: Cambridge University Press.

Zola, I. (1989). Towards the necessary universalizing of a disability policy. *The Milbank Quarterly, 67*(suppl. 2, pt. 2), 401–428.

Zola, I. (2005). Toward the necessary universalizing of a disability policy. *The Millbank Quarterly, 83*(4), 1–27.

Index

Note: Page numbers in italics indicate a figure and page numbers in bold indicate a table on the corresponding page.